UNDER THE MERCY

Other books by Sheldon Vanauken:

A Severe Mercy
Gateway to Heaven
The Glittering Illusion

UNDER THE MERCY

By

SHELDON VANAUKEN

HODDER AND STOUGHTON
LONDON SYDNEY AUCKLAND TORONTO

British Library Cataloguing in Publication Data

Vanauken, Sheldon
  Under the mercy.
  1. Christian life
  I. Title
  248.4   BV4501.2

  ISBN 0–340–38301–1

*Hodder and Stoughton Editorial Office: 47 Bedford Square, London
WC1B 3DP.*

ACKNOWLEDGMENTS

For their kind permission to reprint his letters, poems, and essays, the author thanks the journals that are named where the item appears in the pages of this book.

Chapter II: "Forever England," Copyright © 1970 by the New York Times Company. Reprinted by permission. "After the South Won" was first published in *The Southern Partisan*, 1984. Used by permission. Chapter III: "Conscience Above the Law" first appeared in *The Daily Advance*, January 1983. "An Afterword on the Genesis of *Gateway to Heaven*" was first published in *New Oxford Review*, September 1980. Chapter IV: "Against Giganticism" was first published in *New Oxford Review*. "The Corruption of the Killers" was first published in *The Peacemaker*, 1970. Chapter V: "Reply to the Bishop" was first published in *The Southwestern Episcopalian*. "There was a young man of divinity" was first published in *New Oxford Review*. "A General Rule for New Testament Criticism" was first published in *New Oxford Review*. "The Playwright Incarnate" is reprinted by permission of *Eternity* magazine, Copyright 1978, Evangelical Ministries, Inc., 1716 Spruce Street, Philadelphia, Pennsylvania 19103. Chapter VI: "God's Will" is reprinted by permission of *The Living Church*, 407 E. Michigan Street, Milwaukee, Wisconsin 53202. "The Shepherds' Reformation" is reprinted by permission of *Christianity Today*, Copyright 1978. "Cardinal" is reprinted by permission of *Eternity* magazine, Copyright 1980, Evangelical Ministries, Inc., 1716 Spruce Street, Philadelphia, PA 19103. "Jake's Place Revisited" is reprinted by permission of *The Wittenburg Door*. "Christmas Eve: That Difficult Birth" is reprinted by permission of *Eternity* magazine, Copyright 1978, Evangelical Ministries, Inc., 1716 Spruce Street, Philadelphia, PA 19103. Chapter VII: "The (False) Sanction of Eros" is reprinted by permission of *Fidelity* magazine, 206 Marquette Avenue, South Bend, Indiana 46617. "The Bachelor" is reprinted by permission of *The Hillsdale Review*, Summer 1982, Vol. IV, No. 2. Chapter VIII: "Women's 'Ordination' Denies the Incarnation" was first published in *New Oxford Review*, 1978. "Her unisex temper would worsen" was first published in *New Oxford Review*. "The Queen's English" is reprinted by permission from the April, 1980 issue of *The Christian Challenge*, Copyright 1980 by The Foundation for Christian Theology, P.O. Box 2624, Victoria, Texas 77902; and by permission of *The Wittenburg Door*. "Unisexism" was first published in the *New Oxford Review*, December 1981. Chapter IX: "There were some old clerks" was first published in *New*

CONTENTS

UNDER THE MERCY

This book is dedicated to Saint Luke.

CHAPTER I

A Day in the Life

The late-winter sun rising in brilliance threw long shadows across a Virginian garden. The branches and twigs of leafless trees in all their bare grace were touched with gold, and the banks of early daffodils were aflame. In one corner of the garden, half under a huge oak, stood a tiny cottage. The small, diamond-shaped panes of a casement window glittered in the morning light, and a plume of smoke arose from the chimney.

Presently the blue door of the cottage opened, and a tall man, wearing a tweed jacket and a long green-and-white Oxonian scarf, emerged. He took a deep breath of the morning air. Then he looked around, almost as though he expected a dog, perhaps a light-footed collie, to come bounding up. Under his breath he murmured in a rising tone, "Flurry, Flurry, FLUR-ry!" Smiling a little, he threw his green bookbag over his shoulder and walked off across the garden, zig-zagging to pass close to the beds of brave daffodils. Once he paused and looked back towards the cottage with the slender white birch bending across one of the windows, looked back as though he had heard a call or fancied someone might be standing in the cottage doorway waving. But the door was shut.

He walked on, feeling the stir of spring in his blood as always, anticipating the lilacs and the tiny leaves of April. "Three years," he thought. "Three years ago in a brilliant winter dawn she died; half a year ago, somehow, she was with me as I walked up to Lincoln Cathedral in the sunset; but now...far away...even when the daffodils are blowing. Nothing. Not even tears..." He shook his head a little and walked on.

Beyond the garden were academic buildings arranged in a great oval, the cottage and garden being behind the quiet library. It was the campus of Lynchburg College, where he taught both history and English literature. He walked across the oval towards a columned building with a green dome and mounted the steps to the porch with a word or a grin for the students who greeted him. Once he paused to answer a student's question and again to chat with a colleague. Then he entered his classroom just as a bronze bell outside the building pealed to begin the eight o'clocks.

His lecture this morning in English history was on the seventeenth-century crisis that became the English Civil War, and it was less of battles than of the characteristics of the opposing sides. He began by reading Browning's "Cavalier Tunes", and there were other poets, seventeenth-century ones, scattered through the lecture, as well as pauses for discussions. As he proceeded, a certain sympathy for the Cavaliers and some distaste for the Roundheads, including Cromwell, were perhaps to be inferred—after all, seventeenth-century Virginia had been as Cavalier as Boston had been Roundhead. At intervals he put questions to students or invited theirs. Although he addressed them as Mister or Miss, the atmosphere was one of informality, often humorous. There were analogies to the present day as well as to that re-run of the English Civil War that took place in Virginia, when Jeb Stuart was the Prince Rupert (Stuart) of the Army of Northern Virginia and the Virginian 'Cavaliers' rode against the Yankee Puritans.

The lecturer's accent was perhaps appropriate to the subject matter, being neither altogether Virginian nor 'American' nor English. It was indeed what he, after his Oxford years, and an English friend who had gone to an American University, had decided was in both of them a 'mid-Atlantic' accent.

Towards the end of the hour, he told of the death of King Charles, condemned by Cromwell for treason—which in law was defined only as disloyalty to the King. He pictured the scene: King Charles, calm and graceful and, at that moment, altogether kingly, kneeling to the block, and the headsman's axe flashing downward. And the crowd that did not cheer the death of a king but, instead, felt (in Buchan's words) "the horror of a great sacrilege." The class, like that crowd, was hushed as the bronze bell marked the end of the hour.

Out on the porch behind the Ionic columns, he perched on the side balustrade and smoked a cigarette while talking and joking with three or four students. Then, re-entering the classroom, he turned to Roman history. Today his subject was not, as it had been the previous week, Latin literature and Roman government but the

Legion. He quoted a Greek in one of Benet's short stories speaking to a Roman: "You [Romans] had nothing but an arch, a road, an army, and a law. And yet a man might walk from the east to the west because of it..." Walk in safety wherever the Eagles of the Legions maintained the *Pax Romana* from Londinium to Damascus.

This lecture, unlike the one an hour before, would be about battle itself, a battle between three legions with a fourth in reserve pitted against a huge barbarian horde. With rectangles for the cohorts and different shading to distinguish each legion, he had put on the board a sketch of the curving, ordered, three-legion front of the Romans, stretching for nearly a mile and waiting in grim quiet under the bright Eagles for the barbarian onslaught. He described the disciplined Legions and the yelling, boasting barbarians, and then the barbarian charge. As the screaming horde drew near the silent Roman lines, a Roman trumpet sounded, and as one man the Legionaries poised their javelins. Another trumpet blast and the javelin volley flashed through the air into the massed barbarians. Again the trumpet and the short swords were drawn, flickering between the interlocked Roman shields; and then the battle was joined. As the unbroken forward cohorts tired, the trumpets signalled for the fresh cohorts of the second line to move forward, as with steady discipline the weary cohorts fell back. But the barbarians, too, were tiring, falling back. And the fourth legion in reserve was now advancing to take the horde on the flank. Again the trumpet sounded, commanding the advance.

"And then," said the lecturer, "the calm, terrible legions move forward with short steps, cutting, stabbing, killing. The barbarian retreat begins to turn into a panic rout. The trumpet sounds for the charge, led by the Emperor himself with the Praetorian Guard. Some of the barbarians are still fighting, bravely and desperately. The Romans care nothing for their bravery; they cut them down coldly. The battle is won."

The lecturer paused, and then spoke of the aftermath of the battle: the parade, the awards for courage, and, later, in Rome the Triumph. It was a lecture that always held the class spellbound, especially the boys—they marched under the Eagles of the Legions. But that, indeed, was what the lecturer always intended: that the students should see and hear and smell the scenes of the past: the glitter and tramp and rough jokes of the Legions; the crack and boom of the sails and the swish and lift of the sea when a great ship-of-the-line of the Royal Navy stood out; the coronation of a queen or the quiet death of a king except for the thud of the axe. To see and feel and, therefore, remember.

After the class he strolled towards a nearby building, already thinking of what poems he would read aloud in the literature class tomorrow. There the aim would be somewhat different: to make the students *see* the poet's images, yes; but, above all, to *hear* the power and magic of words in combination—how the poet out of three sounds creates not a fourth sound but a star (to paraphrase Browning). Lines of high poetry flashed through his mind: "Like Ocean on a western beach, / The surge and thunder of the Odyssey." ☆ "Red lips are not so red / As the stained stones kissed by the English dead." ☆ "Dear, beauteous Death! The jewel of the Just, / Shining nowhere, but in the dark." In poetry and literature in general, he sought to say in essence: This is the rose garden that the writers create; you are glimpsing it now—look! the roses!—but you can enter it if you choose and make it your joy for ever. He would be as gripped by the poems as they; and they would know that and sense a magic that they, some of them, might come to love.

The building that he approached and entered going to his office was a curious and attractive one with three porches and three staircases, like an Oxford college, with no interior passages between them. Here for an hour or two he talked with students. During a lull following one of them, who had admitted, in effect, that all he wanted out of college was the degree with as little learning as possible, he composed a limerick to be circulated among the faculty and later published.

> He believed that degrees were *essentia*,
> So he entered the realm of *scientia*,
>   But the books proved arcane
>   And, discov'ring no brain,
> They conferred his degree *in absentia*.

Having read this to a colleague, who laughed and asked for a copy, he walked back across the campus and the garden to his cottage, picking a single daffodil for a vase on the mantelpiece. There another friend came by in the late afternoon for a drink. And in the evening a dozen students came for the weekly meeting of the

Christian group that had begun while his wife still lived. There was talk of the Faith—the faith in the Risen Lord who was and eternally is God Incarnate—and what that meant in one's life. There was coffee, the students on the floor before the glowing coals of the hearth as well as in chairs and on the bed. Towards the end of the evening, after several requests, he agreed to read poetry, with only his reading lamp and the fire for light. He ended with some of the then-unpublished poems of his Oxford friend, the Benedictine monk, Dom Julian [poems now published in *There Shines Forth Christ* (St Bede's Publications)]. The evening ended with silent prayers, all kneeling by firelight alone, only the soft "Amen" of each student as he finished his prayer breaking the silence. One of the girls gave a peaceful little sigh. Then as the students departed into the night, he murmured, "Goodnight. Go under the Mercy."

He stood there on the stoop until they had disappeared, and then he went back into the minute cottage. It was old, said to have been a one-room schoolhouse just after the War of Secession. At all events, it was but a single storey and only twenty feet by twenty, plus a bathroom wing and the stoop. The college had recently inherited it along with the garden and, during his absence in England the previous year, had done it over for him to his own design. So now there was a main room that was twenty feet by twelve, almost a golden-mean rectangle, the interior wall lined with books to the ceiling except for the fireplace in the centre of it—the coal fire that was his only heat. There was always, therefore, a fire in cold weather, banked with ashes at night or during classes but ready to spring to life with a poke or two. On icy mornings the poke was very rapid indeed, followed by a leap back into bed until the fire took the chill off the room. Two of the other walls were windows, five of them; and the rest of the cottage consisted of a tiny kitchen and an equally tiny dressing room and closet. The main room—drawing-room, library, dining-room, bedroom in one—was comfortable and, somehow, because of its proportions and the glowing coals on the hearth, conducive to quiet talk. Its furniture and the Persian rugs were from Glenmerle—Glenmerle, his boyhood home—very old even then, including the narrow four-poster that had been in his room there; and the windows had dark-blue curtains that were drawn at night. Above the mantelpiece were some of Davy's paintings—country scenes—and below them, glowing in the light, was the figurehead from the schooner *Grey Goose*.

This was the Birdhouse, called so not only because of its tininess but because of a tiny house in Hawaii he and Davy had once planned to live in. He and Davy had often walked by this one in Virginia and wished to have it. She had never, in fact, been in it; but she had known it and the books and furniture had all known her touch, so there was for him a sense of continuity. He paid the college the nominal rent of $30 for it; and ten years in the future, when the college would decide to build a library extension back through the garden, he would buy the cottage from the college for the great sum of $200 and have it and its garage trundled down the hill to a lot on the edge of a small park—his new 'garden'—and he would continue—indeed, still continues—to live in the cottage, with the college, behind its mellow stone wall, on the bluff above the park.

CHAPTER II

The Hollow at the Centre

The foregoing 'day in the life' sets the basic scene for what I very naturally think of as the second half of my life, Davy's death, three years before, and the grief having occurred almost in the middle of the three score years and ten. In this second half there will be goings forth—travels and expeditions—but always the cottage, in the garden or on the park, to come back to, to write my books in.

People these days speak knowledgeably about the delights of word processors and laugh at my antique Royal portable that I had in Glenmerle days, but I murmur: "It writes books." —It is, at the moment, writing *Under the Mercy*. There is on the bed a low wooden desk with a slanting top that holds the portable, four headless nails going up into its four paws; and there very comfortably, the desk standing on its own legs on either side of me, I type with two or three fingers. Or, with the desk removed, read over what I've written. As I type the light comes in over my shoulder, and if I raise my eyes I see the wall of books and the fire. Thus it was that *A Severe Mercy* was written.

Or, in terms of the present narrative, *will be* written: it lies many years ahead of the Day that I've just described. The chronology is a bit confusing. For the reader who wants to get things straight, I may say that Davy's death and the grief occurred in the mid-'50s, which is where *A Severe Mercy* ended and this book begins. But the *writing* of *A Severe Mercy* didn't happen until the mid-'70s (as the publication date suggests), and the present book is being written in the '80s. It would, incidentally, appear that, since my novel *Gateway to Heaven* (despite its later completion and publication) was substantially written in the '60s, a book a decade is about my rate. This is borne out by the writing of *The Glittering Illusion*, my Oxford thesis, in the '50s.

Although I suppose most readers of the present book will have read *A Severe Mercy*, I ought perhaps to say briefly what it was about for those who haven't read it. *A Severe Mercy*, its title drawn from a letter of C. S. Lewis to me (and perhaps unconsciously from St Augustine's *Confessions*), was about the first half of my life—what I called "the autobiography of a love". It was a pagan love, a love protected by what we called the Shining Barrier, a springtime love—the little drawing I made for the front of that book shows within the walls the great tree of our love with the tiny leaves of early spring. The story begins and, in a sense, ends at Glenmerle, my family's country home, the dearest and, somehow, the realest place on earth to me, though now destroyed. I saw its lawns and trees and meadows and hills with the remembering eyes of boyhood, and there our love flowered. But the story also tells of the deepening of that love when, in Oxford days, it was invaded by Christ; and then, finally, her death when we were only in our late thirties, followed by the grief and the search for meaning through the Illumination of the Past, aided by the wise counsel of my friend, C. S. Lewis.

A Severe Mercy closes with what I call the Second Death, the moment when the grief comes to an end, as it must, and the tears are dried and the beloved (though no less dear) becomes remote. Whether the Second Death is merely the operation of time or whether it represents a turning away of the beloved towards Deep Heaven, having been allowed by grace and mercy to be, in some sense, still with the bereaved lover for a while, is a question I necessarily left open.

At all events, what follows the Second Death is not a sudden renewal of joy and laughter but a terrible emptiness, a hollow at the centre of one's being: one is, as C. S. Lewis wrote to me, "bereaved of the bereavement itself". There is no more sense of the beloved's presence, yet no more tears for the new loss. The grief and her seeming nearness had lasted for almost three years. A few months before this present book opens I had walked up to Lincoln Cathedral in England, the towers rose-red in the setting sun, with Davy seemingly lightly walking beside me, unseen but felt; but when I found myself in Virginia again, she was gone, along with the light-footed Flurry, and there were no more tears. Only the hollow at the centre. And that is where, with the first hint of a new spring, this book begins.

I feel hesitant, almost shy, at offering the reader a further book with an autobiographical theme, a sequel to *A Severe Mercy*. Externally, at least, the story of my later life lacks the fire and drama of the earlier story, and it lacks, too, a heroine except for the ghost of Davy (not, regrettably, an actual ghost), never far from my thoughts. Moreover, *A Severe Mercy* was so God-commanded (*vocatio*) that I tend to feel God wrote it and whatever was good about it was God's doing.

And yet the sense that I should write this new book, if only to show that *all* my life, not just the first half, has been lived, as indeed I shall die, under the Mercy, may come from God. The title of the book, *Under the Mercy*, is its theme. The phrase comes from Charles Williams's splendid novel, *Descent into Hell*; and Davy and I used it at Oxford and ever after to speed the departing guest. It is fitting that the title of the one book should come from C. S. Lewis and the other from Charles Williams, for their influence upon my thought was great.

If indeed "all men praise some beauty, tell some tale", that is done in *A Severe Mercy*. *Under the Mercy* is, then, a supplement and a continuation. It is not a love story except in that love for Davy continues and love for Christ deepens, and there is here no tragedy and tears. I beg the reader to spare me the comparison, for it has not escaped my notice. One thing the book will do is to answer the questions so often put to me by readers of the earlier one: whether I still love Davy (yes, of course); whether—the female readers ask—I ever married again (no, though once or twice I might have); and whether I have kept the Faith in our Christ (yes, with one wavering I shall touch on). These questions, especially the last, suggest that a pilgrimage is lifelong. *A Severe Mercy* was a pilgrimage book, and this book is the continuation of that pilgrimage—a justification, I trust, for its being written. A love story does not end with the vows at the altar; that is merely the beginning. Similarly, the real pilgrimage to God merely *begins* with conversion. Neither is the time to sit back and coast.

A Severe Mercy was written twenty years after my life with Davy—a *completed* thing—had ended, twenty years of contemplation, of seeing what was really important. It would have been a very bad book indeed if I had written it immediately after her death. Ideally *Under the Mercy* ought to be written twenty years after *my* death and after long purgatorial contemplation of the second half of my life as a completed thing. But publishing arrangements would be difficult. I have of course contemplated the events here to be told, and perhaps I can see the main outlines, the essential shape, as through a glass darkly. Still, unable to see the whole from a distance, I may omit what has abiding significance and include what does not. All books are selective, but right selection depends on contemplation and perspective, when the foothills sink into the ground and the mountains stand forth.

Although the fruit of contemplation, *A Severe Mercy*, many readers said, was written with an immediacy that suggested its events were but yesterday. If that is so, it is because I had our very complete journals, as well as poems and essays like "The Fall", that were written *at the time*. There are no journals for these later years, but there are even more writings that I shall be using, many of them published in magazines of limited circulation. The reader will have to change gears, so to speak, but I think the immediacy of these pieces written *at the time*, put in context by the narrative, is worth it. Moreover, since I wish to preserve the integrity of these essays, I hope the reader will forgive a certain amount of repetition, and, if so inclined, skip over it. These writings are as much the real content of the book as the narrative text, for *Under the Mercy* must be primarily the story of the development of my thought. Life, it has been said, is change; and to lose the capacity for change is to be dead though one still breathes. Thus this is a record of change and development since Davy's death, although there are constants, too, such as my love for Davy, and my friendship once-given, and my faith in the Risen Christ.

If it is difficult for me, without long contemplation, to determine what is truly significant and what is not even with the help of memory, I often speculate on the horror that might be felt by the illustrious dead if they could read the interpretations of their biographers. I, at least, can more nearly know what is genuinely significant than any picklock stranger, or even friend. Kipling must have had the same thought, which he expressed in his "Appeal" (and mine, too):

> If I have given you delight
>   By aught that I have done,
> Let me lie quiet in that night
>   Which shall be yours anon:
> And for the little, little span
>   The dead are borne in mind,
> Seek not to question other than
>   The books I leave behind.

Under the Mercy is a narrative of my life and thought since the Second Death, illuminated by my writings of these years. These writings more often than not challenge the Spirit of the Age: as my editor, Peter Gillquist, jested: "Something to offend everybody." Despite the noticeable wrong-headedness of the Spirits of past Ages (for instance, in the '30s when so many nations welcomed the dictators), we all tend to blind faith in the pronouncements of our own Spirit of the Age or *Zeitgeist*, a secular spirit today that is both egalitarian and feminist; and we are ready to be offended by any challenges to it. Even Christians, as Christians of every age have done, are inclined to confuse modernity, the Spirit of the Age, with the Holy Spirit. This may be the moment to throw my book on the fire.

Now, as we return to the late '50s where this story begins, I remind the reader that the writing of *A Severe Mercy*, even the intention of writing it, lies nearly twenty years into the future. The journals and letters are in a locked suitcase in the dressing-room. Moreover, if there are in that book insights that have seemed to the present reader true and wise, they are insights that perhaps I have not yet attained at the moment of the walk across the campus. In the years that stretch ahead between the walk and the writing—the years to be described in this chapter and the next two—I shall think much of my life with Davy, but, as I shall write in the Afterword of *A Severe Mercy*, I did not at the time of the walk yet see the essential shape of what had been.

> Instead, I reflected upon the past, seeing it anew year by year in sharper if more distant perspective. The foothills, as it were, merged with the plain while the blue mountains stood forth. Our life, including her dying, acquired *form* in my mind. I was, in fact, preparing myself to write a book I didn't intend to write. Just as a sculptor might contemplate a block of stone, seeing ever more clearly what was within it and only then beginning to remove the stone hiding that form, so I, contemplating the past, saw ever more clearly the essential form, moving in time, hidden within the block of seven thousand days. Art is first a seeing and then a revealing.
> [From the Afterword]

The 'day in the life' that was the first chapter was typical of my days, not only in the late '50s but in the years to come. Good days but undistinguished, days full of small pleasures—daffodils and blue sky or new-fallen snow, jokes with colleagues and students, talks with friends, reading poetry and discovering the bright and eager student, parties, and drives up into the Blue Mountains. But what the typical day did not disclose and what those round me did not discern beneath my cheerful demeanour was what I've called the hollow at the centre—the Davy-shaped hollow.

This should not be taken to mean grief—the traditional 'broken heart'. The tears were gone. And *she* was gone, not to return in this life. It was, I imagine, a bit like the loss of an arm; the loss is accepted, new ways of coping are invented, life goes on, but there is an empty sleeve. So in me the emptiness, the hollow, where once Davy had been and all our dreams of *Grey Goose* and Ladywood had been—a hollow that only she could fit. She and I had deliberately bound ourselves each to each with a thousand sharings, not fearing a sundering of the web because we should go together in the last long dive, but now I lived with a thousand severed ties. Or perhaps more accurately, a thousand *un*severed ties stretching into eternity.

She had been the centre of my life, as I of hers, long before I had pledged my sword to Christ the King. And she was the centre in her dying and in the grief and the Illumination of the Past. But now with the Second Death she was gone indeed. I had studied our past during the grief, written a bit about it, and now that past, *as* the past, was, so to speak, in the locked suitcase in the dressing-room. I was not trying to live in the past nor to hold on to her; I had dropped her rings into the North Atlantic. Nothing remained to do—except of course to write *A Severe Mercy* far in a future that was veiled to me.

I had been sustained in the three years following her death by the purpose of understanding the past. If nothing remained to do, if all our dreams of the future were dead, I had now no purpose, no direction in my life. I had thought that God might reveal one when the study of the past was finished, but He had not done so. I was faintly reproachful towards Him. There was nothing that I was working towards. To be sure, I had my job—my duty—as a teacher; but that had always been regarded by Davy and me as a mere prelude to casting off the lines in our schooner *Grey Goose*, and the teaching not only didn't begin to fill the hollow but it wasn't a direction. There was God, of course: I prayed, I sought to do His will; but what *was* His will for me? Where was I going? If He would not provide a direction, then nothing beckoned ahead. The hollow.

I went about the duties and the ordinary pleasures of life, often with enjoyment. I taught my classes with animation and enjoyed that. But there's a peculiar thing about teaching: it uses only a part of the mind, though it uses that part intensely, to the exclusion of all else; and after teaching, there is a sense of coming back to one-self. Coming back, for me, to the hollow. At all events, classroom teaching occupied but two hours a day. I talked with and encour-aged students, and spent good hours with friends. I squired ladies about. I went to church. But the hollow remained.

Unconsciously, I suppose, I was casting about for something to fill that hollow, something to give me a new sense of purpose. Many men in my position would have bounded back into matri-mony, perhaps because it was the *state* of matrimony, rather than a unique individual, they were missing—a warmth in their bed, a sympathetic listener, and breakfast on the table—a woman, prefer-ably attractive. And indeed there was no dearth of sympathetic ladies, often themselves widowed. But it was a Davy-shaped hol-low and the thousand sharings, not just the sympathetic ear and the warmth: it was the incredible closeness, the deep knowing. How could that be with another?

We had worn the grey-goose rings—a grey goose flying over stylized ocean waves under a blue star. We had chosen the grey goose as our symbol because the grey goose, if its mate is killed, flies on alone for the rest of its life. I was mindful of that. But we, in those pagan days, had not intended there to *be* any rest of life: we would go together or follow one another.

But now, in the Obedience to God, I must live. And in my own mind I was not vowed to singleness—a new situation had arisen with Christianity. And there were, in fact, two women I was close to, both about my age. One lady, a lady indeed, linked to the fa-mous first families of Virginia, was gay and charming, and I went with her to many a party and country afternoon. And the other, whom I sometimes called the Blue Butterfly, was a steadfast friend, who had lost her husband in circumstances not dissimilar to Davy's death, making a bond between us; she and I talked deeply and honestly as well as journeying together to places as far re-moved as the island of St Pierre and New Orleans; she was a cheerful, humorous, and valiant companion. I thought indeed of marriage (as they did); but I also thought of Davy, grey goose, and the Shining Barrier. And there was no marriage.

When Flurry, my light-hearted collie, died, I would not have a dog again for a dozen years. By analogy and in proportion I might be ready for another wife in a dozen decades. Or might not.

What I did wish, in vain, was that Davy and I had had a child. A daughter, who would grow up looking like her mother, would have been a delight. But even better a son, with Davy's eyes perhaps, to go adventuring with. Although we intended never to have children, we were in a sense deferring a child in our adventurous days, sailing in *Grey Goose*, travelling to Yale and Oxford. Whether we were right to defer a child, I think now that we were wrong by God's law to *intend* no children. But in my wishing that we had had one, my thoughts adverted often to an incident that I was later to regret not including in *A Severe Mercy*.

It happened when Davy was first mildly ill, before we dreamt that the sickness was to kill her. Her belly was a bit swollen (it was fluid, but we didn't know), and we were concerned. And then one day, there at Mole End, she mentioned that she had not had her period. That and the swollen belly snapped together in my mind, and I exclaimed: "Good lord, Davy! Could you be *preggers?!*" And in that moment, looking at each other with a wild surmise, we believed it. *That* would explain her mysterious malaise. What were we to do about it? At Oxford in becoming Christian we had known that all our pagan ways had to be re-examined, including our stand on no children. That's what Ladywood was to be, a re-examining. But now re-examining was upon us in the matter of a child. It was done in an instant. Abortion—for Christians—was unthinkable. We accepted that supposed baby as God's will. We would have it and *keep* it. It was a decision, an act of will, a submission to God. Even though the pregnancy was a brief delusion, I am glad we so decided. Was it a sort of atonement?

When I now look back to those years immediately after the Second Death, they seem both pleasant and purposeless. I could laugh and joke and enjoy myself, and I cared about the integrity of my teaching. But what I search my memory for is anything that stirred my mind beyond the pleasant pattern of my days or the performance of my duty; and I do not find much, not even little things, that made me want to act—that made me care about something.

There was one small thing, I remember, that stirred me a little. I became impatient, even angry, with the widespread misuse of the terms 'England' and 'Britain'—references to "Shakespeare's Britain", instead of England, for instance. Behind the anger was my love for England—the great name of England—a love that began when I was taken there as a boy, a love that deepened through English books and English poetry. And of course through Oxford— Oxford was England. And Britain was the name of a province of the Roman Empire; and Britons were chaps that painted their faces blue and worshipped the mistletoe. 'Britain' wasn't even the correct geographical designation, which was *Great* Britain, and even that didn't include Northern Ireland. It made me very sad that the splendid name of England was being forgotten, though no one forgets Scotland or the Scotch (the *English* word for the folk of Scotland). I was, I recall, stirred enough to deliver a fiery lecture to all my classes on what is England. It's a small thing, not nearly so important as sanctity or church reunion—but it was what stirred my interest. I repeated the lecture in other years, and finally condensed it into a letter to the Book Review of *The New York Times*:

Forever England

To the Editor:

I write to you in behalf of England...a country south of Scotland and east of Ireland commonly called Britain. It is mentioned in Shakespeare and in other ancient writings. It is thought to have some connection with our language.

Your reviewers are in no danger of forgetting the name of Scotland. They wallow in the name of Ireland. But the great name "England" is in danger of being swallowed by "Britain." The Irish are always "Irishmen" (even when they're Anglo-Irish). The Scotch (a perfectly good English word) are always "Scotsmen."...But who is an "Englishman" anymore? When I see Shakespeare called a Briton, or see a reference to "British cockneys," or read that a lady traveled in Scotland and then in Britain, I know it can't be long before someone will raise the battle cry, "St. George for Merry Britain!"

Although the Act of Union occurred in 1707...England remained the national designation (except in formal documents) until well into the twentieth century. Nelson's signal from HMS *Victory* at Trafalgar was that "England expects every man to do his duty." In 1914, the headline in your own newspaper read: "ENGLAND DECLARES

WAR."...Now, a book published in London as "England Expects" appears in the United States as "Decision at Trafalgar"—apparently, on the assumption that the average American no longer knows where England is.

It is ENGLAND, not Britain, that is the Mother of Parliaments: Parliament is as English as the Kirk is Scotch, which is what Charles I didn't understand. It is England that "muddles through," as well as losing every battle but the last one.... There are, of course, colorful, fascinating things that derive from "the Celtic fringe": the pipers and kilts of Scotland, the song-and-poetry festivals of Wales...and (Mother of God!), the Irishness that is Ireland. No one is in any danger of forgetting them. *Those* things are never called "British." What Churchill described as the "self-denying ordinance," seems to apply only to the English.

We in America are not bound by that ordinance. In Heaven's name, let us remember what is forever England...the Beefeaters at the Tower, the lovely gentle country, the pub, the Rolls, the bells of London, the vicar on the village street, Oxford...the deep sense of fair play, the stubborn love of freedom...the thousand other things that belong to the country that shaped us.

Such a flicker—or perhaps a flash—of love and anger, while it represented a slight involvement in and caring about something in the present, was not of course filling the hollow place except momentarily. Still, it was a sort of promise of the future—not that I thought of it in that light. I did think at times of writing a novel—I had long had it in mind to attempt to create a living, breathing heroine—but I was not yet interested enough to embark on any major literary enterprise. Perhaps I never should be.

There was another stirring of my literary imagination in this period—my imagination and my sense of humour. At Oxford in the early years of this same decade I had written my book—*The Glittering Illusion*—on *English Sympathy for the Southern Confederacy*.* In it I had sketched out a little fantasy on what might have happened if that intense English 'Southernness' had led England to intervene on the side of the South, as might easily have happened. I myself had been a 'Confederate' since boyhood, as suggested in *A Severe Mercy* by the Confederate battleflag in my room at Glenmerle. This strong Southern sympathy was not lessened by the ex-

* The Southren Press (*The Southren Partisan*), P.O. Box 11708, Columbia, SC.

perience, when I was in school at Staunton, of meeting an old man who had been one of the valiant VMI cadets who fought for Virginia at New Market forty-five miles away, and hearing his stories. And at school my Georgian roommate and I had defended the South against the Yankees.

Now it occurred to me to turn that little fantasy into a mock-historical, mock-scholarly exercise in 'whatifery'; and this I did, with a grin, though I made no effort to publish it. (It was published years later in *The Southern Partisan* as "The World After the South Won.") Although it has little to do, seemingly, with the pilgrimage to God, I think it ought to be included in this book as another side of the pilgrim, and a smile along the way. Anyhow, I think the line between the secular and the sacred is not as sharp as is sometimes thought. And the Confederate side of me, not elsewhere shown, makes my later thoughts on the racial struggle more meaningful. Moreover, it shows that, despite the hollow, humour and imagination were not dead.

Davy and I had laughed at the original sketch in Oxford days, and I hope the reader will smile with us. Most people like 'what-if' stories, especially if told with straight-faced humour. And if there's to be "Something to offend everybody" in this book, I may be able to offend a die-hard Yankee or two.

In the story that follows, the reader should note that the short Part I describes the actual state of English sentiments without exaggeration, and the then-not-unlikely 'what-if' fantasy is in Part II. It is, we shall imagine, a British historian of our day writing in Oxford, well known to be (in Matthew Arnold's words) "the home of lost causes and forsaken beliefs...and impossible loyalties." But 'our day' is very different because, with the assistance of Great Britain, the Confederacy won her independence and the subsequent history of the world was changed.

The quotations in Part II, like those in Part I, are genuine; but see the notes for the context.

After the South Won

Richmond Enquirer

| VOL. XXV | JULY 4, 1863 | NO. 5 |

LEE WINS AT GETTYSBURG
WASHINGTON FALLS
NORTH SUES FOR PEACE

Part One: The Historical Position in 1862

In that year the balance of the bayonets on the battlefields of North America was plainly falling on the Southern side, owing to the genius of General Lee. In England, watching with the absorbed attention that had never waned after *The Times'* vivid account of the battle near Washington at Manassas and the passions aroused by the *Trent* affair, everyone knew that English recognition of the Confederate States and even intervention were more than a possibility.

Many of the "educated million", deeply sympathetic to the South, expected action by the Government at any moment. Powerful men, who believed that the traditional English way of life would be endangered by a Northern success, endeavoured to force the Cabinet to ensure Confederate independence. Others, deeply stirred by the valiant struggle of the South, urged England to help it as they had helped freedom fighters in Greece and Italy. Countless appeals stressed the same points: The South is English, unlike the North which has become mongrel through immigration. Moreover, the South is led by gentlemen—English gentlemen—and the war is (as one columnist summed up the general sentiment) an affair of "Gentlemen vs Cads." The Southerners, our kinsmen, have proved by their indomitable spirit that they are worthy of independence; England must abide her traditions and help them.

A. J. B. Beresford Hope, the brother-in-law of the Marquess of Salisbury, wrote: "I declare that the cause of the South is the cause of freedom, the cause of those principles of constitutional government which we desire to see prevailing all over the world...If we made allowances for Italy, should we not be willing to make equal allowances for our own flesh and blood...who are trying to raise up a new English nation...? They have passed the Red Sea—shall we never give them a hand that they may reach the promised land?"[1] Such an appeal, it would seem, could not be made in vain. Indeed, that keen French observer of the English scene, Louis Blanc, wrote for his paper in France early in 1862: "I say...without hesitation, because I think it to be a fact, that everything here [in England] is preparing for a signal recognition of the Southern States."[2] Thus when Gladstone, one of "the Triumvirate" that led the Cabinet, told the wildly cheering crowd at Newcastle that Jefferson Davis had made, not only an Army and a Navy but a *Nation*, it was held to be tantamount to Recognition. As the pro-Northern *Spectator* said: "We cannot...blame the Cabinet. They have only followed the lead of the people, and followed it at far distance. The educated million in England, with here and there an exception, have become unmistakably Southern...[T]he Cabinet has made up its mind that the American struggle is over, and that henceforward two nations must exist on the American continent."[3] Far from disagreeing with *The Spectator*, Louis Blanc was inclined to suspect that Gladstone was "courting popularity" by appealing to the universal Southern feeling; Gladstone's words, he said, "went straight to the heart of the nation," which responded with a great cry of "Down with the North! The South for ever!"[4] All England awaited the next move.

Part Two: The Then-Probable

All England awaited the next move. There was not long to wait. The Cabinet, after, in Lord Acton's words, "taking one of the most momentous resolutions ever adopted by a Ministry,"[5] were now prepared to move swiftly. The Newcastle speech was delivered on October 7th, 1862, and on the first day of November England and France, which had long advocated such a joint move, proposed mediation to the warring American nations. It was a favourable moment, for, as

Gladstone had observed in his Memorandum to the Cabinet, "fortunes have been placed for the moment in *equilibrio* by the failure of the main invasions on both sides."[6] That the Confederate States would gratefully accept the good offices of the European powers and the United States belligerently refuse them had been expected by the Ministry. Both the acceptance and the rejection were by the 25th of November in the hands of Lord John Russell, the Foreign Secretary. But, as he himself had said earlier, if the North refused mediation, England would have no alternative but to recognise the South. On the first day of December, therefore, the Queen's Proclamation recognising the Confederate States of America was issued, to be followed by that of France and other powers. It was at this juncture there occurred the famous dialogue between the Foreign Secretary and the United States Minister in which his lordship endeared himself to generations of schoolboys by uttering what has become, by reason of its brevity, his most memorable remark. Making his final call before sailing, Minister Adams said stiffly: "It would be superfluous in me to point out to your Lordship that this is war."[7] Rising to show that the interview was over, his lordship said: "Damme! Quite!"

The events which followed are familiar to everyone. The welcome tidings of their recognition reached the Confederate States on December 12th, and on the following day Lee's army, no doubt heartened by the news, crushed the enemy at Fredericksburg. Nevertheless, the United States, refusing even in defeat to accept what all the world could see must be accepted, declared war—with a courage that was as admirable as it was foolish—on both England and France. It was regrettable but, as Lord Palmerston, the Prime Minister, said, "not perhaps a very formidable thing for England and France combined."[8]

And the editor of *The Times* wrote to Russell that "the whole Army, Navy, and Volunteers are of one mind and all mad for service in America. For once, the Navy has been found ready when wanted; as to the Army, we might recruit each company into a battalion if necessary."[9] The Government, though, intended to leave the operations on land in the capable hands of the Confederates, merely reinforcing the troops in Canada. But there was work for the Navy. As Winston Churchill observed in his study of this war, "The Northern blockade could not be maintained even for a day in the face of the immense naval power of Britain"; and, as he also wrote, "The Northern forces at New Orleans were themselves immediately cut off and forced to capitulate."[10] This event caused huge celebrations in London, less because an old defeat was thus avenged than because of the summary hanging of General "Beast" Butler from the yardarm of the Royal Navy flagship.

We need not linger over the subsequent events of the war. Despite another grave defeat at Chancellorsville in the spring of 1863 and a growing peace party in the North, the United States continued to resist and even to make preparations to send an expedition into Canada. The Cabinet, therefore, decided to avert such an invasion, if possible, by reinforcing the Confederate armies. Two months later General Lee led his veteran army across the United States frontier into Pennsylvania, and the British Expeditionary Force, which had just been landed in Virginia, were sent to join him. Before they reached the scene, Lee had joined battle with a large American army near the village of Gettysburg.

Winston S. Churchill, in his thoughtful study, "If Lee Had Not Won the Battle of Gettysburg," has shown how close an affair it really was. The crucial moment came on the third day when Lee ordered an attack on the strong Northern centre. Pickett and the Virginians swept forward into their deathless charge. But, gallant as it was, we know now that the Union fire would almost certainly have so cut down the Virginians that they would have been unable to hold the position if they had gained it. But in one of those timely arrivals that suggest the workings of Providence, the British brigades, having been apprised of the tactical disposition by units of Stuart's cavalry, were, just at the moment of the launching of Pickett's charge, driving into the Union rear, led by the Coldstream Guards. The resulting panic of the entire Union left as the English and the Virginians joined hands, cutting the U.S. army into two, led to Meade's surrender. The field was won—and the war as well. The formal surrender was on the fourth of July—Confederate Independence Day—even as Stuart was riding into Washington. Three days later the Allies entered Washington unopposed. And a fortnight later the United States Government at the new Capital in Portland, Maine, yielded to the universal cry for peace and capitulated.

It is not necessary to examine the generous terms of peace that the Allies imposed. Our concern is rather with the effects of the victory on the Allies themselves. The Confederacy was now independent, and England had now a firm friend in the new world. As Churchill put it, "Gladstone achieved not merely the recognition but an abiding alliance between Great Britain and the Southern States."[11] It was an alliance destined to become even closer when the South became, somewhat later, a member of the British Commonwealth, and its President became Prime Minister, with a Royal Governor to open the Parliament at Richmond in the name of the Queen.

In England one of the first effects of the victory was that John Bright and indeed the "Manchester School" lost such influence as they possessed. It was widely recognised that they had supported the brutal attempt of the United States to conquer the Confederacy in hopes of gaining power through the working classes. But these had not been much impressed; the great heart of England was sound in this struggle between Northern conquest and Southern freedom. One historian has, we may notice, suggested that the failure of the working classes to raise a cry for Government action in the great cotton famine might be interpreted as sympathy for the North or for the doctrines of John Bright; but the fact that in Liverpool—the most Confederate city outside the Confederacy—no sympathizer with the United States could even hold a job—tells against the interpretation. It is surely far more probable, as most historians agree, that their quiet was simply the proverbial patience of the British working man and his trust in the Queen's Government—which, as the event demonstrated, was very well founded indeed.

The decline of the "Manchester School" was but a sign of the underlying reality of the discrediting of the doctrine they had preached: the universal suffrage that must lead to that tyranny of the majority de Tocqueville had warned against and the Southern States had suffered from. The general recognition that it was a dangerously unsound doctrine was decisively shown in England by the overwhelming failure of the Reform Bill of 1867. We today who perceive the fatal flaw, the lack of balance, in the doctrine that three dockers should outweigh the duke and the don—that, so to speak, the pawns should take the knights and the castles—may wonder how some Englishmen in the 1860s could even have considered it; but it must be remembered that the United States before the War of Northern Aggression had held forth a beguiling if specious promise of prosperity as well as proclaiming a spurious "liberty" that was, in fact, not liberty but equality. And our present concept of a balanced society in which the major elements—the business interest, the working classes of the cities, and the rural people—are equally represented, regardless of numbers, which may be called true equality, and each with that veto upon the others that is so sure a protection to minorities: such a concept was then scarcely a dream.

It must indeed be regarded as one of the fruits of that great victory upon the plains of Pennsylvania, a victory now regarded as the most decisive since Waterloo. Some, in fact, believe it to be *more* important: Lord Acton, more aware than most people of the corruption of power, including that of the majority, said that he rejoiced more deeply over the stake won by the South at Gettysburg than that saved at Waterloo.[12]

Another result of that victory has been the firm establishment of the principle of self-determination, to which even the United States and Russia now give assent. An equally important result of the victory was, as the Confederate Commissioner to London, J. M. Mason—Sir James as he became—had promised, the gradual ending of slavery. It was in 1875 that the Southern Prime Minister, Lord Arlington—or, to use a more familiar designation, General Lee—announced that the several states had agreed that all slaves born after the last day of 1879 would be free; and the Confederacy thereupon embarked on the benign programme of slowly raising the Negro to the limits of his ability. A few years later the United States also emancipated the small number of slaves in their territories. We can only be grateful that emancipation of the slaves in the South came about in this way and that the sinister Emancipation Proclamation of President Lincoln—an invitation to the slaves to rise against their masters, or more precisely their mistresses, since the men were with the army—had no effect. Lincoln, himself, an inherently kindly man, has confessed in his *Apology for My Administration* (Portland, 1871) that he was deeply thankful that the slaves did not rise.

One more result of the Allied victory at Gettysburg must not be neglected: the complete discrediting of that barbarism in warfare that marked the efforts of the Americans to subdue the Southerners—the barbarism of Generals Sherman and Sheridan and "Beast" Butler. It is to be hoped that no civilised nation will again make use of such methods. There is, indeed, reason to hope that no civilised nation will again resort to war of any sort. In the nearly fifty years of world peace which have followed the Great War or One Year War of 1914-1915 when the Allies so completely defeated Germany—a victory, incidentally, that might not have been so swiftly won but for the Confederate divisions under the second Marquess of Arlington—the Kaisers appear to have relinquished their dreams of militaristic glory.

These, then, are some of the things that such far-sighted Englishmen as Beresford Hope and the many other supporters of the South fought for on the lecture platform and with the pen while General Lee and the Army of Northern Virginia fought so gallantly in the field. The world owes them a great deal. Had these dedicated English supporters of the South not perceived what was at issue, England might not have acted; and there is a real possibility—though many historians will disagree—that if England had remained neutral, the United States with their vast resources might have conquered the South and occupied it as an inferior province. All in all they had a remarkably clear vision of what was at stake. And these things were at issue when Lord Palmerston's Ministry took their most momentous decision. They were at issue when, in Winston Churchill's resounding words, the Allies "by a deathless feat of arms broke the Union front at Gettysburg and laid open a fair future to the world."[13]

Notes

I   1 Hope, *The Social and Political Bearings of the American Disruption* (London 1863) pp 5–6, 42.

     2 Blanc, *Letters on England*, 2 vol (transl.) (London 1866) vol 1, p 263.

     3 In J. F. Rhodes, *History of the United States*, 8 vol (N. Y. 1920) vol 4, p 340.

     4 Blanc, *op. cit.*, v 2, pp 176-178.

II   5 Lord Acton was of course referring to the Ministry's decision not to act.

     6 P. Guedalla, *Gladstone and Palmerston* (London 1928) (Letters) p 244.

     7 Adam's oft-quoted remark was made on a later occasion in connection with the naval rams built for the Confederacy. Russell no doubt made his remark to somebody.

     8 E. Ashley, *The Life of...Palmerston*, 2 vol (London 1876) v 2, p 210.

     9 *The History of The Times*, p 373.

    10 W. S. Churchill, "If Lee Had Not Won the Battle of Gettysburg" in *If It Had Happened Otherwise* (Ed., J. C. Squire) London 1931.

    11 *Ibid.*

    12 D. S. Freeman, *R. E. Lee*, 4 vol (NY and London 1935) v 4, p 517, quoting a letter from Lord Acton to Lee in which he, in fact, said that Lee had fought the battle of English freedom and concluded: "I mourn for the stake which was lost at Richmond more deeply than I rejoice over that which was saved at Waterloo."

    13 W. S. Churchill, *op. cit.*

An Afterword:

Why Didn't the British Intervene?

A German general, von Bernhardi (quoted by W. A. Dunning, *The British Empire and the United States*, London, 1914, p xxxii) said: "England committed the unpardonable blunder, from her point of view, of not supporting the Southern States in the American War of Secession." Few historians, either English or American, now suppose England's neutrality to have been a blunder in the way they regard England's passivity to the rise of Hitler as a blunder; but it must be supposed that had England ensured Southern independence, that action would now be celebrated in London and Richmond and largely approved by historians. The most that can be said is that from the point of view of the "educated million" of *that* England of the mid-19th century it was a blunder. The War of American Independence was won because of the assistance of France. The War of Southern Independence could almost certainly have been won with the assistance of England. Whether that would have been for the better or worse, in the long run, no man can say—only opine, more or less fiercely.

An equally intriguing question that may be raised by this exercise in what might have been is this: if the "educated million" in England were, as described by Louis Blanc and *The Spectator* and as shown by Beresford Hope and Lord Acton, so passionately Southern, and if Lord Palmerston's Ministry (with the firm support of France) were so close to action, why didn't they? This writer has pondered that question in his Oxford thesis, *English Sympathy for the Southern Confederacy* and is convinced that the brilliant success of the Southern army under Lee convinced the Ministry, *The Times*, and much of the "educated million", that the South must inevitably win anyway. "The Glittering Illusion" is the title of the referenced thesis; and it is precisely the illusion, held right up to 1865, that the North's effort to reconquer the South was doomed.

The most significant bit of writing of this period came about at the very end of it—almost by chance. Although I was an Anglican, I had begun to go to the small ecumenical Church of the Covenant (although continuing to go to my Anglican Church for communion) because it seemed to me that there was in it a lively life in Christ that reminded me of Oxford days and the Studio: a real interest in talking about Christ and the meaning of the Christian walk.

One day the minister, the Reverend Beverly Cosby—he was known to some of us as the 'Rev-Bev'—asked several of us to write a page or two on how we became Christians or became alive Christians. I don't know whether the others wrote more than a paragraph, but I became interested and wrote at considerable length about my still-recent conversion at Oxford—thus preserving for the far-in-the-future *A Severe Mercy* memories that might otherwise have been forgotten.

The paper was entitled *Encounter with Light*, and the 'Rev-Bev' was sufficiently impressed with it that the Church had it printed as a small, thirty-page book or booklet, anonymous and uncopyrighted, after I had written to C. S. Lewis and got his permission to use the first three of his letters to me in it. Some thousands of these little books were given away by the Church of the Covenant, and people wrote from as far away as India for copies. (It was later published also by Wheaton College, still uncopyrighted though no longer anonymous, and more thousands were given away.) Since, with regard to my future writings and with regard, even more, to the building of the Kingdom, this is my main writing of the period, I shall quote the first few paragraphs from the first of the three tiny chapters of *Encounter with Light*. These paragraphs represent the real beginning of the pilgrimage.

The Light Obscured

The beginning of conversion was, I suppose, the moment that I abandoned my childhood Christianity and became a small, fierce atheist—in the name of truth. There seems to be in the lives of many rather thoughtful and independent persons a progress of three steps: first, abandonment, often rebellious, of an imperfectly understood, childish Christianity, held only on adult authority; second, reacceptance, very gradually, of many of the moral principles and some of the insights of Christianity; and, third, conversion to the faith. But, of course, each step may be one's last. The necessity of this process is explained by the aphorism: 'To believe with certainty, one must begin by doubting.'

By doubting, then, and by abandoning a seemingly inadequate Christianity that I had never, so to speak, believed on my own, I had taken a first step towards real belief. Perhaps any belief that one has not thought one's own way to is inadequate. But, in addition, there were four specific inadequacies in the only Christianity I knew: it was not exciting, not positive, not big enough, and not related to life.

It was not exciting: The Greeks in history, with their passion for truth and beauty, lucid as a sunlit Doric temple above the wine-dark sea, were exciting; astronomy, with its blazing stars and icy distances, was exciting; poetry, reaching for beauty in words of splendour, was exciting; but this Christianity, with its fragmented accounts of dark and incomprehensible deeds in Palestine and its solemn, humourless voices, was too stuffy for excitement, too dull for tears.

It was not positive: The Christians dying in the Roman arena had died *for* something; the crusader knights riding under the cross of gold had fought *for* something; but this Christianity did not preach the crusade—the cross led only to respectability. Indeed, the message seemed to be, mainly, that one was bad if one did any of quite a long list of things, such as saying 'Damn!' or missing church or drinking any of the joyous, sunny wine that Our Lord had made at Cana—indeed, the churches 'improved' on the innocent Jesus by rejecting the glowing wine that was His chosen symbol of the Eucharist in favour of solemn tinned grape juice. It was all negative and on the whole repressive; one was not working for something, except perhaps new chairs for the Sunday School and, of course, a rather dull Heaven—though the occasions when someone presumably attained Heaven were ones of unmitigated gloom.

It was not big enough: This Christianity was simply not big enough to include all the worlds that swung about our sun and all the worlds that might swing about a million racing suns in the chilling immensities of space; how could the redemption of Earth, in so far as it was redeemed, be related to Aldebaran or the spiral nebulae? This Christianity, then, was too little to be the truth.

Finally, it was not related to life: Outside the church doors beat the turbulence and crookedness and splendour of life. What had the churches got to say about it? With respect to war and arms, the voice of this Christianity was a feeble mutter. It was against sin, to be sure; but the businessmen who practised a dog-eat-dog ethic six days a week were well received at the altar rail—and at the collection plate. Nor was anyone ever rebuked for coming to the altar when she was well known not to be on speaking terms with someone else in the church. Nor was anyone ever turned away for pride. On the other hand, to be fair, it was clear that one oughtn't to say 'Damn!' And there *were* some people who would not be welcomed at the altar rail: the dark-skinned. Who could believe that here in this stuffiness, with all the beauty and laughter and pain of life held at bay outside the church—who could believe that here were the truths of life and death? I could not, and I doubted whether anyone else did. I turned away from this religion and declared for atheism.

Such a relief! What freedom! And atheism was exhilarating: if the gods were dead, then man was the highest. Glorious! And it was a belief totally opposed to that impossible Christianity—a strong, bold creed. But *what* had I said? A belief? A creed? There was the flaw in atheism: one must *believe* in no-god. It, too, is a faith. There is no evidence and, certainly, no revelation; and, by the nature of the case, there can be none. So—I renounced atheism.

From the renunciation of juvenile atheism to agnosticism—not knowing. But with the not knowing, I found—Davy and I found—a truly pagan worship of love and beauty that became, more and more, a theism, a belief that Something underlay the universe. And then at last Christianity. The three full steps of *Encounter with Light*.

The great dream that Davy and I had held and worked towards in our pagan years was that of a schooner under the wind, the schooner *Grey Goose*; and we had not abandoned that dream when we became Christians. Our little ship, wandering the seven seas, was to us, not only a way to the beauty of the world of nature but a step towards the timeless: the time-free life we longed for. We had the schooner indeed, just before Oxford, but we considered her to be the last forerunner of the off-soundings *Grey Goose* that would be our home afloat. The coming of Christ into our lives had caused us to feel a little confused about the relationship of Christianity and the *Grey Goose* dream. We could see no obstacle to their being united, yet we felt that we must talk it through in the new light of the Faith—but death intervened before we could do so.

Now, after the grief had passed, the question sharply re-presented itself to me. Should I go sailing? *Could* I ever sail again—it was *our* dream—without her? Would it be breaking the faith or keeping it? At moments, passionately, I said, "Without her, no, never, never!"

But the grey goose when its mate is killed flies on alone: that is, it doesn't stop flying; it does fly on. And I had a sort of longing for salt water and a tiller in my hand and the great sails above. Should I go sailing? I remembered the peace in the time of sorrow that came out of doors in the country and the wind. Should I have *Grey Goose* again? Should I cast off the lines of the academic life and head for the blue horizon and the far islands, outward bound? All that—the finding of the ship and readying her for sea and then the going forth—would it not fill the hollow, fill it with beauty and adventure?

Long years before I ever met Davy, when I was still in boarding school, my roommate and closest friend, Johnny, was a soft-speaking Georgian. He and I talked as boys will of high adventure. Sometimes it was of high adventure in the past, fighting perhaps for the Confederacy. One afternoon, both of us booted and spurred after a cavalry charge on the school horses, we talked of how great it would have been to ride with Stuart and the Virginian cavalry. But mostly we talked of adventures we might find in our present world. I still see his grin and enthusiasm, met no doubt by my own. Masefield has a phrase that fitted Johnny, "a laughing fellow rover"—and we were resolved to go a-roving.

Finally, we decided to run away from school. We would steal rides on freight trains and trucks and make our way to Mexico where, without a doubt, grand adventures would befall. And so we laid our plans. And then one night, with all adventure in our hearts, we did it. We stole out into the night and moved stealthily along the lake front. A half mile away a road approached the lake, and there at two o'clock in the morning we were to rendezvous with a sympathetic taxi driver, who in our innocence we trusted (of course he told the headmaster), and he would drive us to a nearby town where we could find a southbound freight train. But when we arrived at the rendezvous, some husky masters leaped out of the bushes and collared us; and a day or two later we were sent down from school—and Johnny, best of friends, to his death, diving a few months after he got home into icy water to save a small boy. He might as well have gone adventuring.

As for me, I was met by my father who greeted me in a decidedly old-fashioned manner (though, as I learnt long after, with a private chuckle). I used this time of rustication—I was to return later to the Academy—for various sorts of naughtiness. My main activity was to learn to fly, very secretly (I had saved tips from uncles and grandparents) in a highly maneuverable Waco F biplane.

After I had gone back to my school in order to leave it in a more orthodox fashion, I entered college; and there I found a fellow flyer and comrade, Bob. We promptly constituted ourselves as Squadron 13, and entered upon a brief career of somewhat reckless aerial deeds. These consisted of stunt-flying, hedge-hopping, barnstorming, and all but rolling our wheels along the tops of speeding express trains, culminating in our diving three or four times into a football stadium and scattering cards in behalf of our college team. This led, after a stiff interview with our Dean, to our being, very properly, grounded for half a year by the federal authorities. But what we actually did is not so important, since we killed neither ourselves nor anybody else, as what we dreamt of doing.

Bob, the co-commander of the Squadron, was another laughing fellow rover; and our talk was all of adventure in far places. We longed to hit what Kipling called "the long trail"—the trail that led to the far places, the primitive places, the places back of beyond; the trail that was the disappearing wake of a tramp steamer heading for the Southern Cross. Then, before World War II, the places back of beyond still existed. And our own symbol was a plane, a biplane that could land on any beach or meadow—wings over the Andes. Adventure beckoned. To many of our college friends, heading for business careers, we were mad; but we meant it: we were going to take the long trail.

But then Davy came into my life, and I was falling in love with her. What now of the Squadron and the long trail? She thought it romantic and wanted to come, too; but I knew that couldn't be. I wrote an anguished essay called "Squadron versus Apron Strings". Davy didn't care for it. Neither did my unsympathetic professor who gave it a lower mark than my essays usually got. It has long since deservedly perished: but the title says all. A conflict that many a man has wrestled with. Davy of course won.

So did I; but something perhaps was lost, too.

Davy and I discovered the *Grey Goose* dream—a little sailing vessel wandering in the far places. I persuaded myself that the long trail could happily be combined with marriage. Davy, surely, was a laughing fellow rover, in so far as we roved. This was a better thing.

Undoubtedly it *was* a better thing. But it was not the *same* thing, *not* the long trail. Nor was Davy, dear and brave and cheerful though she was, a laughing fellow rover as Masefield meant the words: he meant the comradeship of men. Friendship.

C. S. Lewis in *The Four Loves* says that *Eros*—inloveness—is *like* pure *agape* in that, for the moment, the lover puts another in the centre of his being, but it is *not* pure *agape*: Heavenly love is not so easily won. Similarly, inloveness contains something that is *like* friendship, but it is *not*. Lovers, marvelling, gaze at one another; friends stand shoulder to shoulder gazing at what absorbs them both, which may be fishing or chess or a vision of art. Or the hazardous quest for a lost gold mine or blowing up an enemy redoubt. It is where the gaze is that determines inloveness or friendship. No doubt friendship may exist between a man and a woman, who are not attracted to one another, but it is apt to be superseded by *Eros* at any moment.

Now, in this time following the grief, I thought about the long trail again and the laughing fellow rover. What I thought was that it *cannot* be combined with marriage or indeed with women as fellow voyagers. One can be reckless with one's own life, but not with the life of a beloved—and frail—wife. She, as a female, is vulnerable, terribly so; and her lover, therefore, is vulnerable through her. A beloved woman is the Achilles heel of the adventurer. Davy and I might have sailed the seas together, but not to adventure, except inadvertently. I should have steered away from danger that with a friend I might have risked. The sort of thing Johnny and I had boyishly dreamt of, and Bob and I had planned, is a thing for two or three men. Comrades, not lovers. Men in the pride of their strength, each risking his life on his own. Women may not like my saying this, but it is so. Even a woman who is not one's beloved is in her vulnerability—her frailty and her femaleness and her otherness—a call to the male protective instinct or chivalry to shield her or rescue her, not infrequently at the cost of men's own lives. Indeed, deep down, she—even if she's a feminist—*expects* protection. We, both sexes, are unwise to deny anything so basic.

Females in peril, of course, are the very stuff of high romance—Sir Lancelot thundering through the dawn mists to snatch Guinevere from the flames. But her *being* there in peril may ruin the quest for the lost gold mine or the Golden Fleece or bring down the towers of Camelot. The knight or the adventurer or the expedition turns aside to rescue the female who, often enough, shouldn't have been there to be imperiled. Not, certainly, as a comrade on the long trail.

Friendship, to be sure, is also a great love; and a man will risk or lay down his life for a friend in a tight place. But no man wants a woman even to get near a tight place. The long trail is a man's thing. Men's comradeship. No matter how people delude themselves—as I did in thinking that our *Grey Goose* dream was the same as the long trail, and as women constantly do—it is a man's thing.

But now, Davy being ineluctably gone from me, it was no longer a choice, no longer 'Squadron versus Apron Strings', no longer men's friendship versus the deep closeness of spouses in union. Should I now take *Grey Goose* to sea, outward bound? Should I be able to support myself by teaching here and there or by writing? Was I now, having turned forty, too old? Above all, would the adventure and beauty and comradeship of the long trail fill, or partly fill, the hollow at the centre of me? I knew, sadly, that the world was becoming more and more a world without unspoiled far places and without innocence. After all, a far island with TV sets and cokes and snarled traffic—or a Marxist government—hardly beckons. Still, it seemed to me that a few corners remained for the wanderer.

I seriously considered it. The small double-ender surfboat from Hawaii that had been our dinghy hung in the garage, the fine liquid-filled compass of *Grey Goose* waited, and the graceful figurehead was above the mantelpiece looking as though she were longing to dip her breasts into the waves. In letters to C. S. Lewis I joked about the "drastic step" that I was contemplating; and, reading one letter over again, I added a postscript that the "drastic step" was not suicide—to his relief, he replied. But I did not tell him what the step was; I would wait until I decided. He would hardly approve, I thought, of a life that was so turned away from libraries.

But that life was beckoning me strongly, and it was the only life, the only life in the realm of the possible, that did beckon me at that time. Glancing over our Yale journal one day, I was compelled by something I had written there:

Somewhere, beyond the buildings that loom against this lowering winter sky, the trade-winds blow, the long blue rollers crash upon the reef in white foam, and a rakish schooner swings, tugging at her anchor. God! what are we doing here?

But of course I never did it. I came very close. I have wondered since—I wonder now—what would have happened if I had taken that "drastic step". That was the moment. What if I had left the college and the Birdhouse and the quiet life of books and set sail, the fine compass by the tiller, the figurehead beneath the pointing bowsprit, and the sails asleep? I firmly believe that God was to command me to write *A Severe Mercy*: would I then, have written it under a palm tree in Tahiti or the Tuamotu? If it were God's will that I write it? But I have a will, too; I might have refused. Yet I could have refused here in the Birdhouse as well as aboard *Grey Goose* swinging at her anchor in a lagoon of *les îles sous le vent*.

At all events, it is a question that cannot ever be answered. I prayed of course about whether to go or stay. I had no inkling of God's will in the matter, but I did not go. Was God's hand in that? And as to what would have happened, as Aslan would point out, it is never given us to know what might have happened on the road not taken. I *might* have written *A Severe Mercy* (inevitably a somewhat different book) under a palm tree not too far from the sounding surf; or perhaps, long before I could have written it, there might have been "a ninth great peaceful wave to drown and roll me under."

I never did finally decide one way or the other between the two roads—"I kept the first for another day" and "way leads on to way"—so I came to a bend that was the '60s, and the hollow was partially filled.

CHAPTER III

Putting the Neighbour First:
The Idealistic Years

These were the wild years—the '60s—wild in most of the senses of that word. Rebellious years, stirring and alive, idealistic and hopeful in the beginning; but later angry, and ugly, and dangerous. The young president with his Peace Corps and his call to ask ourselves what we might do for our country appealed to idealism; and the appeal was in the young voice and songs of Joan Baez; and Martin Luther King touched the chord of idealism. But we shot the young president, the symbol of the laws, and his compassionate brother, and King. Idealism turned to anger and violence and the rip-off and shrill feminism, yet the idealism was there, however obscured by anger, from first to last.

The '60s were that surprising bend in the road that somewhat filled that Davy-shaped hollow. I was caught up in the '60s, involved in the '60s from first to last—though I mightn't have been, or not so completely, but for the hollow.

The decade began properly with its first year, 1961, but (in an idiosyncratic determination of my own) didn't end until 1973: two periods with a good deal of overlapping, and a curious tail. First there was what I call the Idealistic Years until about 1965, then the Angry Years until May of 1971, and then the tail, which was the flight to the country. Of course some people were angry from the first, and others were idealistic and gentle to the end, redeeming the time.

What unified the whole of the '60s (and early '70s) was the people, the same ones all the way, and their strong sense of identity with each other. Once in the later '60s I was driving to Richmond with a friend—a former student—named Bruce, and, as we passed a long-haired, blue-jeaned chap who gave us a wave or a V-sign, Bruce murmured, "One of Our People." That is what unified the

'60s for us who were involved—Our People. And, in very different words no doubt—"One of Them"—unified the folk who were hostile to us.

The Idealistic Years

A fortnight before the '60s actually began, in mid-December 1960, six students from two Lynchburg white colleges and one black one seated themselves at a segregated lunch counter and asked to be served. A sit-in. Service was of course refused, and the six would not leave without it. Consequently they were arrested and dragged off to jail. I had known about it beforehand from the two boys, Terril and Jim, from this college. Indeed, Jim Hunter was to become a permanent friend, one who in youth and in manhood thought independently as well as morally. I went down to the jailhouse to tell them the Dean's ruling that they should not suffer academic penalty for their absence. I also had a big argument, frustrating but finally victorious, with the jailor who was unable to comprehend how they could each need half a dozen textbooks. They could only read one at a time, he pointed out, and they could have that and change it when it was completed.

The Idealistic Years of the '60s had thus for me begun, along with arguments with duly constituted authority and the beginnings of alliance with students: we laughed together at the jailor. In January 1961 I wrote a letter to the Lynchburg newspaper, evidently following one to the college paper. What is written at the time is not subject to the distortions of memory; and this letter was not only a justification of the sit-in but of the whole protest movement of the '60s. The first sentence is extremely ironic.

Editor, *The Daily Advance*:

Sir: It cannot be supposed that *The Advance* would intentionally create a false impression of a person or event in its news columns. Nevertheless, inadvertently, it has done so by describing in summary form a letter of mine that was in the Lynchburg College newspaper. *The Advance* stated that I "took a stand comparing the sit-in movement to the trial of Socrates who was condemned to death for 'not believing in the gods in which the City believes'." This, surely, would suggest to your readers that I took a stand in favour of the sit-in movement (or, just possibly, in favor of serving a cup of hemlock to sitters-in). In point of fact, I did not so much as mention the sit-ins, and I did not imply support of the movement (or of hemlock).

I do, quite firmly, believe that justice *must* be done to the Negro; but my letter was not about the means of obtaining it. My letter dealt with the greater question that has perplexed mankind down the ages: how to deal justly with just men who break the law in the name of justice. Socrates, of course, sought only to lead his fellow citizens to truth and justice. My own position has come to be, after much thought, that a committed, believing Christian *must*—and a true patriot *should*—stand ready to put conscience above the law, if necessary. Surely it is clear by now that the whole crime of the Nazi officials and the German people was, precisely, that they did *not* put conscience above the law. For that they will answer as there's a God in Heaven.

I should like to take this opportunity to say that I have the deepest respect for the English common law on which our law is based and a deep respect for the too-often-abused rights of private property. I abhor lawbreakers. And yet, as a professor of history, I cannot forbear to add that but for massive lawbreaking we should all be both Roman Catholics and subjects of the crown of England. This might or might not be a good thing; but those who hold that it is preferable to be Protestant or American or both are simply *not* in a position to condemn wholeheartedly lawbreakers who put conscience above the law. To be sure, a distinction can be made between safely dead lawbreakers (such as the early Christians, Martin Luther, Thomas Cranmer and Sir Thomas More, John Bunyan, Tom Paine and George Washington, Henry Thoreau, Mahatma Gandhi, and Mister Jefferson) and the live ones who are still dangerous fellows. This distinction would run, as follows: dead—good: live—bad. As a position, it has a certain logic, and it has the supreme merit of being comfortable. Thus those in the past who put conscience above the law and were duly jailed or beheaded may be retained as harmless saints and heroes; but the dangerous ones who do the same thing today may, since they fail to meet the simple requirement of being dead, be roundly condemned. How else, indeed, without this useful distinction, can we of the present day provide heroes who have suffered for their beliefs for the future?

I have the honour to be, sir,
    Your most ob't s'v't

Another student who became a friend was a girl, a senior of much brilliance who was in my classes and came to the Birdhouse with the Christian group. I often thought of her as Helen—the name seemed to fit her somehow. She was tall with luminous eyes and a level glance. In the English history class there had been a good many references to Oxford, and at my house anecdotes about it. Then one day in my office when she was speaking of graduate school, I said casually, "How would you like to go to Oxford? I think we might get you there, you know." She didn't speak—she said afterwards she couldn't—just looked at me with all her eyes. The very thought of Oxford—that remote magic—had overwhelmed her. But she would do anything to get there. And I was inclined to feel that I would do anything to get her there.

So we became dedicated to that end, and we talked and planned all that final semester of her undergraduate years. I liked her immensely and respected her mind. Beyond that though, as a believer in women, I loved the idea of passing on Oxford to a girl—a girl who would appreciate it. Owing to our enthusiastic talks about it, we became very close. And then still closer when she became, after much reading of C. S. Lewis, a believing Christian in March, being confirmed, with the gift of a Prayerbook from me, in my (Episcopal) parish church. We said that she was my daughter-in-Christ (as I referred to her at the end of *Encounter with Light*). To glance ahead, I may say that she did get to Oxford. She won a scholarship, partly no doubt through my eloquent letter of recommendation, that took her, according to our Plan, for the M.A. to a northern college headed by an Oxonian I knew; and then with recommendations from him as well as me, she won another scholarship that took her to Oxford for the D.Phil. But all that lay in her future.

As spring came on, we began to take long drives into the lovely Virginian countryside in the Jaybird, my Triumph two-seater, still talking of Oxford and now of Christ Our Lord. I can't remember a year when there was such a flame of red roses, rambler roses, as there was that May. They were everywhere, particularly along one winding country road that we named the Road of the Roses—indeed, since they lasted all summer and into the autumn, that year could be well named the Year of the Roses.

That spring and that flame of roses lingered in my mind, and when, a year or two later, I began my novel, *Gateway to Heaven*, I brought them into the story. Since that book was written in (and of) the '60s—my major writing of the time—I shall have occasion to quote from it more than once in this chapter and the next. The following excerpt is written by the heroine, Mary (not modelled upon Helen)—she and Richard take turns telling the story. The description of the day, though, fits the actual Maytime.

Then Daddy got out and told us to take the car and enjoy the Maytime. So Richard came round and we drove away, stopping at the gates for the perfect, clear-red rose, and then driving on through the shining Virginian countryside, lovely with new green and red roses and tiny bright-blue indigo buntings flitting across the road like bits of sky. And ahead of us rose the Blue Mountains.

Soon we were climbing the road into the mountains, heading for our meadow where the spring trickles down. The day was fresh and shining, we were in love, and—I was winged! I would run and dance. Not today, but soon. My heart was bursting.

There was the meadow, unchanged. There we looked at the pure lines of the two mountains sweeping up to make the Gateway to Heaven.

In real life that spring, Helen and I marvelled at the beauty of the Maytime and at the goodness and beauty of the Virginian earth as we wandered about in the Jaybird. And we marvelled, too, at what good friends we were, despite two-thirds of a generation separating us. It did not occur to either of us in that lovely May, but I expect we were a bit in love. We saw a friendship based on Oxford and England as well as Virginia, and, even more, on Christianity. Everything seemed to be touched by the Sacred.

In early June she was graduated, pausing for an instant as she came down from the platform to give me, seated among the faculty, a radiant and lovely smile. Whatever I had given her towards her future, she had given me something, too: she had filled for the moment that hollow in me—partly filled: nothing could fill it entirely. And she had given me something else. Not only did she and I relate to one another as though we were the same age, but I had come to know, through her, a number of her closest friends in the same way. And through them, in later years, *their* friends, relating to them less and less as 'a professor' but simply as a fellow voyager through life. And the protest movement, as with Jim Hunter, the chap who went to jail, gave us something to be friends about. Beginning with Helen and Jim, there was a sort of chain all through the '60s and, in many instances, beyond. Old comrades.

The people God gave me to love at this time and place.

In that merry month of May, Helen and I thought we ought to strike a small blow against the one most unforgiveable sort of segregation—at the altar of Christ, He who loved the outcasts of society. Accordingly, we invited a black couple, whose black Episcopal church had warmly welcomed us when we went there, to come to ours. Our sympathetic Rector, whom we warned, asked only not to know the day. When we did bring them, he quite by chance preached powerfully on the evils of segregation. But some of the congregation tip-toed out before the end of the service to avoid greeting the blacks, and some (not all) of those who remained were frigid and hostile.

Next day friends in the church told us what was being said—that we were 'nigger-lovers', that the Rector had put us up to it, that the famous 'outside agitators' had put us up to it. Consequently I wrote to the Rector, a letter to be read to the Vestry. I said that if there was an 'outside agitator' it was either Christ or the Devil. Which did they think it was? The letter continued:

Let me say this clearly: I brought these people because I firmly believe that segregation before the altar of Christ is sin—an offense against Christ's holy laws. It is just possible to make a case of sorts for segregation elsewhere, but it is totally impossible without 'doublethink' (intellectual dishonesty) to believe that Christ would have tolerated it in His Church.

St Paul says (Gal 3:28) that "there is neither Jew nor Greek, neither bond nor free...ye are all one in Christ Jesus." All one—except blacks? Is that what he meant? If you can believe that, you can believe anything. You can believe that black is white—and that will solve the whole problem. St Peter says (Acts 10:28): "God hath shewed me that I should not call any man common or unclean." No man except a black one, he meant? Why not burn your New Testament? The Christian poet Hilaire Belloc wrote a little poem that is worth remembering: "He served his god so faithfully and well / That now he sees him face to face in Hell."

Christ, Our Lord, chose His apostles from among the poor and He loved the outcasts. Respectable society crucified Him because it was offended by Him, as it always is by the *real* Christ. He was not a tame little suburban god, and we must take care that we don't worship false gods. The real Lord Christ, who passed through the world like a flame, would no more have tolerated segregation than He tolerated the money-changers in the Temple. Would you really want to be defending segregation on the day the Lord strode in? Would you want to be tip-toeing out to avoid a black man? How if you met *Him* at the door?

Think, please, of that most terrible verse in the Bible (Matt. 25:45): "Inasmuch as ye did it not to one of the least of these, ye did it not to me." Think of it—and then go on with your icy unwelcome.

We must welcome the Negro in our church with smiling eyes—and we shall have welcomed Jesus. Or we pierce the Negro with the nails of our hostility; but we do it in Hell's name, having helped to crucify the Lord.

If our church is to be a private club of the respectable, then for God's sake let the *Christians* know so that they, black and white, can find an old barn or catacomb and raise there the altar of the crucified Christ.

Despite the letter, one of the Wardens came to call. If we brought those blacks again, he said, it would break up the church. I wanted to say—or perhaps I did—that in that case the real Christians would remain. What I did certainly say was, "All right, I'll give you a choice—you speaking for the Vestry. You all heard my letter. Now, which would you prefer: that I should bring my black friends when they want to come? or that I should leave the church?"

He looked at me with unhappy eyes. Finally he said: "If you put it that way, we have to say that it would be better for you all to leave than to wreck the church." So we did not return to Grace Church, though of course in later years it had to bite the bullet of integration. But it was not the Church showing the way.

At almost this moment, by contrast, a Catholic bishop in North Carolina, a Virginian, simply ordered the black churches there closed, its members to come to the white churches.

Earlier, in connection with my little book, *Encounter with Light*, I mentioned the ecumenical, but deeply Christian, Church of the Covenant. As far as I know, it was the only 'white' church in the city, then in 1961, that warmly and genuinely welcomed black folk, not only to the church itself and to luncheon afterwards, but to its day camp and (shockingly) its swimming pool and to its coffee house, the Lodge of the Fishermen. This provoked much hostility among the citizenry and from the newspapers. I had been there a few times with my daughter-in-Christ, finding the talk of life in Christ deeply appealing.

Now, rejected by my old church for my stand in behalf of the black brother, I began to go regularly to the Church of the Covenant, although since I was a believer in the sacraments and the Apostolic Succession I went on occasion to a (different) Anglican church for early communion. Nevertheless, I became a member of the Church of the Covenant; and, since the Covenant was a promise to be a *functioning* member, if only a finger, I worked in the Lodge, waiting on tables. There, at the drop of a question from a guest, one of us would sit down and explain why the coffee house existed or why we welcomed blacks. I still think this was *the* way, although slower, to bring about an end to segregation, not intervention by the federal government.

Eventually I made and illustrated by hand—and the church had printed—several small leaflets to hand out to explain the Lodge and the church itself. Since these give an idea of my Christian thinking, apart from the segregation issue, I shall give two of them.

The Lodge of the Fishermen—What's that?

The Lodge of the Fishermen is neither an association of ardent anglers nor a club. It is a Christian coffee house, open to all. The next question is, what, then, is a *Christian* coffee house? How is it different to, say, a Turkish coffee house? For one thing, of course, we don't have Turkish coffee. But the difference may go a bit deeper.

A *Christian* coffee house, as we conceive it, is a coffee house maintained by Christians, that is, by people committed to the service of the Lord Christ. (We really believe all that stuff.) But the Lodge is *not*, please notice, a meeting place *for* Christians only, or even mainly—it is for all who come.

Well, then, are we trying to raise money for some church or some good cause? No...Making money is no part of our purpose. Actually, everyone who works in the Lodge is a volunteer, serving you because of a belief in the purpose of the Lodge, and any profits go back into the Lodge. Just possibly we *are* in business for our health.

But, you notice, we have slyly admitted we have a purpose. And it is not the 'natural' one of making money. Decidedly odd. But, really, Christians have always had a purpose, haven't they? Rest easy, though; we are *not* about to tap you on the shoulder and say, "Brother, are you saved?" We shall not look askance if you haven't seen the inside of a church for ten years. We shall preach you no sermons nor bend upon you any holier-than-thou looks. Our haloes are quite undetectable, even by us.

What we shall, in fact, do is serve you as best we can—with coffees (naturally) and teas and pastry. And provide music for you to listen to and paintings and sculpture and sometimes drama for you to look at. We do not charge you for all this.

On the other hand, quite simply, we continue to exist through your contributions. Only through your gifts do we buy more coffee and country ham and lemons. Yet remember, too, that we all serve you without pay; so even if you do drop the odd fifty-dollar bill in the bowl, you are still in a very real sense our guest. We are very much aware of and pleased by this, and we hope that you will be, too. We want to make a place where you can come comfortably, alone or with friends, to talk and laugh or sit and think. You are wholly welcome if you only order water.

But you're still not very clear why we're doing it, are you? "—Damned funny kind of Christians that aren't raising money or ramming something down people's throats!" Even the coffee—you have to drink it yourself.

There are two things that may explain why we do it. One is, if we are a group of Christians with a purpose, we are the Church. And if so, then you *are* seeing the inside of a church; and taking of it what *you* want, too. If you ask for coffee, we give you coffee. If you ask questions, we try to answer. We give you what you want, as nearly as we can. *You* do the ordering. So you can think about that.

The other thing is, we're *doing* this. We like serving you, of course. But *why*? Why do we? You can think about that, too, if you like. Or not.

At all events, this is what the Lodge of the Fishermen is. We who run it are the fishermen, and you—if the thought is not too dismaying—are the fish. But we, oddest of fishermen, merely feed the fish what they choose.

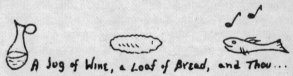

A Jug of Wine, a Loaf of Bread, and Thou...

What's So Special *about the Church of the Covenant?*

You've been there, perhaps. Not much to it really—just a chapel in a big, old house. Can't have many members. Usual sort of service, hymns and a sermon. Nothing you'd call really *special*. You did think once you felt something...something—well, kind of special, actually—in the air. But you couldn't pin it down. Imagination, probably.

It could so easily be like that on a first visit, and it's always hard to pin down things like the love of a country or a person—or the love of God. So maybe we should try to say what *we* think is special. It has to do with the Covenant that gives us our name. It's a covenant we each make with God, not just once but every year over again; and we, for our part, agree to pray a lot and read the scriptures—well, every day, really—and give more than it *feels* like we can afford. Not only that but it usually takes months, even years, of study and association with the community of the church even to be ready to covenant. Thus you were so right: there *aren't* many members. And there's *still* something more, perhaps most important of all and most difficult to explain. The member must, in his commitment to Christ, have a willingness to *act*. We don't mean just busyness or being a church-worker; but, rather, a constant awareness that Christ's Church *exists* by mission, by acting in the world with purpose, even as a fire *exists* by burning. Thus the member *as* a member exists by being on fire, also. Or at least smouldering.

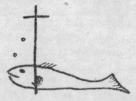

If you ask us *why—why* do we make it so tough? *why* must we require this integrity of membership?—we can only reply that it comes down to what the Church *is*. Our Lord didn't spell it out exactly, but He did say, didn't He, that His Church was His *body*? He said we must eat His flesh and drink His blood; and we must become His body. Hard sayings. He, the head; and we, the body. Right, then: now consider the relationship of an actual body—yours, for instance—and its members, that is, its muscles, fingers, ears, legs. Each member with a specific function in the whole. Each member related to all the other members, depending on them and being depended on. And what happens if an actual member of an actual body ceases to function? If circulation stops and gangrene sets in? It has to be cut off, doesn't it, before it infects the whole body? (What a thing for a *church* to talk about! But is it certain that Christ wanted His Church to be, precisely, *nice*?) Anyway, this is the way we see the Church: Christ, the head, the will; the Church, His body; and we, the living functioning *members* of that body, carrying out that will.

Are we all that perfect? Don't be silly! We know just what your response is, about now: "Join such a church—me? No fear!" So it was, friend, with *every one of us*: "God, no!" But for some of us it became at last: "God, yes." We don't suggest you join; but maybe you'd sort of like to come back now and then and see if there actually is anything special. You'd be so welcome! Many in the congregation, while loving the 'specialness', are, quite comfortably, sure that they'll never be foolish enough to join. Of course, there's a slight risk; but you're tough, aren't you? We trust you to know what's important.

The marks of Christ's Church are not, we think, soaring spires and gothic windows; even less are they riches or hugeness. A vast congregation with crowds of non-functioning members is, we think, sick or dead. Better a lively mouse than a dying elephant. The mark of the Church is *life*: the living body carrying out the will of the living head. Every member living. He may be only a finger—but that may be the finger that turns on the light—for someone. And, remember: behind that finger is the hand and the arm and the shoulder. The member is linked not only to the head but to every other member. And the thing that thrills through all the fibres of the living body, making them one, is Love—that common word, that difficult and frightening word, that Word that is the centre of all.

This, then, is what's special about the Church of the Covenant. If you thought you 'felt something', perhaps you did. A sort of a tension of life in Love. Friend, what you felt, maybe, was yourself being loved as a person; for that's another way of saying what's so special about the Church of the Covenant.

There was nothing in those leaflets about our welcoming the black man, nor was that a deliberate omission. It was simply that we welcome *everybody*—any sort of outcast—and meant it. That was what the Church *was*, a hospital for sinners, a hope for the rejected. Nevertheless, the racial struggle underlay everything in the early '60s. The minister, the Reverend Beverly Cosby, the covenant members, and most of those who worked in the Lodge were Southerners; but Southerners, by and large, have never hated blacks (with the hate that can be found in the big northern cities), and the time had come to remedy the old wrong of the 'system'. The Church of the Covenant, as well as the people who came to the Lodge, were the cutting edge in our town.

But though the racial issue was in the air (and news) in the Idealistic Years, it wasn't a full-time activity for most of us. That summer of 1961, when I began to work in the Lodge, along with Helen and the Rev-Bev and a number of students, was a merry one, with times for drives in the country and in the Blue Mountains. At the end of the summer, I drove Helen up to her new college that was to be the stepping stone to Oxford; and we paused in New York to see *Camelot* and dine in the Village and, by happy chance, to see *A Man for All Seasons* on the night after its opening—before the rave reviews made it impossible to get a seat. Then we drove on to her college where I left her at the door, the doorway to her future.

When I look back to those years, I see, sometimes with no past or future, scenes that linger in memory. This one is in Washington very late on a summer night. With a student friend I wandered into DuPont Circle about one or two o'clock. He and I looked at the fountain and then noticed little groups scattered round under the trees. We went over to one and were welcomed with smiles, so we sat down in the grass. A young man was playing a guitar—folk music—softly. Sometimes someone would sing or everyone would. One or two of the people were black, and it seemed to me that love drifted round the little circle. That remains in my mind as what the early '60s were all about.

The letters to the newspaper and to the Rector indicate my stand on the racial issue at the very beginning of the decade. And yet I grew up, as most of the members of the Church of the Covenant had done, taking segregation for granted. There were black servants at Glenmerle when I was a boy; some of them I loved very much. But servants, waiters, jolly porters on trains: that was what black people *were*.

Curiously, it was on a train that my personal 'conversion' came about. It was a troop train in World War II, and I wore the uniform of a naval lieutenant. At lunch time white personnel were coming into the dining car from the front of the train, black ones from the rear, white men being seated on one side of the car when there was a vacancy, the blacks on the other side. But when I got to the head of my queue, the black stream had dried up, and there were, in fact, two or three vacancies on that side.

I waited a few minutes. Suddenly I thought how silly the whole thing was, and I marched in to where a black naval quartermaster-first was sitting alone. "Do you mind, sailor?" I said, while the headwaiter fluttered about in ineffectual and shocked protest. "No, *sir*!" said the quartermaster with a grin, so we lunched together and had a good talk about how stupid segregation was.

From that day I rejected segregation for myself. And yet, believing in freedom of choice, I didn't object—and still don't—to chosen segregation: a black club, for instance, or a white one (or a men's club). I shouldn't even have objected to a segregated restaurant, *provided* that there were *three* areas, one for blacks, one for whites, and one for both. —But of course a church is not a private club.

While it was still 1961, I wrote another letter to the newspaper. It was about a black man named Douglas Johnson, a poor man, who found $250,000 in the streets of Los Angeles. He could have kept it but he returned it: and he was mocked and vilified for being so stupid—so honest—as to do so. Meanwhile all honour was being paid to Commander Alan Shepard, the space hero, for doing what he was keen to do. I concluded the letter by saying:

> Unless my reading of history is at fault, the greatness of a nation rests at least as much on its Douglas Johnsons as on its Alan Shepards; and I am wondering what is presaged for America by its very different responses to two kinds of virtue.

However impassioned I was about the sin of segregation in Christ's Church, and however accepting I personally was of blacks, I attempted to keep a degree of balance. As always in this country, perhaps all countries, political differences and social ones of every sort lead to polarisation and adamant refusal to see any side but one's own. I saw virtues, a deep kindliness between the races, in the old system, basically unjust though it was. But the spokesmen, male and female, for the extremists, most of them northern, were all for erasing the Southern past in the manner of Orwell's *1984*. Joel Chandler Harris's marvellous *Uncle Remus*, although perfectly true to its time as well as wise and amusing, must be burnt, along with the Battleflag of the Confederacy. On both sides the extremists called for force, police with fire hoses stopping Martin Luther King or troops enforcing integration and compelled bussing. Naturally, since I had taken a stand for the black man, I was expected to be an extremist. The *either/or* mentality. Thus, when I published the following letter—*against* the banning of "Dixie" that the extremists were calling for—both my allies and my opponents were shocked, the latter pleasantly.

> The playing of *Dixie*, even in the Southland, is objected to by extremist reformers because it might offend black citizens whose an-

cestors were owned by (some of) the men who fought and died for Southern independence and the doomed Confederacy. It might be thought that I, in view of my radical stance on contemporary political-moral issues, would be the first to favour banning *Dixie* totally. But I do *not* favour it. Otherwise, I should have to urge the banning of *The Star Spangled Banner* because of U.S. wrongs to the Red Indians and the banning of the *Requiem Mass* because of the (Spanish) Inquisition.

The Greeks who fought at Marathon and the Virginians who fought at Manassas alike held slaves and alike fought for freedom. General Lee fought for Virginia. *We cannot judge yesterday by the convictions of today*. The wartime words of *Dixie*—how many have ever heard them?—were: "We'll take our stand / To live and die *for* Dixie." Not for keeping our slaves. Indeed the Confederate States Ambassador to England offered to free the slaves for England's help in winning independence from the United States. Brave men who loved their native land sang *Dixie* and died embattled. It is, if you please, a freedom song.

I submit that censorship and bookburning/songburning is not the way—ever. It is too bad that men in other ages held slaves or discriminated against Jews. (It is too bad that we neglect Appalachia.) But we cannot change history by banning *Dixie* or *Uncle Remus* or *Oliver Twist* (because of Fagin the Jew). The right way is to keep *Dixie* with all its overtones of valour but give it new meaning: a new Dixieland of freedom and justice for which we shall all take our stand.

The letter to the Rector and Vestry, and the leaflets I wrote for the Church of the Covenant may have established that I was firmly Christian as the '60s began. This chapter is "Putting the Neighbour First", but so far I have not put him, the black neighbour, first—not ahead of God.

It was in 1962 that I began to write my novel *Gateway to Heaven*, most of it written in that year and the next and substantially finished in the later '60s: it belongs to the '60s, and is my best 'source' for the period. Since I wish, as far as possible, to tell the story of my later life in the words written at the time, I need to say something more about the novel; and that is best done by including its "Afterword" which deals with how it came to be written and its link to Davy.

An Afterword on the Genesis of Gateway to Heaven

Readers of *Gateway to Heaven* have sometimes inquired how I came to write a story of such complexity with, they are kind enough to say, such insight into my heroine.

The genesis of the book is to be found in my earlier-published work, *A Severe Mercy*. There it is told how my wife and I, to enhance our closeness and understanding, endeavored to see through each other's eyes in order to appreciate what it is to be in the world as the opposite sex. This effort, though necessarily incomplete, did indeed give us an immensely deepened empathy. It also gave me the thought of someday using these insights to create a female character in a novel.

Almost idly I contemplated this idea from time to time: and gradually the female character—she was Mary from the beginning—took shape. A novelist must of course imagine himself into his characters: almost *be* them. This was not at all difficult to do when, later, I created Richard. But it was different with Mary: not only must I imagine the subtleties of feminine response to men and to other women but also imagine such revolutionary novelties (since I am 6' 3") as looking up at people instead of way down, or going about in skirts; and I decided, first of all, that she must be one for whom ordinary things would be full of wonder. She would, therefore, be young—she would be a girl—in order to have freshness of perception. But even girls, today, are often too blasé to have that freshness and wonder; and I further decided that Mary would have to have been so crippled as to be cut off from life until the time came for her to experience it. Thus the Disaster, as she calls it, came to have happened, leaving her twisted and motherless. To make up for it, she would have a truly wise father—so "Daddy" came into being, along with Jolly, her devoted old nannie. Moreover, Mary would be a reader, not a television watcher, for nothing so destroys all freshness of experience as TV. She would be a deep reader and consequently highly literate: advanced intellectually beyond her years but younger than her age in experience, especially emotional experience. Her father would be comfortably well-off and himself widely read and civilized, for he must be the shaper of his daughter.

Thus Mary, a unique personality modeled upon nobody I'd ever known, came gradually to exist in my mind, though not yet on paper. I don't know how many novels begin with only a character, but this one did. I knew that if, finally, I embarked upon a novel about her she would be healed or—her word—"winged"; but I didn't know how the healing would come about or what would happen after: plot was still nonexistent. Yet she herself, the crippled girl with her books in the household of Daddy and Jolly, was becoming ever more real to me. Then one day, picturing her reading in her quiet house, I imagined her suddenly throwing down her book and, passionately, desperately, longing to leap out of her wheelchair into life: and I was moved to write a poem for her (or perhaps she dictated it to me): it was "Wind Song." Now she was indeed intensely alive for me.

And now I knew that I should write a story about her. A novel in the ancient form of separate journeys, to be brought into a degree of unity by a central crisis and by the resulting development of character. Both Richard and Peter came into being, and I began to write down adventures Mary would have once she was winged. But the final birth of the novel was interrupted by the necessity of writing *A Severe Mercy*.

Curiously enough, all the early Journeys were written before there was any thought of the last three, and an early version of the Journey to Tintern Abbey was the first of all. The incident of Jacqueline, the adventure of the Bull of the Mountain, and the story of Mercia were most certainly not written to prepare the way for what happened with Deirdre. Later, Richard would speculate about them and find them, especially Mercia, significant. But they were not written so that he might find them significant; he found them significant because they had happened—almost the haphazardness of life.

Something should be said about the central crisis of the novel. Back in the 1960s, whenever I went to New York, I used to stay at the house of a young woman, a remote cousin, who was of the same persuasion as Deirdre (though nothing like her). She was thoughtful and intelligent—and a friend—and I, like Mary's father, held that if God had a word for her He would not speak it to me. By being sympathetic, then, and by being on the scene, I gained considerable insight into her and her friends' vision of things. Consequently, when I decided that I must have a central and unifying crisis to make what I had so far written into a novel, I chose to draw upon that New York experience because it seemed to me that our times called for something of that sort.

None of the characters, as I have elsewhere remarked, is anybody I have ever known—except for Mercia, dead before the time of the novel. Mercia is, a little, my wife, Davy, of *A Severe Mercy*. Since it was from her that I derived the understanding to create Mary, it seemed fitting that she should be in my book as a sort of guardian spirit of my heroine. Once during the war with Japan at about the time when I might be hitching a ride in a bomber back to the Islands, Davy wove in her imagination a little wartime horror story. She would be swimming off a lonely beach and be caught by a current that must inevitably cause her to be smashed on the black rocks. At the last moment she would cry out to me in our old playful words, "O Aroha!"—and at that very instant, hundreds of miles away, I should hear her voice as the broken-winged bomber drove into the sea. When I wrote of the death of Mercia, I remembered the poignant little tale Davy had told me when after all the bomber came safely home.

This, then, is how *Gateway to Heaven* came to be written.
[From the *New Oxford Review*]

Gateway to Heaven didn't deal extensively with the racial struggle since Richard and Mary were in England, at Oxford, during most of it, but there are sympathetic allusions to it. And there is an account of one imaginary demonstration in 1965, again told by Mary, when they were visiting her father in Georgetown. She, too, has kept a sense of balance.

Also while we were there, Martin Luther King tried to lead a march on Selma that was stopped by Alabama troopers. This civil-rights or freedom struggle is something that Richard and I have in fact thought about, with a great deal of sympathy for the black people. So when an acquaintance told us that there was going to be a demonstration at the White House about the Alabama action, we decided to go. I found some old paints and painted a picture of a Confederate Battle Flag—a valiant flag for which we have love and respect, for the South, too, fought for freedom. But underneath the flag on the big card, I lettered in the same red: CIVIL RIGHTS IN THE C.S.A.!

So, carrying our placard tacked onto a stick, we went to the demonstration, along with maybe a couple of thousand others, both black and white. People shouted, "Freedom! Freedom!" and we sang. Some of them looked at my card with a scowl until they took it all in, and then they smiled. One big black man said, "Right on, sister!" The great moment for Richard and me was when we all joined hands and sang "We Shall Overcome." I had chills going up and down my back, as Richard said later he did, and, at the end, I had tears in my eyes.

The writing of *Gateway* was halted by a grant for travel in Asia plus a sabbatical in England. I departed in the autumn of 1963. A month in France, a month of croissants and awful coffee, was enough to make me long for what made England great: the English Breakfast of bacon and eggs, toast and tea, and *The Times*.

Besides the English breakfast, there were friends to visit and long hours of good talk, and a good deal of wandering about. Once with a friend I was driving over Dartmoor when we ran into a fog so dense that we could scarcely see the side of the road. We decided to spend the oncoming night in a village we were approaching—but it took us three passes to find it. The grassy road's edge would give way to a kerb, and we'd creep along looking for a crossing street or a light; and then we'd find ourselves on the moor again with invisible sheep bleating in the fog. Nothing to do but turn round and try again.

I went to Oxford of course; and the first thing I did was to write a note to C. S. Lewis at the Kilns, asking if I might call. I didn't know he'd been gravely ill during the summer. He invited me to come to tea, and, on the appointed day, I took a bus to Headington. There was some way to walk from the bus stop. It was raining a little, and blowing hard—a blustery west wind that threatened constantly to blow my umbrella inside out. A typical November day. Shelley's "O wild West Wind, thou breath of Autumn's being" kept running through my mind.

Jack met me at the door of the Kilns. We hadn't met since my last visit to him at Cambridge six years before. He didn't look at all well; and, indeed, the first thing he did was to tell me of his illness in August—out of his head part of the time—and of the kindness of his doctor. He spoke of his having to resign his Cambridge chair, and of the help Warnie, his brother, had been since the first of September, taking care of him and helping with correspondence. I said something about his needing a secretary, and he said, "Not yet," or something to that effect. He had warned me at the very beginning that he would doze off momentarily during our conversation and not to be alarmed. He, in fact, did so, and I *was* alarmed—uneasy, anyway. They couldn't operate, he said, until his heart grew stronger; but he seemed both cheerful and confident.

We talked of everything that afternoon while the wild West Wind blustered about the house and the rain splatted against the windows. During the talk we shifted into the kitchen and made our tea: lots of buttered toast and some biscuits. I was relieved to see that he ate with a good appetite. We spoke of Davy and Joy and missing them—and of still feeling union with them. He mentioned his liking for my little *Encounter with Light*, which I had of course sent him; and he joked that its small print (in the Church of the Covenant edition) was appropriate to my "minuscule handwriting". He also told me about his recent article, "We Have No 'Right to Happiness' ", which was to be printed in *The Saturday Evening Post*. I told him a little about my role in the racial struggle, particularly the story of my Anglican church: he, of course, agreed with my stand that no Christian church might exclude blacks.

Finally, reluctantly, I took my leave, after he had urged me to come back in a week or so: we set a date. Then I left the warmth within and sallied forth into the blustery evening. That tea remains vivid in my memory.

The day that I was again to go to the Kilns, I saw a small headline in the Oxford *Mail* as I was eating my breakfast sausage and eggs: "C. S. LEWIS FUNERAL TODAY." He had died two or three days before at 5:30 in the afternoon. I hoped he had had his tea. I did not have the heart to go to the funeral, even though I was, so to speak, an invited guest: *he* would not be there. But I did walk over to the Eastgate and stand there a few minutes, looking across the High and remembering, a decade past, his great shout from the other side: "Christians NEVER say goodbye!" And his grin. And I thanked God with gladness for the meeting we had had. It was a rather wonderful last meeting—the rain and the wind without and all snug within. Later I learnt that he had died under the Norman Christ I'd given to him and Joy: it was above his bed.

The reason I'd not heard of his death was that it was swallowed up by the enormity of the assassination of President Kennedy on that same November 22nd: no one talked of anything else. Shopkeepers there in Oxford came out in the street when they saw Americans they knew to express their sorrow; and the Oxford M.P. was unable to go on with a speech when a note was handed up to him. He tried but couldn't. More than a month later, on the long flight to India, I fell into conversation with two other men, a London jazz musician and an English mercantile marine officer rejoining his ship in Singapore. The three of us had little in common except the grief we all felt at the death of the hope that Mr Kennedy seemed to embody.

My months in India and later along the Ionian shore of Turkey—Troy and the ancient Greek cities—and later in Greece itself were simply a pleasant interlude in the real story of the '60s. I taught Greek civilisation and had made some study of Indian history, including the Greeks in India; and now I was seeing something of the actualities. At Delphi the lord Apollo seemed still to brood from the fastness of Parnassus, but he did not speak. Earlier in India I was befriended by an Indian professor at the University in Bombay and by a pleasant Parsee family with two charming daughters. It was pleasant to be addressed in hotels and shops as Sahib, and I mourned always the disappearance of the British raj. I liked India and the Indians, except for the dreadful poverty—the swarming people who had no homes but shop doorways or the pavement itself, and the begging children with enormous eyes and matchstick arms. I survived a light-plane crash, though another did not. I saw the beauty and power of a Bengal tiger, and once as I sat on a bench an Indian beside me pulled out a flute and tootled: out of his basket by my foot arose a swaying hooded cobra. I retracted my foot.

One strange thing happened that I remembered when I got back home to the racial struggle. The Indians, of course, are as Aryan as the Germans; and, at lunch one day, over my invariable curry with lots of chutney, I found myself looking at a table of four Indian businessmen and thinking that one voluble one looked Irish, and the quiet one English—quite forgetting complexion. The Indians no longer seemed dark, and a chance glimpse of my own face in a looking-glass would startle me with its paleness. When I left India for the "holy city of Byzantium", I took away a warmth for its people and a sense of the incredible complexity of the country.

In London later I saw a perplexing reference or two to something called the 'Beatles'. A typo? A new kind of insect?

Then I was in Virginia again, after nearly a year: the Road of the Roses and the blue mountains of home. Faculty friends, particularly the cheerful and valiant Belle Hill. And student friends—a quiet, sensitive girl, Betsy, whom I sometimes thought of as a white witch in her perceptions. She seemed touched with the sacred. She was later to marry my friend, Jim Hunter, thus uniting two of my dearest student friends. A boy named Dexter, and Nancy of the long copper hair. And the racial question again.

My dark-blue Triumph, the Jaybird, had a little flagstaff affixed to the right-hand fender, like that from which an admiral's pennant is displayed. Mine on occasion flew a small flag, too: a Confederate Battleflag on which was lettered: CIVIL RIGHTS IN THE CSA. Some of the segregationists were displaying a distorted, oblong version of that flag (it's a square flag) on a licence plate, and I wasn't about to surrender it to them. My pennant earned some dark looks from blacks before they looked more closely, then great white smiles.

One more vignette of the racial struggle. I was driving up a steep hill from Main Street, top down, and traffic was causing me to creep. Walking down the hill on my right side was a young, strong black man holding his head up proudly. He gave me a direct proud look, perhaps slightly hostile or at least tough. I did not avert my gaze but looked back at him, with possibly the slightest hint of a grin—but also tough. For an instant we crossed swords, then suddenly we both smiled, wide smiles. A man and a brother.

The '60s—the early, idealistic '60s. Red roses and black faces, a girl to Oxford, and student friends. A church with a conscience, a last tea with C. S. Lewis, and a Parsee family in India. Letters to newspapers and a 300-page novel.

CHAPTER IV

Putting the Neighbour First: The Angry Years

The Angry Years of the '60s more or less coincided with the shift of Movement concern from racial injustice to the expanding war in Vietnam. The blacks themselves were taking over their struggle with massive and sometimes hamhanded federal intervention—compelled bussing and enforced quotas were not the way in a land of individual states, once proud of being a free country.

In 1964 Lyndon Johnson was elected by a landslide, ironically because his opponent allegedly would expand the Vietnam War, which Mr Johnson, with Tonkin Gulf as an excuse, rapidly proceeded to do himself, becoming one of the most hated presidents. In 1965, the year of Selma and Richard and Mary's little demonstration at the White House, Mr Johnson sent 3000 marines to Vietnam. In that same year, a bit later, came the marathon 'teachin' at Columbia, followed by other universities. The anti-war movement was launched.

One curious aspect of the Movement was that the so-called 'radicals' that made up its ranks—the SDSers and the rest—were more contemptuous of the *liberals*, seen as weak and dishonest, than of the outright conservatives. After all, it was the liberal Democrats ("the brightest and best") who had led us into the Vietnam quagmire. I have wondered whether that distrust of the liberals may not, in later years, have led many former Movement folk into the ranks of the Republican Party.

There was a clear and compelling Christian justification for seeking justice for the black man, but it was not immediately clear that the intervention of our forces in the Vietnamese civil war was wrong. After all, we were supporting the legitimate government of South Vietnam against rebels, rebels supported by the Communist

North Vietnamese, and therefore, probably Communists themselves. Or were they only innocent democrats? In any case, was it any of our business? I wasn't certain, and so not committed either way. But I read a lot about it, and, right or wrong, didn't like the way we seemed to be fighting the war. There was a photograph of a U.S. troop carrier dragging a bound Vietcong behind it, obviously killing him. In the end I became committed against our participation in the war.

I am now, many years later, after the Boat People, not certain I was right. But then I was. I spoke against the war, and, therefore, despite four years as a naval officer in World War II and frequent stands for freedom (not highly prized by Communists), got myself called a Communist. Someone even burned a small cross about one inch inside my property-line—when I was away and the house was dark. Brave fellers! The thing was, while I had taken no very active role in the black freedom struggle, I came to take a much more active part in the anti-war one—becoming what was, not very precisely, called a 'radical'. So our extremely reactionary newspaper—it was called "Lynchburg's Daily Shame" in a magazine article—hinted broadly and often that I was under Communist influence.

It was the silliest of charges. I like Communist totalitarianism not a whit better than Nazi totalitarianism. And the paper had only to get a (free) *Encounter with Light* from the Church of the Covenant—although that church was in the paper's black books (Red books) itself—to discover that I was under the influence of Jesus Christ, not highly regarded in Red circles.

In the anti-war movement I again attempted to keep some balance, trying not to blame those who, patriotically, supported the war, including U.S. servicemen. After my years in the Navy, I was not willing to condemn the men who did their duty and wore the uniform. On the other hand, I didn't blame the conscientious objectors and draft dodgers.

Since the war was a political issue, and since I took a stand on it, it might be worth while to say something of my political philosophy, if it can be dignified by so resounding a title. If I was a radical—one who wants to go to the very roots—I was so only on certain specific issues, such as the hitherto-unquestioned pattern that had kept the blacks in a servile status; and I was, in fact, a moderate. But not a sheep. Perhaps, more basically, I was (and

am) an old-style conservative of the Southern Agrarian sort, as defined in *I'll Take My Stand*. This includes an abiding belief in the
value of the landed gentry—far from the usual connotation of 'radical'.

And, to look ahead to the present day, I am neither a whole-
hearted Republican (big-business conservative) *nor* a whole-
hearted Democrat (big-government as well as government-inter-
ventionist liberal). Nearly the only cause I whole-heartedly support is that of the environmentalists—a basically conservative
(conservation) cause supported mainly by liberals—conserving,
that is, the air and water and forests and critters, *including* the babies slain by the abortionists, as valuable, surely, as whales and
minnows.

It seems to me that anyone who has thought at all deeply about
politics—not just the issues of the moment—must realise that in the
long run conservatism exists to curb or modify the extremes of the
liberals, and liberalism exists to sink its spurs into the stagnation of
the conservatives; and, therefore, both ought to be appreciated.
But it ain't so. Most Americans seem to believe that, if only everybody of the opposing party were to perish, Utopia would be at
hand. The sad part of this single-minded righteousness is the fac-
tional hate and polarisation between the Left and the Right. My father—he was a Jeffersonian Democrat—told me to trust the people,
trust their inarticulate common sense. But neither party does. The
liberals who ought to, since they claim to be for the people, are, in
fact, involved in imposing their own ideas *on* the people, whether
the people want them or not. And the big-business conservatives
are involved in persuading the people to buy what they don't really
want. Nobody trusts the secret wisdom of the people, unless the
people do what they're told or urged to do.

Many years *after* the '60s I expressed in a letter to the *New Oxford Review* a political philosophy arrived at many years *before* the
'60s.

Against Giganticism

Implicit in this letter is the assumption that man is indeed fallen
and will exploit and thus dehumanize his fellows if given a chance.
Long ago at Yale, two thoughts fell into my mind and remained

there. One was in a book of medieval history to the effect that then a man might appeal from nobles to king (or vice versa) or from either to Church: three great forces more or less in balance. The other came from the intellectual historian Ralph Gabriel who said that what we faced in this country was the uncomfortable choice between "giganticism in Business and giganticism in Government." (The Church, once a third force, was through division and factionalism muted.) These two statements put together constituted what I was pleased to call my political-economic philosophy thereafter. I was never tempted, despite the specious attractiveness of the theory, to embrace socialism, even less Communism, for that way led inexorably to un-opposed giganticism in government. But capitalism, with govern-ment in its hip pocket, would lead, if unopposed, to the other sort of giganticism. In America the Democrats, rightly fearing big business, sought to give too much power to government, and the Republicans, rightly deploring huge government, tended to give all to business. An alternation of the parties seemed safest. . . .

My purpose in writing is only to urge Christians in thinking about the ordering of society to keep in mind the idea of competing forces in balance: a balance of powers, not between the arms of government but between the great forces in society that aim always, if unopposed, at giganticism with concomitant exploitation.

Regrettably that political philosophy of balance didn't prevent me from becoming a bit less than balanced on particular issues, notably the war and feminism, and from sharing the general anger that pervaded the Movement—and its opponents—on these issues. My feelings on the war began with a perception of American bru-tality, though that may have been matched by the Vietcong.

My actual involvement began with a 1966 demonstration that was not precisely anti-war but rather support for religious COs (conscientious objectors), in prison for their faith. Though not a pacifist myself, I was willing to support those who, like the pre-Augustinian Christians, were. Contingents of students from a number of Virginian colleges were to meet at the prison and dem-onstrate their sympathy. And student friends urged me to come along. Suddenly, with slight astonishment at myself, I decided to go, kicking the professorial pedestal entirely away—though resolv-ing to turn my face from any news photographers that might be about. As it turned out some of the contingents from other colleges got lost, and there were only about thirty or forty of us. All the same we made a brave show, first driving down the main street of the town, with my Jaybird, top down, in the lead. Fortunately, I felt, the crazy blonde beside me was standing up, waving a sign and uttering occasional shrill whoops, and she, not I with my cap pulled down to my nose, was the cynosure of the slightly stupified gaze of the townsmen. Then the prison where there appeared to be more Commonwealth troopers than demonstrators. But we were allowed to hold the demonstration on a grassy knoll outside the barbed-wire fence where a few prisoners gathered to watch. We shouted support and we sang, our voices frail in the wind; and we finished, hands clasped, with "We Shall Overcome." And then we went home from the wars.

The next demonstration, the huge March on the Pentagon, I didn't even hesitate. I went. I may possibly have worn a drooping false moustache—I did on some occasion, looking, I thought, very fierce. There was something light-hearted and even humorous about this march. A considerable contingent from Lynchburg College went, as well as contingents from scores of colleges, some all the way from the west coast.

In my novel, *Gateway to Heaven*, Richard and Mary, having come over from Oxford to teach in the (imaginary) college, Holywell in New England, also go to the March. Although the novel is not at all autobiographical, Richard is in some ways not unlike me (since I created him); and in this particular event I gave him my own vision of the great March. The anti-war poems that I myself wrote at the time are also given to him. Indeed, the whole account is written at the time and, consequently, undistorted by memory.

If, then, the reader will change gears slightly, he will find *my* March on the Pentagon (along with my poems) described more vividly than I now could do by my character Richard. It begins at Holywell, a month or so before the March with an account of how the anti-war sentiment began.

This Holywell period has been the time, especially, of our being caught up in something rather different to anything else we ever experienced: the anti-war movement and all that goes with it—protest, rock music, drugs. We were of course somewhat prepared for it. Mary's father had long ago predicted an expanded war, and we ourselves had done a bit of predicting when we dined in the wardroom of the USS *Randolph*. Oxford itself had become aware of the war, and there was considerable feeling against it. And in the summer before Holywell there had been a demonstration in London that we had played a small part in—the Angry Arts protest. Still, nothing had quite prepared us for the major upheaval that was happening in the States.

We arrived there in late August of 1967, I on leave from Worcester College, Oxford, to teach a year at Holywell. It seemed good to us both to be there again. The professor whose place I was taking for the year had rented us his fine old house on the edge of campus—high-ceilinged rooms and a beautiful New England doorway and fanlight.

And almost at once we became aware of the intense feelings on campus and, indeed, in the whole country about the undeclared war in Vietnam. The opposition to the U.S. involvement seemed to be based mainly on the idea that we should not be interfering in another country's civil war. Then, too, the U.S. had pledged to hold free elections in South Vietnam and then refused to allow them, supposedly because of a secret CIA report that Vietnam's George Washington, Ho Chi Minh, would win hands down. If this was true, the U.S. position was fatally corrupted. Fair is fair; and if the South Vietnamese would choose Ho at the ballot box, then we had no right to prevent it. We listened and, increasingly, felt that America was fighting an unjust war. We sided with the protestors and then, little by little, were moved to active protest.

Once in my sophomore year at Holywell, way back in 1959, Jim Cosby, who was then a midshipman at Annapolis, came up to visit me. I was at that time rather anti-scholarship—that is, people who wrote footnotes instead of poems or novels. On a trip to New Haven to visit a common friend I held forth, to Jim's amusement, on scholars; and when we got back to Holywell I wrote a poem on footnotes, which, in view of all the footnotes on poems, is a rather man-bites-dog sort of thing. I have digressed into this anecdote because I now—in 1967—took out that old poem and altered and polished it into my first poem about the sixties.

Footnote[1]
[1]Spectacled little scholar
Scribbling away in the stacks
Walled off from life in the library
Turning out lifeless books
Books about books that live
Forming the learned footnotes
Concepts to classify
Label but never believe
Sonnets and songs to dissect
Muting both music and meaning
Adoring nothing at all

> Not life or the Christ or the poem
> Branches and trunk without leaves
> Lost in a lifeless limbo
> Of ambiguities
> While kids cry freedom and cops
> Strike blood at the barricades
> And about the buttressed towers
> Is the roar of the rising wind

Mary approved of this. The thrust of the poem had now become, not against scholars—after all, I was one myself—but against the timid and, above all, against the sort of scholar who never connects up ideas and life—who talks about freedom without believing in it, who deals learnedly with the New Testament accounts of Jesus but thinks his objectivity would be impaired by belief. Strangely enough, he never supposes that disbelief mars objectivity.

The faculty at Holywell were divided, as I suppose faculties everywhere were. The older men, the majority in fact, were shocked at the disloyalty of the protests, the decline of patriotism as it seemed to them, and the questioning of authority. Not to mention the long hair. Many of the younger faculty as well as a few of the older ones were beginning to believe that America was fighting a war of aggression that was inherently unjust. Moreover, they—I should say we—believed that there was a higher ideal of patriotism than acquiescence to injustice.

We were sounded out, by students and faculty alike, from the moment we got settled in at Holywell. We could not have avoided the question had we wished to, for everyone was talking about the war one way or another, even if they seemed to be talking about long hair or the Beatles. Actually, the anti-war people asked us point-blank where we stood. The other party didn't ask in so many words, or even state a position; they simply grumbled about the long-haired types or the decline of patriotism, meanwhile peering at us to see whether we would grumble back. The old idea that America was always righteous—always the 'good guys'—was one that men who had fought against the genuine evil of Hitler found it hard even to question. It was, I suppose, one of America's most deeply rooted fundamental assumptions.

Anyhow, we answered roundly that we thought the war was wrong. Then, when "Footnote[1]" was printed in the *Holywell Holler*, our position was made quite clear; and we were at once drawn into the anti-war group. There was a chapter of SDS on campus, and I spoke to them one night about the Angry Arts thing in London and the vigorous anti-war feelings in Oxford.

It was a strange thing all the same for Mary and me to come from Oxford, which somehow always remains serene and civilised despite Roundheads or Reformers, into this American storm. We were, in a way, prepared. We had been sympathetic to the black Freedom Movement—or black and white, I should say—and had even been involved in that small demonstration in Washington at the time of Selma. And of course our friends in the States, not to mention the newspapers, had kept us in touch with what was happening. But in Oxford the bells rang as always and people went to tutorials and what was happening in America seemed very remote. Not so in Holywell. Peaceful New England town, yes, and nothing like Yale or Wisconsin or Berkeley, but compared to Oxford it was the eye of the storm.

All the threads of protest came to our ears: the whole case against the war—and against the government. Speakers came to Holywell, including SDS leaders and black leaders. Mary and I talked a great deal about it. If anything, she was more angry, more eager to take some sort of action than I was, possibly because she was closer to the students. But there was no disagreement between us. The thing was, it—the war, the whole 'sixties thing'—took so much of our time. Somehow, we read poetry less, listened to music less, took fewer walks. And that may be significant.

The bombing of those hapless people in Vietnam especially filled us with anger. And the anti-war protests, however spirited, did not seem to be accomplishing anything at all. Out of my anger—our anger, I should say—I wrote a darker, angrier, bitterer poem.

Faith

"In God we trust" our coins proclaim.
Only, what God? what holy name?
The great Apollo, lord of light?
Wisdom, thou of the triple helm?
Jesus, loving his enemies?—
The Christ who healed the cop's slashed ear?
Is there, I wonder, a lord of bombers
That don't turn into butterflies
In shaken skies above Vietnam?
A god whose heaven is falling flame?
Old Mars would do, or some beast-name—
Moloch perhaps or the Lord of the Flies.
"In God we trust"—and in his name
Devote our billions to his claim.
Credo: we believe in, not

> —Not the owl and not the light,
> And not in Him whose "Father, forgive"
> Haunts still the blood-stained centuries.
> Ours is a different, darker spell,
> The pattern of a pentagon:
> Conjuring the power but not the glory.
> Is there a god of murder to proclaim?
> —In his name.

That poem was widely reprinted in the so-called 'underground' press, and I was right pleased one time, on the occasion of calling at the office of a theologian in another college, to see it, framed, on his wall. He must have been a Christian. More important, perhaps, for this account of our journey to Holywell, the poem does suggest how we felt—where, as they say, we 'were at'—when it was written. I remember vividly Mary's fierce approval when I first read it to her. I may speak of it further later, but it is important to note that, although we weren't going to church much, we both thought of the world—and the Vietnam war—in a context of solid Christian faith.

We realised increasingly as time went on, as I suggested earlier, that the anti-war movement was not a thing in isolation but, rather, tied up with a number of seemingly unrelated things. Long hair for men, for example, is almost invariably a clear signal of an anti-war stance. But it is also a signal of defiance of constituted authority. All, then, are part of 'the Movement'. But the whole Movement is closely linked to folk music and the stirring rock music of the sixties. The long hair was almost certainly triggered by the Beatles in England, and their songs breathed a cheerful defiance of authority. The lovely, soaring voice of Joan Baez, whom we heard in concert soon after coming to the States, seems to express the highest ideals of the Movement, first as Freedom Movement and now as Anti-war Movement. Mary adored Baez and said she had a winged voice. But no less a part of the Movement are the great songs of Bob Dylan, whether hauntingly sung by Joan Baez or, with somewhat raucous impressiveness, by Dylan himself. Mary and I tend to see the music of the sixties as the key to the decade, so far at least. The reason that so many older people have seemed pathetically bewildered by what's going on is their refusal to avail themselves of that 'key'—the music. Finally, as part of the sixties, tied up with all the rest, is what's called 'the drug scene'. It is important, as is the music, to the story of Mary and me; but I shall come to it later.

One other aspect of our emotional involvement was, and of course still is, the very real possibility, if the war continued to expand, of me being drafted. I had a deferment as well as a wife and had reached the ripe old age of twenty-eight—twenty-nine last month—but still there was the spectre. Mary was terrified of it, and I myself didn't much care for the idea of stumbling about the rice paddies shooting at folk I felt rather friendly to in behalf of a cause I didn't believe in. Thus we could join in with spirit to the shout, "Hell, no! We won't go!" as well as other, less printable chants.

We had scarcely got ourselves settled-in at Holywell and become known as anti-war people when the massive March on the Pentagon began to be planned and talked about—a great and peaceful march on the center of the warmaking activity, the Pentagon, which had become a symbol of aggression. The idea was, of course, to show the American people how great the opposition to the war really was. A considerable contingent from Holywell planned to charter a bus or two and go, along with other contingents from Yale and Dartmouth and Smith and Mt Holyoke and everywhere else. And of course Mary and I planned to go, not only to express anti-war sentiments but to have fun.

Thus in late October, on a beautiful Indian-summer day, we found ourselves near the Reflecting Pool in Washington, along with tens of thousands of others, waiting for the march to begin. The sky was a deep October blue and the pure beauty of the Doric columns looming above us on the Lincoln Memorial lent something of their austere majesty to the scene. There were banners and signs everywhere expressing anti-war sentiments, often with humour and always with vigour, and signs also identifying groups, such as Harvard Divinity School or Indiana University. The mood was lighthearted, not grim; and everybody was friendly to everybody else. It remains in my mind as a fine thing: to march, not to a war shouting Hurrah but against a war shouting Peace. Mary said she wondered if perhaps Jesus might be here, walking around in blue jeans with a merry smile on his face.

We sat about in clusters on the grass with the shining Doric columns above us, and sometimes we took little tours among the various groups. There was so much affection and comradeship that it was, I imagine, quite like one of the be-ins or love-ins they were having out on the west coast. Hand-rolled pot cigarettes—joints—were being smoked and passed about freely. We smoked our first pot there—everyone was doing it—and got high in a sunny sort of way and enjoyed it. It seemed to make the sky bluer and the columns purer in their splendour. We felt that it made us see more: the individual twigs and leaves of the tree, and the bird in the tree, too. There were lots of speeches, but we knew all the arguments and soon stopped listening. The march had by now begun, though our turn was a long time away. One of the things I remember most vividly was the long ranks, ten or more abreast, swinging out gaily with their banners and signs, laughing and shouting.

It looked as though Holywell might not march for hours—there must have been over a hundred thousand people there—so finally I rallied our group and we watched our chance and slipped into the march, forming two or three ranks. We had a golden banner with "Holywell for Holy Peace" stencilled on both sides of it, and it floated above us as we marched onto the bridge over the Potomac. We were all shouting, "Peace—*NOW!* Peace—*NOW!*" like a chant, and then we began to sing about how we all lived in a yellow submarine.

There was a delay of some kind up ahead on the Virginia side, and the long column, marching on the left side of the bridge, slowed and stopped. After awhile there were immense cheers from behind us, but we couldn't see what the cheering was about. Soon the cheering came nearer—and louder. And then up the right side of the bridge came the tread of marching men, real marchers keeping the step, and the sight of the nation's flag. We could see, first, a proud little man, stern-faced, carrying the colours, then a sign in the first rank of the briskly marching men: "Veterans of the Abraham Lincoln Brigade Against Vietnam!" They went by like heroes, eyes front, to immense cheers. Soon after, we began to move again.

At the Pentagon the scene became grimmer. There were troops everywhere, and U.S. Marshalls with armbands arresting everybody. We couldn't get anywhere near the door and tried to circle round the crowd. But across the road was a line of troops with rifles at the port-arms position. We tried to persuade one unhappy looking soldier to let us through. He evidently wasn't allowed to answer, but he rolled his eyes in the direction of his sergeant. Mary talked to him a moment or two about how wrong the war was, and then she reached up and put a flower in the muzzle of his rifle. I heard later that a couple of soldiers—perhaps Mary's soldier was one of them—had flung down their rifles and leaped into the ranks of the demonstrators and disappeared as people gave them coats and shirts to hide their uniforms. Other soldiers were less sympathetic....

After the great march was over and we were back at Holywell, I kept thinking about the meaning of the day—people marching for peace. A month or two later I had occasion to be in Washington again, and I walked back to where the march had begun. All was quiet except for a few winter tourists, and I sat down on the steps of the Lincoln Memorial and wrote a poem trying to tell how it was and what it meant.

March on the Pentagon
Retrospect: Lincoln Memorial

That October was a sort
Of Indian Summer. We lay about
Here on the sun-warmed grass beneath
The radiant columns, smoking pot,
And still we hoped for America.
Then with the long ranks moving out
We raised our banners: home-made signs
For Peace held high into the blue
October air, and laughed, and stepped
Out lightly towards the Pentagon.
"Peace—*NOW!*" we shouted, and we sang.

Let these be famous: let men raise
In bronze these blue-jeaned brigadiers
Amidst the clubs: let history praise
Not only endless ranks of spears
But those who marched for peace with cheers.

That is the way it was—to resume the narrative in my own voice,
not Richard's. That's the way the anti-war movement arose and the
way the first great march took place in 1967. And how we felt at
the time. People change and the times change: it would be hard to
catch that immediacy of experience, or to convey it, now—especially for those who didn't experience the '60s themselves. That,
of course, is why I turned to the novel written in that time.

There were many marches and demonstrations in the next four
years. The great march on Fifth Avenue in New York at the same
time as the Columbia sit-in followed closely upon the March on the
Pentagon, though they needn't be described in such detail. The one
thing that needs to be said about them is that they became less
light-hearted, ever more grim and angry. There is a hint of that in
the poems by 'Richard', especially the one called "Faith" which
was actually written a couple of years after the March on the Pentagon—and the anger is in it. I speak of Jesus's "Father, forgive"
that "Haunts still the blood-stained centuries"—it is a Christian
view but not truly Christian. It is angry and, in fact, unforgiving.

Some of the readers of *Gateway to Heaven*, not themselves '60s
people, enjoyed the rather idyllic first half or more of the book but

didn't like the jolting descent into the harsh realities of the Angry Years. Life is like that, though—the perfect summer and then the guns of August. Moreover, the novel mirrors the '60s: the idyllic parts were written in the Idealistic Years; the rest in the Angry Years. And the anger of the late '60s: it was there, it was in the air, it is in my poem: a gentle clergyman framed it and put it on his wall. The poet, Stephen Vincent Benet, in his "Apology" defended what was in his own writings. "Pardon, after poets," he says, "if I have written / Not of the moon and roses but of...the nightmare.../ Pardon me, then, for mentioning the bombs / Which happened to be around."

I speak of this because I have got the strong impression (partly from readers' letters) that there are rather a lot of Christians who shut their eyes to harsh realities, including sin. The good people of my Episcopal church, despite my letter, were doing just that sort of eye-shutting. No doubt the Christians I'm speaking of hate sin (when they can see it), but they are unwilling to look at unpleasant realities—unwilling, indeed, even to look at, let alone love, the sinner. It would be sad if the world saw Christians as so many ostriches with their heads firmly buried in the sand. But many *do* see Christians that way. That's not the faith that will overcome the world.

We are told to *hate* the *sin* and *love* the *sinner*. That, I think, is one of the very hardest things for Christians to do: to keep the two parts in balance. One set of Christians hate the sin *and*, in effect, hate the sinner as well by refusing to understand and love him. The other set of Christians love the sinner—the homosexual, for instance, or the woman who has an abortion—so enthusiastically that they love the sin also by denying it to be sin. Both sets deny the Lord.

If I said that I was sinless in the '60s, the Christian reader, knowing his own sin, would rightly be sceptical. If I say, as I do, that my sin in the '60s was real and terrible, I hope the reader will take my word. Almost without knowing it, I drew away from God. He ceased to be first—and He *must* be first or nowhere. Movement goals became first. The anger was in me. Moreover, my own goals—what *I* wanted, following the devices and desires of my own heart—were more important than God. C. S. Lewis in *Pilgrim's Regress*—I, in fact, was a pilgrim regressing—describes his hero's search for the 'Island in the West' as he runs away from God. And I was wanting illusory joys more than I wanted God. Earthly joys. Chimerical joys. Worse, I *used* people—at least once, a sort of emotional blackmail. I have long since repented and confessed—but the compunction remains. As I said, the sin was real and terrible. I was not a sinner because I committed sins. I committed sins because I was a sinner. Infected with sin, as we all are.

I did not ever, blessed be He, renounce the Faith. At Oxford I had deliberately *chosen* to believe on the balance of the evidence; now, when people all round me were ceasing to believe, I felt that I could not in honour renounce it without thinking it through again as deeply as I had done then. But I was impatient with God and anything but close to Him; I didn't want to be bothered. I was neither the servant of God nor His friend. I didn't *feel* sinful—one never does—but there is no doubt in my mind now that I was falling into grave sin and was in peril of losing my faith for ever. And withal feeling right virtuous.

As Chesterton's Father Brown says, "The one spiritual disease [is] thinking one is quite well."

What of my Christian friends? Why were they not doing something? Dom Julian, from his far away monastery, tried. And he *did* do something: he prayed. How much that had to do with my return to God cannot be measured. But the one person who knew my heart—Davy—could not come to me, though she, I do not doubt, was praying too. And if prayer is a channel for grace, it is the most effective help. At least I didn't renounce the Faith, even though I was tempted to do so. Certainly I remained, at worst, theistic—not totally meistic.

It must be remembered, too, that initially it was the Faith that pushed me into action in the '60s. A church closed to the black man was an offense against Christ. And the war, less certainly, seemed so, too. But the danger of social action is—well, what happened to me. First, a generous and loving *Christian* response to injustice and suffering. Then, putting the neighbour *first*—ahead of God. And finally, putting goals and victory first, ahead of both neighbour and God. Hating one's enemies. Feeling virtuous, as the social activist always does. Finally, the feelings of virtue leading to pride, even arrogance. In some respects it's a noble sin, but it may lead to Hell all the same, as putting something else ahead of God does.

To return now to the narrative, at about the time of the great march in 1967. The summer before that, I spent in England, exploring among other things Hadrian's wall in the north. I also got a new car, a Morgan 4-seater that I picked up at the small factory in the west of England, creeping away towards London running it in. Its name became Morgan le Fay, and sometimes, later, Colonel Morgan after the Kentuckian Confederate. It might well have been Penny Lane, though, after the Beatles' song that seemed to be playing everywhere. Home to the fall term and the march. Someone gave me a kitten about then, and she was named Dimity Jane Pentagon—Dimwitty for short. I need not describe the later marches and demonstrations that I was in on, angrier demonstrations, along with the arrests and the whiffs of tear gas.

The last of the great demonstrations, again in Washington, was the one on Mayday in 1971, actually three days long with mass arrests. I was not, more by luck than by design, one of those arrested. On the second day several hundred Movement people were sitting in a side street by the Department of Justice, occasionally shouting "Jump! Jump!" when Attorney-General Mitchell and others came out onto the balcony above us. The day before, I had arranged that anyone who had earlier been arrested and released would be met at a different corner of the Justice building at a certain hour. Consequently, a few minutes before that hour, I told the others that I'd be back in a minute; I'd just step round and see if Jake, one of our contingent, had got out of jail. One of the girls came with me, and, sure enough, there was Jake. We exchanged hugs. But it was, as it happened, the police hour, too, for suddenly about a thousand gas-masked cops charged by to arrest our companions in the street. We couldn't get through the police lines if we wanted to. We tried. We, therefore, got into the Morgan and drove around the scene, exchanging V-signs with fellow demonstrators being carried off in paddy wagons.

Later, as Morgan le Fay turned her bonnet southwards out of Washington, I announced that I wasn't marching anymore. Apparently everybody else was deciding the same thing in that May of 1971, for there were no more big demonstrations. That was the way the active '60s ended.

But the glance at this last big demonstration was a look ahead. We must go back to 1967—the year of the March on the Pentagon—when the anti-war movement struck the Lynchburg College campus. First there was a faculty anti-war petition signed, I think, by about a third of us. And then I was instrumental in bringing into existence a chapter of SSOC ('sock'), the Southern Students Organizing Committee, which was in the South rather like SDS in the northern states—both very idealistic in their inception despite the fact that SDS more or less went mad later.

SSOC had a button that was one of the best of that age of ten thousand buttons. It was a Confederate Battleflag with a black hand clasping a white one across it, summing up for me the whole of the '60s. One time at a New York march a reporter spied it on my shirt and came up to me saying, "Aren't you in the wrong place with that button?" I said, "Look again, friend." He did—and offered me five dollars for it. I gave it to him, having three more buttons in my pocket.

The college administration, though, were not admirers of the button or of SSOC itself and tried to ban it as a 'radical' organisation. SSOC remained, nevertheless, active and embattled. I published in the college paper a Socratic (or SSOCratic) dialogue, in which SSOCrates in conversation with a student leader asks him how precisely SSOC differs from the 'radicals' who dumped the tea in Boston harbour or those who ran the 'underground railway' for slaves. I also became involved in draft counseling, sometimes going with some student to confront the Draft Board. Once at least half the SSOC people came, too, and, being denied entrance to the draft-board room, sat in shaggy ranks outside on the floor.

One of my closest student, or ex-student, friends was a physically frail young man—no chance that the army would induct him—with a first-rate mind. His name was Tim, and he and I had wandered about Resurrection City, the black encampment in Washington; and we contrived to bring *The War Game* (a British film of nuclear attack, far more haunting than *The Day After* was to be) to campus. Tim, despite his gayety and wit, was an idealist: and he decided after that film that he could not—and *would* not—carry a draft card. He sent it back. Despite the fact that he was 4-F, the Draft Board decided punitively to draft him. Tim and I went to the Draft Board to argue that punishment, not for refusing to fight but for refusing to carry a card, smacked of Russian totalitarianism; but they were determined to do it. So we went to Richmond to the 'high command', again without success: the law must take precedence over freedom and conscience.

Next day, after a night of thinking, Tim announced he would go to Canada and renounce his American citizenship. It was his own decision, but, as he knew I should do, I supported him and, in fact, drove him up to Toronto. He was my friend. Later, I went up again taking his record player and the Beatles records he and I had listened to with immense enjoyment. Also, his record of *2001*, which we had seen together in New York, afterwards going out with a girl we knew to ride the Cyclone roller coaster.

When I went up the second time, he was living in rooms (without furniture except a couple of mattresses on the floor) in one of four row houses, all full of draft-resisters from the States; and it was the time of the Battle of Chicago, the police clubbing demonstrators in the streets. We listened to it on the radio; and I listened to Tim describing it on the air—he'd got a job as an announcer (as he'd been in Lynchburg). We both felt we ought to be in Chicago.

And it was also at this time that we decided we ought to try LSD. We obtained two six-hit caps and, recklessly, decided to drop the lot, though asking some other people to keep an eye on us. This we did, slightly scared but 'going with the flow', listening to the music of *2001*, and having terrific 'trips', mine seeming to be a magnificent experience of God—not seen but pouring love into people. (Richard's trip in *Gateway* is, very exactly, mine.) Then I drove down the states to Virginia, leaving Tim to marry a Canadian girl, and myself resolving that an occasional 'trip' was good for the mind.

In the following year I was invited to give a sermon or talk in the college chapel, a talk that was then printed in the college magazine. Reading it now, I see that it is very much a '60s thing, but it also seems to indicate that my Christian faith was still alive—at least when I thought about it—however coloured by the embattled times. But the reader may judge for himself.

The Image of Jesus

It is said that actors of Hamlet dread the line "To be or not to be" because everyone knows it and has hammed it. How can anyone say it naturally? In a talk about Jesus there's a similar difficulty in the very name. Jesus. How do you say it without either dropping into a stained-glass solemnity—or sounding like you just hit your finger with the hammer? Jesus. Jesus who was called the Christ, the holy one of Israel.

There's an even worse hangup about the image. When I spoke the name of Jesus, what came into your mind? A large black book? The

smell of Sunday School? A solemn figure in robe and halo, arm up-
raised in benediction? The meek and mild Jesus who couldn't hurt a
fly that hangs over a million mantelpieces? —What a bore! And nothing like Jesus. It is we who have made him a bore—he who assuredly
never bored a soul in his brief vivid lifetime. What I want to do is try
to correct and humanize the image. Not in depth—I'll leave that to
the priests. But with the assistance of Dorothy Sayers, I'd like to have
a look at the way Jesus must have appeared when he was a living
man, walking into Jerusalem, annoying the authorities. He was
also—I happen to believe—God. Very God of very God. But it didn't
show much, if at all. Definitely no halo.

All right, then—a young guy, about 30, wearing bluejeans.
"What!" you say. "He did not wear bluejeans; he wore, like —well,
like a bedsheet." You're right, of course. He didn't wear bluejeans.
And yet, he was poor and travel-stained; he must have looked like the
equivalent of bluejeans. So just for a few minutes, let's take that one
liberty and have the bluejeans. Okay, then—a young guy with long
hair and a beard, wearing bluejeans. You probably wouldn't give him
a second look if you met him on campus. He certainly wouldn't be
solemn and Sundayish. He'd probably grin and say "Hi!" Actually,
one of the things we know about him is that he was a Sabbath-
breaker. He said the Sabbath was made for man. Sort of like: The
streets belong to the people. Another thing we know is that he was "a
gluttonous man and a wine-bibber, a friend of publicans and sinners." To translate that out of the stately Elizabethan, it says that he
liked to eat a lot and drink even more—a 'wine-bibber' is someone
who likes to sit around and drink all evening—and it says he associated with fringe types, petty law-breakers and hippies and disreputable chicks. Now, this is the last thing—a guy like this—that most
good church-people today would approve of. They get around it by
cutting it right out of their image. They cut a lot more out of their image, too.

Next I would suggest to you that he was in his own world rather
like the youthful radical in ours. Not, of course, because of the beard
and long hair. Still, keep on picturing the young guy in bluejeans, the
wine-drinking and hippie friends, the Sabbath-breaker. Not 'nice' at
all, but undoubtedly a really nice guy. Probably gay and humorous
over the wine. We know that he was tender to the unfortunate and
very patient with honest enquirers. Today's radical is also likely to be
kind and gentle to the poor and unfortunate—and willing to talk all
night to honest enquirers.

The government, however—the prominent men in church and
state—regarded Jesus as a threat, a disturber of the peace. He talked

too much and brought out too many unpleasant truths. They considered him a political trouble-maker, a threat to law and order, an actual danger. No question about that—and fits the radical image, doesn't it? And that's why they bribed one of his friends to turn him over to the cops. Nothing like that could happen today, of course. And they tried him on the rather vague charge of creating a disturbance, and executed him like a common criminal. They had to have really wanted him shut up.

Let's glance at some of the things that he did that annoyed the government and the establishment. He spoke of the king (Herod) as 'that fox'—very much like some of our references to LBJ or Tricky Dick. He insulted respectable clergymen—definitely establishment types— by publicly calling them hypocrites. He enjoyed himself at parties and drank a lot: he even made wine to keep one party going. He showed no respect at all for wealth or social position. In fact, he implied strongly that the kingdom of love that he was building would have no room for riches and property and repressive laws. There is nothing more revolutionary than love. Nor anything more of a threat to special privilege. You can be sure that nearly all the prosperous respectable people, including the clergy, were against him. He broke all sorts of regulations and defied all sorts of sacrosanct customs. I'm not sure he would have lasted very long at this College...or anywhere else. Because, of course, the sort of thing he did—breaking rules and flouting authority—is really contagious. Spreads fast. —We are, by the way, pretty well out of the stained-glass bag with our image, aren't we? We have a guy who is very human and very likeable and very dangerous.

Another thing about him: He had a sense of humour. He always kept his cool, but you can see that a lot of what he did had to have been done with a smile or at least an inner grin. Calling the king 'that fox'. And the clergy 'hypocrites'. And when those pompous clergymen set neat argumentative traps for him, he'd answer with some paradox that they couldn't work out or with some frightful pointed question that they couldn't answer by the book.

Now, there's just no way at all around the fact that he was a peacenik. Blessed are the peacemakers—he said—the makers and maintainers of peace. True, there were no 'Godless Communists' in those days, but his country was under the domination of the 'Godless Romans'—and Jesus gave no support to those who wanted war. He said we had to love our enemies. There isn't the slightest doubt, or the slightest grounds for doubt, about where he would stand on what we're doing in Vietnam. I can't even begin to see how anyone can favour the war and yet claim to be a Christian. Only by cutting this hard truth out of their image. He stands for peace. He said some very tough things about haters and about those who took the sword perishing by the sword. And when they finally busted him and Peter cut a cop's ear off, Jesus healed it.

Just about the surest way, then as now, to get into real trouble is to fail to respect private property. And Jesus showed no respect at all for private property or vested interests or free enterprise or any of the really important things. In fact, he was more than a little casual with other people's property, including pigs. And that rich young man—remember?—who wanted to follow him. Jesus really liked him, but he told him he'd have to sell all his property and give the money to the poor. The rich young man couldn't make it; he went sadly away. And we—well, we shut this out of our image, too. Think of all the men of property sitting in all the rich suburban churches, shutting it out. The last thing they'd like is for their minister to say: "Now, will the *real* Jesus please stand up!" And what about the money-changers in the temple? They were perfectly legit business men, respectable and law-abiding, converting currencies. And this radical Jesus literally took a whip to them, and threw them and their property down the steps. Not meek and mild—at all! And what shall we call this happening with its disrespect for law and private property? Civil-disobedience? A demonstration like against Dow Chemical on campus? The same sense of outrage, certainly.

Although the government and the church people and the wealthy hated him and put him down in the end—or *did* they?—he had a liberating influence on people who weren't too set in their ways. Mostly young people. The way he broke laws and customs, for example, and called the stuffy clergymen hypocrites. And that great saying: "You shall know the truth and the truth shall set you free." There's an old legend—it's told in Dostoevsky's *The Brothers Karamazov*—about how Jesus came to Spain in the Spanish Inquisition and was immediately arrested. That night the Grand Inquisitor comes to his cell and sadly explains that Jesus had made men free, and it had taken the authorities all these centuries to stamp that freedom out again, men being too frail and weak to be allowed freedom. Now Jesus must be again put to death so he can't again set men free. That's worth thinking about. All over the world governments are secretly agreeing with the Inquisitor that freedom is too dangerous and must be suppressed.

But—we still have Jesus. He lives. He is alive and well. Only: *Don't* let him slip back into the respectable, dull Jesus, meek and mild, supporter of the status quo, and comfortable. He's *nothing* like that! If you have a comfortable Jesus, it's not Jesus at all. He's a lot *more* than I have said, but he is not *less* than I have said. And let us all remember: If we're going to follow him, it's got to be *his way*. As the rich young ruler found out. It really means laying your body on the line. Make *no* mistake about that. Prison or death—it may be—for us as for him. How long do you think they'd let him remain free in *any* country you could name today? Maybe you're wondering why I'm not in prison. A lot of my sisters and brothers are. Maybe, like the rich young ruler, I just can't make it. But at least I know, a little, where the way leads. It's beautiful, baby—but dangerous!

Well, if anything lingers in your mind from this evening, let it be the image. The young merry bearded guy in bluejeans—radical, defiant of authority, contemptuous of property and respectability, witty, loving, life-affirming, and brave. No wonder the early Christians died with a song. The one thing he assuredly *wasn't* was dull. He went through the world like a flame.

And if he was God—then, by God, God isn't dull either.

When the year in which I gave that talk ended, a day or two after the students went down for the summer vacation, the President of the College, saying that I was a Sword of Damocles hanging over his somewhat balding head, threatened me with firing—despite tenure—if I didn't cease my 'radical' activities both near and far. My first reaction was amusement at the timing, after the students—who might so easily occupy his office—had gone for the summer. I had no belief that he would, in fact, fire me; and he didn't, despite my continuing my activities.

But in the autumn, I was presenting an account of the threat to our chapter of the AAUP (American Association of University Professors) when a more serious crisis, or series of crises, arose that put my case on the back burner. First, someone rushed in with the report of the actual firing of an alleged homosexual teacher on the testimony of a student he'd given a D to. Then a very able professor of political science, who had been rather caustic in criticizing the administration, was fired (under the guise of a reorganisation of his department) causing all the rest of that department to hand in their resignations in protest. Finally—and in some ways worst of all—the much-liked college chaplain, a wonderful chap, understanding and sympathetic with everyone, was to go. Instantly the entire faculty was up in arms. An emergency faculty meeting, without administrators, was called, a committee was formed, and the rebellion was underway. Perhaps a third of the faculty were resolute, and a third were pro-administration, and the largest 'third' were sympathetic but timid. In the end, the President, after, we thought, running scared for awhile, won by frightening the middle third about their jobs. It was a spirited year, though the faculty were a long time recovering from it. My own contribution, apart from satirical verses in the college paper, was mainly urging the committee to more resolute, even drastic, action. The 'Faculty Rebellion' of 1969-70.

On the national scene, violence and the threat of violence were increasing; it was not only the burning of draft files but actual bombs in police stations and the blowing up—with the death of a late worker—of a weapons research centre. And in their anger, the Movement extremists were urging greater violence as well as the rip-off. This latter, of course, was plain stealing, justified as a 'right'—as so many immoral acts have been justified ever since—a 'right' because it would be plundering the 'wicked' system. I could not go along with either the violence or the rip-off, pointing out in Movement papers that the rip-off didn't hurt the 'system' but only the inoffensive little grocer or bank clerk. As to violence, I wrote in a Movement magazine called *The Peacemaker*, in one of my last Movement papers in 1970, a rather grim warning that concluded:

What I am concerned about is escalation. Our peaceful protest has escalated into the destruction of such property as draft files and, in a major escalation, into the destruction of police stations, Bank of America branches, and weapons research centres. What will be the next step as increasingly violent repression comes down? Will we, like revolutionary movements elsewhere, move on to the killing of men who, like us, are mixtures of good and bad but who are involved in the system's evil? And, if so, what will it do to *us*? And would *we* then be able to build an America of justice and love?

I reflect on Lord Acton's familiar words about power: "*All power tends to corrupt and absolute power corrupts absolutely*"; and think them relevant to our decision. The hard corrupted men who carried out the Stalinist purges were idealistic young revolutionaries once. If someday *you* go forth to kill a man—a man who maybe loves his wife and maple trees but is Chief of Police or chairman of Dow—you will, in the moment when the trigger finger is tightening or the knife is poised, have absolute power over him, another human being; and you will be corrupted absolutely.

Reading that now, I see that a mother, deciding about aborting her unborn babe, has precisely that same absolute power in the moment of her decision to kill.

As Richard remarks in *Gateway*, the anti-war movement could not be seen—or understood—in isolation. The protestors and the hippies (protestors in their own way) grew together, flower children and protestors, be-ins and demonstrations, blended into one thing, moving to the sound of rock music with the aroma of pot or 'grass' in the air: the '60s thing. And with the rock, the songs of Bob Dylan and Joan Baez. One thing that must be remembered about the '60s, if one 'went with the flow', is that, danger notwithstanding, it was all rather a lot of fun. Indeed, the danger of arrest or of being busted—"Hark! what's that sound?"—added a sort of zest to the times, the fillip of danger. The same sort of fun that can occur in the far more deadly game of war: a common cause, a brotherhood (with sisters as well, adding further zestfulness), and a uniform (long hair and blue jeans). And I was fully into the '60s thing, long hair and grass and rock, the lot.

I have, in fact, often reflected on the experiences of the war and the movement—the early '40s and the late '60s—not without amazement that I should have been so thoroughly into both that I *could* compare them as to humour, comradeship, and mood. I decided once that the humour of World War II was better. But the comradeship was in both.

Something should be said about the 'drug scene', as it was called. Of course pot is no more (and no less) a 'drug' than tobacco or coffee or wine, and even the hallucinogens, apart from LSD—that is, mescalin and the 'sacred mushroom'—are natural substances. At all events, the '60s were an open-to-anything, adventurous decade. And the official statements about pot—that one puff enslaved the puffer and turned him into a crazed killer—were so obviously false that people tried it out for themselves. And how could I say anything to students about pot or, indeed, LSD without first-hand knowledge? When I did try it, pot seemed a harmless 'high' without even the possibility of a drunken stage.

C. S. Lewis in *Screwtape* speaks of pleasures, all produced by God, in their "healthy and normal and satisfying form," and Screwtape goes on to say that all Hell can do is tempt people to take those pleasures "at times, or in ways, or in degrees, which [God] has forbidden." This could suggest that pot at the right times and *in moderation*—which applies also to wine or whisky—was indeed a harmless pleasure. Today, it appears to have been discovered that its frequent (immoderate) use may lead to the dulling of mind or will. As to LSD, despite the impressive Canadian experience with it, and a few others, I never could decide whether I *liked* tripping. There can be intense beauty, but there is also what I can only call a vibration along the nerves that is unpleasant—one would like to turn it off, but of course it can't be turned off until it has run its course. In the end I decided that, although I was glad I *had* tripped, I didn't want to do it again. Besides, the '60s, which included LSD and pot and rock, came to an end. All aspects ended for me.

One other aspect of the late '60s, which, perhaps regrettably, *didn't* come to an end for me, was feminism. After sleeping since the '20s (no one had time to bother in the Great Depression), the new feminism was born out of the anti-war movement. And I, who had held Davy to be an equal partner in our marriage and had de-lighted in getting that girl to Oxford because she *was* a girl, sprang at once into the as-yet-unnamed Lib thing. In late 1968 I wrote a more or less flaming tract or booklet, published in that year, called "Freedom for Movement Girls—NOW!!" in which, to my present regret, I invented the rather ugly words 'sexist' and 'sexism', de-fining them as one who believes or the belief that one sex is supe-rior to another. Since Women's Lib is to go on, I shall defer my later and deeper thinking on it until a subsequent chapter.

But there are two aspects of it that I should like to comment on here: Lib in relation to '60s idealism and anger; and Lib as an anal-ogy to black freedom. With respect to the first of these, the black-freedom movement began (and largely remained) deeply idealistic (and Christian), *appealing* to idealism. The anti-war movement, however angry it became, was at least born in idealism—the teach-ins and the peace vigils. But the women's movement was born in the years of deepest anger, and it was itself angry from the begin-ning—my booklet was full of anger. Lib didn't ask; it demanded with shrillness and rage, and there was little of idealism and less gentleness. The shrillness and rage, it seems to me, has marked Lib in all the later years.

It has been said that people who shout, "I'm as good as you are!" never, in fact, really believe it. The blacks dropped that line and proclaimed the more effective "Black is Beautiful!" Perhaps if women would cease to cry, "We're just as good (men) as you are!" and turned to "Feminine is Beautiful!" there would be universal agreement.

The black movement was born out of obvious and great injus-tice, and it was born of itself. But the female movement was based on a false analogy with the blacks. Women were not down-trodden and impoverished and made to say, "Yassuh!" They shared their husband's prosperity, and, by and large, as wives, didn't have to work as hard as he did. Indeed, women controlled more wealth, left to them by dead husbands, than men did. There were, to be sure, inequalities of pay for working women; but many women— editors, scholars, doctors—were brilliantly successful: success was open to them, as to few blacks, even if it wasn't easy. But, above all, blacks were excluded in America merely because of their colour—literally a skin-deep difference. And women, not just in America but everywhere—in *all* times and in *all* places—were held, not to be inferior but to be *deeply* different, different through and through. The deep difference was the basis of role differences.

Lib's analogy with the blacks is false because it assumes (assumes without proof) that a soul-deep difference is the same as a skin-deep one.

But I was caught up in the Spirit of the Age; and in leaping into female lib, I was neither asking what God's will was nor doing the sort of deep thinking I had done about the black cause and, to a considerable extent, about the anti-war one.

Before it ends, one more vignette of the anti-war movement: Morgan le Fay with two or three passengers and a van with many more had travelled to Nashville where the SSOC headquarters were. The meeting was about the oncoming Mayday demonstration. The long journey back was slowed by car trouble, and we didn't arrive until about 2:30 in the morning—too late for some, especially the girls, to get into the dorms. So everybody spent the night in the Birdhouse, which took on some resemblance to the Black Hole of Calcutta. A couple of people spread their sleeping bags under the bed, someone had the couch, and others were littered about the floor.

I lighted one candle on the mantelpiece and left it burning; and on the record-player a Joan Baez record turned down to a tiny, silver trickle of sound. So, because of a single candle and that little voice associated with the idealism of the '60s, a vivid memory. And not far ahead, Mayday in the streets of Washington: and then the SSOC buttons stowed away in bureau drawers.

It ought to be said that, while these various actions were going on, so, too, was what might be called ordinary life. I taught my classes faithfully, with no compromise of standards, and I talked to colleagues and friends about ordinary matters. There were trips to London and New York and Washington just to see friends. Once when I was visiting two women in Washington, we even played miniature golf which they'd become enthused about—what could be more 'square', more innocent? They beat me, incidentally, quite overwhelmingly in the first game; I tied one of them in the second round; and beat them both in the third. Satisfactory.

When the active Movement ended after Mayday in 1971—except for a wild-eyed remnant (the Weathermen) of SDS—no one knew it had ended. The embattled stance continued for awhile. But what now began was that curious tail of the '60s, the flight to the country, like a migration of bees. Everyone seemed to discover country roads and old farmhouses and a vision of bucolic bliss at the same moment, and they flocked there in couples or communes. I don't know what the real farmers thought of this invasion of long-haired youth, but they probably took it calmly and taught the newcomers how to make gardens. And the invaders were really falling in love with the country.

It was perhaps a little like the rediscovery of nature by the Romantics at the end of the 18th century. I imagine that these ex-Movement people had a lot to do with the later environmental movement, for they were zealous to protect their new-found-land from littering, from suburbia, and from every other threat. Many of the communes, unwilling or unable to impose any rules, broke up in much acrimony; but the commune folk, now back to the natural order of couples, with, increasingly, babies, didn't forsake the rural life.

I, myself, bought with a friend a roomy log cabin in the mountains of Amherst county with 150 acres around us, rising up to Cedar Mountain; and we named the place the Rock. No other house or road could be seen from the cabin. There was a spring of pure and delicious water, and a stream came down the mountain to a pool where we could swim, and there was a waterfall. In the cabin a great fireplace with a kettle to swing over the flames. It was a fine retreat, and a dozen friends dwelt round in our part of the county. In the early spring there was a magical beauty of tiny leaves and pink Judas trees and dogwood.

I wrote a number of letters to newspapers concerning the protection of the unspoiled countryside, and I shall include here the briefest of them: "A Postscript" to a longer letter the week before.

Dear Sir:

> The Developer grabs the green dell,
> First the trees, for his profit, to fell,
>   Then the ranchhouse and curb
>   Of the plastic sub-urb—
> May he mar his next landscape in Hell!

When I look before and after the '60s, the period seems a strange interlude—a digression—in my life; but I am a part of everything I've seen and known, including that adventurous time with its ever-present sense of the new. I learnt the language of the '60s, not the slang only but its very way of thinking, which would influence *A Severe Mercy* towards truer communication. Strangest of all, associating with, accepted and accepting, the collegiate generation of the '60s, I had what was in many ways a second youth. If Davy had lived—or if I'd sailed off in the schooner—it wouldn't have been so. Beyond question, the hollow had much to do with it. Perhaps the truest thing I ever wrote of the '60s is a retrospective paragraph in the "Afterword" of *A Severe Mercy*, and I shall end the chapter with it.

To say how I came at last to write the book, I must explain that I was one of those caught up in the mood and action of the 1960s, especially the Peace Movement. Christ, I thought, would surely have me oppose what appeared an unjust war. But the Movement, whatever its ideals, did a good deal of hating. And Christ, gradually, was pushed to the rear: Movement goals, not God, became first, in fact—not only for me but for other Christians involved, including priests. I now think that making God secondary (which in the end is to make Him nothing) is, quite simply, *the* mortal danger in social action, especially in view of the marked intimations of virtue—even arrogant virtue—that often perilously accompany it. Some may avoid this danger, perhaps. But I was not obeying the first and greatest commandment—to love God *first*—nor is it clear that I was obeying the second—to *love* my neighbour. Hating the oppressors of my neighbour isn't perhaps quite what Christ had in mind.

CHAPTER V

Putting God First:
The Vocation

At the beginning of September in 1973—the '60s having ended by my reckoning in midsummer—Watergate Summer—four friends of movement days invited me, rather urgently I thought, to come over to their farm. We sat about in the grass beneath a spreading tree. And then they brought forth a gift, a small, mostly black object that rose to stand on four wobbly white paws: a six-week-old border-collie pup. She wobbled off towards the tree and barked a small, shrill bark. We looked—a copperhead. One of the girls snatched up the defiant puppy, and another chap and I killed the snake. We all congratulated the puppy. That was the coming of Nelly.

I had not wanted a dog again after the death of the beloved Flurry a dozen years before, but my friends thought otherwise. I tried in vain to create a name for the puppy out of my friends' initials—RDTL—and then, since she was a border collie (the Border between England and Scotland) I took a name from the north of England, the old nurse in *Wuthering Heights*, adding a reference to the year of her birth, so the puppy became Nelly Dean Watergate. She was to be just such another as Flurry—obedient, gentle, loving, and a lady. She is beside me as I write.

The '60s were over, except for a few belated bishops and Jesuits just arriving with 'with-it' yelps: they would continue to trouble the air—and the Church—throughout the '70s. And of course there were the left-over hippies, hairy and forlorn, unable to adapt—one saw them along the roadside. But the '60s were *over*. I knew that well; and I'm thankful I saw it and made an end. Nelly Dean marks for me the beginning of the future.

There was in my life a post-'60s lull—no clear direction except away from the '60s. My cottage had now been moved down the hill from the campus to its new location by the park. The people who had known it as the Birdhouse were mostly gone. People referred to it as "Van's house", and I would murmur, "Van's *cottage*." Finally, to symbolize the new location and the new era, its name became *Vancot* (as one says dovecot or sheepcot). But it was changed in more ways than name and place: I restored it to a gentleman's residence, as opposed to the '60s pad—painting inside and out, Glenmerle furniture refinished and softly glowing, and, after a fascinating study of Oriental rugs, some new Persians, including an exquisite little Nain.

I also, as I put it to myself, 'rejoined the faculty'. My long hair was cut, and—a day's wonder—I appeared in a necktie. And there were a series of colleagues and their wives coming to Vancot for sherry and biscuits. I never do things by halves. There was a sense of coming to myself again.

All the same, I was remote from God, much more so than at the time of that chapel talk, and I was not going to church at all. I had not renounced the Faith, perhaps couldn't have, but I was quite able to ignore it, making it a nearly dead faith. I didn't want to think about God and so did not. Although I had immediate interests—studying carpets, restoring Vancot, patiently training the small eager Nelly—I was not thinking about the deep things. It may be that I was vaguely aware that some day I should have to—but not yet.

It was to be sooner than I knew. 1974 was ending; and 1975 was to be one of the most remarkable years of my whole life.

The Year of the Nudges. Nudges from God, that is, or twitches upon the tether. Nine or ten of them, all having the effect of making me think about my distant God. It was really very odd indeed.

First of all—the first nudge—I discovered, belatedly, that the Book of Common Prayer was threatened by revisionists. Why should I care, since I was not going to church anyway? But I *did* care. "WHAT?!" I cried, in effect. "Revise the PRAYERBOOK? That lovely thing? Vandals!! Not one hair of its grey beard shall be touched, not one!" It would be like modernising the west front of Chartres Cathedral. It *was*, in fact, like the disastrous 'improvements' the nineteenth century wreaked upon Oxford, now regretted by everybody. But even they didn't touch the Prayerbook. I fired off long and eloquent letters to the vandals (revisers) and to Anglican journals and even to local Rectors. And, in thinking hard about the beauty and power of the Book of Common Prayer, some of its meaning—meaning about God—sank in.

The second nudge came about through the Prayerbook-letters to local Anglican clergy. The Rector of the little country church of St Stephen's—the church Davy and I had loved and where, in the churchyard, her ashes were scattered—came to see me. If I were going to fight for the Prayerbook, he said, I needed to have a church base and be a church-going Episcopalian. This made sense. Accordingly, with Nelly in Colonel Morgan (the car, newly painted in Confederate grey), I turned up at St Stephen's. What I hadn't reckoned on, though, was being overwhelmed by the dearness of St Stephen's itself—the sense of coming home. If I was coming home to it, was I not, having erred and strayed from His ways like a lost sheep, beginning to come home to God too? I didn't think of it, but the coming home—that was the nudge. And soon the people, some of whom I remembered affectionately from the old days, became dear, too. Indeed, one of my closest friends from the college, Shirley Rosser, and his wife and children were going there now.

It was perhaps that first Sunday that I noticed an old lady, in her mid-seventies, but slender and somehow elegant. When I first saw her, she was skipping gaily on the arm of her daughter, frisking in the early-spring sunshine. I was charmed. And more charmed later when we talked a few moments. Her name was Frances, and her fine-looking husband was Barney: when they went up to the communion rail, I fancied he ought to have had a sword at his side. They lived on down the St Stephen's road at Elk Hill—an eighteenth-century house both spacious and beautiful that reminded me again and again of Glenmerle, especially when, having been there to dine, I came out among the trees with the bright stars overhead—the sense of wide acres round and the sheltering trees of the country. And her border collie frisking round as well as Nelly.

One time in the British Museum I was walking down a wide corridor to the Greek wing. On either side of the corridor were Roman statues that I wasn't especially noticing, but one of them caught my eye: a woman, calm-faced, with a battered nose. I stopped and looked at her, later getting the Museum to photograph her for me. She was unmistakably a lady: she would have a low, a quiet voice, and she would never have to raise it for a servant: she would speak gently—and be obeyed. It was this elusive quality of ladyhood, the quiet—never shrill—*feminine* authority, the mistress, the sensitive perception of her world, the graciousness to guests. Ladyhood, rare and becoming rarer: I knew it when I saw it and was charmed by it.

This was the quality that Frances had. From the first I called her, in my mind, not Frances but Lady Frances. I was to be at Elk Hill often in the next five years, and I adored her. She mothered me a little; and then, too, the reminders of Glenmerle from the moment I turned into the avenue.

I continued, with Nelly, to go to St Stephen's; and Nelly, waiting patiently in the Morgan, as she had been taught to do, though the top was down, became everybody's darling, especially the children's. But once her obedience wavered (I forgave her, as I hope God forgives me). On Rogation Sunday in May, everybody brings animals to be blessed. The people and animals led by the Cross parade about the bounds of the churchyard, blessing the air and the water and the fields and the beasts therein—the cows in the adjacent meadow all looked round when they were blessed. Then a picnic, the tables under the great oaks. On this occasion the church ladies prayed me to allow Nelly, back in the car after the parade and looking longingly at the festivities, to come out for a heaping plateful of meat scraps. So I shouted "Abandon ship!"—the only command for leaving Morgan—and she came running. She took one look at the plate, possibly close to fainting with joy, and whiffled it up in an instant. Then everyone petted her—she has an infinite capacity for loving and being loved.

Next Sunday Nelly marched in with the Rector and choir. Everybody smiled, especially Lady Frances. Still, I took her out and had a few words with her. But she didn't have to explain. It was that plateful of meat and all the loving. She remembered, and she thought: "If this is Christianity, it's for me. Oh, boy!" So she came to Church. —Perhaps my coming home to St Stephen's was a bit like that.

The next nudge was that of mortality. My brother Paul had died at the very end of the '60s; and both my return to St Stephen's with its memories and the coming of Nelly were making me think of Paul. Now I received word that my cousin Ann had been killed in a wreck out west. A second or third cousin really, she was much younger than me, young with sea-blue eyes. We had come to know each other in the '60s when she had often been in Lynchburg, even living once or twice in the cottage when I was travelling. Now she was dead and would be, for me, for ever part of the '60s, as Paul a part of Glenmerle. Now I thought of Ann's bright spirit and Paul's loyal brotherliness. And the Christian hope.

The former chaplain of the college, 'Fig' Newton, whom some of us had fought for in the Faculty Rebellion, was now teaching in Kentucky, whence he had sent me a book. It was by Clyde Kilby at Wheaton College and was called, *C. S. Lewis: Images of His World*. Now I picked it up: glorious scenes of Oxford and rural England. I don't know why it hit me so hard, perhaps it, too, was a coming home after being 'away' in the later '60s from that side of myself. Anyway, I read it with tears in my eyes—Lewis and Oxford and England—and it, too, was a nudge.

And it contained a greater, more powerful nudge. In the book Kilby, along with the pictures, had used numerous excerpts from Lewis's writings. One of these, some lines from *Pilgrim's Regress*, which I had of course read, now—by reason of its being separated from its context—struck me very forcibly indeed. Here it is, the underlining being mine in the book:

> ...if a man diligently followed his desire [for Joy], pursuing the false objects <u>until their falsity appeared and then resolutely abandoned them</u>, he must come out at last into the clear knowledge that the human soul was made to enjoy some object that is never fully given...in our present mode of subjective and spatio-temporal existence.

I stared at these lines for minutes on end—a nudge indeed, almost a punch. Then I typed them on a card and set it on the little shelf by my 'bed-office' and stared at it some more, then and all that spring and summer. And thought.

I had followed that desire for Joy. I had sought an earthly joy that was, despite its first loveliness, as illusory as a wraith. I had been, I thought, not unlike a small boy in the park where someone has blown a large and shining soap bubble, beautiful in the sunlight, that goes drifting off in the gentle breeze. The small boy—me—runs after it, arms outstretched, longing with all his heart to catch it, to possess it. Suddenly it is gone, burst, leaving *nothing* behind. Gone soundlessly in an instant. Looking at Lewis's words, I realised that *all* bubbles end so. But the "some object that is never fully given"—the thing our soul was made to enjoy—*that* was what had to be thought about.

The next nudge—one would scarcely think *it* could be called a nudge from God—was a bit uncanny. I'd been visiting friends in Indiana and Kentucky, including 'Fig' Newton who'd sent me that book. Now I was in Cincinnati with one of my oldest friends, George—he and I had been young radio announcers together and in the Navy together. In later years he had become a newspaper man, a feature writer. On this occasion, he wanted to interview a man named Greener who called himself a clairvoyant and lived over in Kentucky somewhere. After much searching and telephoning, we finally found him, living in a trailer with his plump wife.

George had suggested I talk with Greener first—have a 'reading' as Greener called it—for my comments would be useful in the article. I agreed, expecting a lot of claptrap; and I went with Greener into a tiny trailer room with a table. There was nothing the least bit spooky or wizard-y. He spoke plainly in a soft Kentuckian voice, and I looked out the open window at the chickens scratching about in the yard. Greener wanted to hold something of mine, and I gave him a watch, once Davy's, that I was carrying whilst mine was being mended.

The first twenty minutes *was* claptrap—auras and previous incarnations and that sort of thing. Once I asked him if he could tell my zodiacal 'sign'; and he said I was such an advanced soul that signs were not important.

"Aha!" I thought. "He can't do it."

"But," he added, "your birthday must be about—" and he named a date only one day off. And he also remarked, correctly, that I had been in Hawaii and it had meant rather a lot to me. Two marks for Greener. Still, it was mostly nonsense.

Then he said, "Oh! I see a great bird flying over the sea." Of course I instantly thought of the grey goose. He went on, "This bird is your highest symbol."

"Good lord!" I thought. "Is it just coincidence? Not only the bird—a big one—but the sea. And I *wasn't* thinking about the grey goose."

"Oh! oh!" cried Greener. "I am seeing a woman. The bird has made me see. Her name is Jean, and I see her surrounding you, filling your being. She is your soulmate, the love of your life; no other love can ever take her place. Oh! oh! Now I see! She is dead—she died of something rare; the doctors didn't know what it was."

All this—the bird flying over the sea, the woman linked to it, the love of my life, her name (her real name, not the Davy nickname), her being dead, the doctors (even after a *post-mortem*) not knowing why—was absolutely accurate; and along with my own near-birthday and my having been in Hawaii, it amounted to eight facts that he could not any way at all have known (*A Severe Mercy* wasn't even thought of yet).

But Greener had not done. Now he said (as I continued to scribble down his seeing), "Her birthday, or possibly her deathday, was near July 27th." (She was born on the 24th, and it was near that date that, years later, I learnt from the doctor that she must die.) He added that she was now totally fulfilled. And then:

"I don't understand this: somehow she *chose* to die...she didn't take her own life and she didn't want to die...but in some way she chose her death. I don't understand how this can be."

My blood ran cold at this. *I* understood. But I had never told a living soul of Davy's offering up her life in prayer. This was clear-seeing indeed, whatever clairvoyance precisely is. Either he plucked it out of my mind, though I was not consciously thinking of even one of his ten truths, or he saw truly in some other way. Certainly he did not read anything in my deliberately immobile face. It was quite fantastic; and I do not doubt the existence of his power. From now to the end, though, the power, I think, faded. He said whatever came into his mind, but nothing seemed significant.

I count it a nudge because it pushed my thoughts towards Davy and Heaven. What he said while the 'seeing' was in him included, not only the facts that I knew but also that she was totally fulfilled and that she "surrounded" me: perhaps, I hoped, that was true, also.

The question might be asked, what of the legitimacy of clear-seeing? I don't quite know. The Church, without denying the possibility, forbids any efforts (mediums) to communicate with the dead. But this was not that. As I remarked, he said a good deal earlier and later about previous incarnations and auras, along with predictions about my future. I didn't believe it—claptrap, I called it—but the gullible might, so there's some danger. I expect he was just giving me my money's worth—but his own excitement indicated when the power really got turned on; something, I suppose, he couldn't fully control. I now cannot disbelieve that the power exists: and that leads me to wonder whether the prophets and possibly some of the saints may not have had that power, disciplined by the faith.

After I had returned to Virginia, a young man I had known in the past came to see me on his way to New York. When he'd gone, I found he'd left his copy of *The Lion, the Witch, and the Wardrobe*. I had never read the Narnias, so I decided to read this one (and, later, the lot). Needless to say, it was a nudge.

Next there came a letter from Dr Clyde Kilby, the author of that *Images* book that had so moved me. The letter had to do with the reprinting of *Encounter with Light*—he was giving copies to every visitor to the Wade Collection of C. S. Lewis, Charles Williams, and others. Naturally, in replying I spoke of *Images* and Oxford, and a correspondence began, leading in the end to my writing a little account, at his suggestion, I think, on what our group of Christians at Oxford had said about Lewis. This was not only to be helpful when I wrote *A Severe Mercy* but it turned my mind to the lively and living faith of those Oxford days. Another nudge.

When the fall term began, there was a new chap on the faculty, an Englishman named Jim, who rapidly became a friend. More important, though, in the story of the nudges was his wife, Margery. She was newly Christian, partly through the C. S. Lewis books, and she was eager to talk about the Faith. Her enthusiasm, her fresh faith, fitted right in to the Studio group I'd just been writing to Kilby about. The nudges were coming thick and fast. Everywhere I turned.

And of course I was doing what I'm pleased to call thinking about them. Or perhaps not exactly thinking on a conscious level: mulling them over. I didn't consciously think they were from God (nor did I think they weren't); and I didn't feel impelled to *do* anything about them. As far as I can remember, I didn't think I was or wasn't a Christian. I was just receptive. I did think a lot, peacefully, about Davy-Jean—the clairvoyant partly and the influx of Oxford memories had a lot to do with that. St Stephen's, too, and even having Nelly (reminding me of Flurry).

But I was thinking about Davy in a new way—here the clairvoyance certainly had something to do with it. I was not so much summoning up memories of her: I was thinking of how she saw *me* and how she had seen me in the past. There was, for some reason I can't guess, a recurrent image from the past: my father and I out with the guns on a frosty autumn morning at Glenmerle and coming back to the house with a couple of rabbits. Davy would be sitting by the drawing-room fire with a book, and she would look up with a happy smile. I thought about how she saw me in that moment, almost seeing through her eyes, and I somehow knew she was seeing truly—and if I were indeed seeing through her eyes, then I was seeing truly also. That was not the only image; there were many more—me looking down from the bridge of the destroyer as she approached in the motor boat, or me committing my ways to my Lord, the Christ. The thing was, I was seeing myself more clearly and honestly—through her loving eyes—than I possibly ever had done. I'm not sure that seeing oneself truly is a step towards God, but I think it is.

At all events, by reason of the nudges and the thinking and the mulling over—not forgetting that C. S. Lewis excerpt on the card—I was not the same man I had been at the beginning of 1975. And now comes the slightest and most compelling of the nudges, nothing in itself and yet in effect rather like being that mule who is whacked over the head with a two-by-four—just to get his attention. I had gone to bed one October night and was cheerfully reading a murder mystery. Quite suddenly in the middle of it, I had a powerful impulse to re-read C. S. Lewis's *Out of the Silent Planet*, the first thing of his I had ever read. The impulse was so strong that, cursing myself for a fool, I climbed out of the warm bed and went over to the bookcase and got it. Back in bed, not knowing or destined to know for a year who done in the squire, I read the first page of *Silent Planet*.

That page has *nothing* of the least significance on it, not even a mention of God—just a walker at sunset after a rain looking for a village and a pub for the night's shelter. One paragraph and three lines of the next. A hundred English mysteries begin in just the same way. And yet—I don't know how it was—but in the course of that single page, it happened.

At the beginning of the page I was not close to God, not on speaking terms with Him. At the bottom of the page, with as little fuss as the falling of an autumn leaf, I had returned to the Obedience—God was first in my life. His will was to be my will. I knew this suddenly and totally. I prayed. Christ, I thought, looked at me with forgiving eyes.

This, I later thought, was what all those nudges were leading to. There certainly were a lot of them. I was not very quick. At all events, I was not able to believe that the nudges and that strange return to the Obedience, like hearing a distant bell at night and knowing suddenly where you are, like catching a whiff of salt in the breeze and knowing suddenly the ocean is near, were not of God. He pulled me back. That meaningless page of *Planet*—surely it was used as a channel of grace. Plainly it was a great mercy. I was under the Mercy.

I did not ever go back to that mystery until I had re-read or, in a few instances, read for the first time everything that C. S. Lewis ever wrote. And Charles Williams to boot. And others. And the very next day, I think it was, I sent to the Bodleian Library at Oxford for copies of the Lewis letters I had given them. I came home one evening from late classes to find the parcel from Bodley's; and I didn't even take off my jacket and scarf till I had read the lot, not without a tear or two for so great-hearted and dear a friend.

I contemplated that invisible line I had crossed on the first page of *Planet*. What a difference between thinking vaguely one is a Christian and suddenly becoming one! Not unlike thinking one may be in love and *knowing* one is.

That was the Year of the Nudges. On Christmas Eve, with Nelly cheerfully beside me, I went to St Stephen's as dark came on for our lovely carol service, the last carols being in the churchyard, everyone holding a haloed candle in the misty night: "God rest ye merry, gentlemen." And then Nelly and I followed Lady Frances to Elk Hill to dine and to sing more carols by the tall candlelit tree.

In January of 1976—destined to be, if possible, an even more significant year—I learnt what the nudges and the recall to the Obedience may have been pointing towards. In that month one day, sitting by the fire, I re-read Lewis's letters to me. When I had done, I sat there in the silence thinking of Jack and the Faith, wishing Jack might appear to me as he had done to J. B. Phillips—appear in the chair and give me a grin and be off again. But no burly and amiable ghost turned up. Something else happened. At one moment nothing was further from my mind. Thirty seconds later I was *going* to write a book that was to be named *A Severe Mercy*.

I recall no process of thought or decision, certainly no Voice or Presence. The intention, calm, clear, firm, was simply there—a *fait accompli*—and thirty seconds before it had not been. That is all I *know*. But I *believe* as I believed then that God had commanded me to write the book. It was, precisely, a vocation. In the Afterword of *A Severe Mercy* I put it thus: "Beyond knowing, I *believe* (and did then) that, having been recalled to the Obedience by the nudges and, finally, by irresistible (or, at least, not-resisted) grace, I was now commanded to write: *vocatio*."

The Year of *Vocatio*. That is more impressive to me than it may be to some readers, for I have never considered that anything I have done, including my academic career, was a vocation—something I was called to by God. I do not normally ask whether something I may decide to do is God's will, though I may ask for guidance. But generally I rely on what I call Christian wisdom: seeing how in the circumstances and with one's talents one may serve the Kingdom.

Nor am I given to seeing ghosts or to having direct experiences of Divinity. I have always believed that what I called the Oxford-Vision Dream (in *A Severe Mercy*) was granted to me *and* Davy by God, yet it came in the form of a dream and may, therefore, have been merely a dream (though the only such dream of my whole life). Again, I believed that Davy was sometimes with me during the grief, yet I never saw her or heard her voice, much as I longed to.

Since what I'm talking about is my credulity in relation to the particular vocation to write *A Severe Mercy*, the question of my previous experience with the unseen is relevant. The matter of the clairvoyant does not bear on the question, though; that was simply reportage of *his* 'seeing', though it may be noticed that the clear seeing I accepted was merely what I knew to be true, not the stuff about other incarnations and auras. But I have had one and only one experience of the unseen, a rather odd affair at Oxford. What happened was that a chap, whom we had known but slightly before he went down, came back to Oxford not long after we had become Christians and paid us a visit. He told us with what seemed sinister enthusiasm of a spiritualistic group he'd got into in Southampton: they had a 'guide' and were in touch with the great powers that really governed the earth, and they scorned Jesus. It all sounded like *That Hideous Strength*. And he wanted us—we couldn't think why—to come to it, wanted us very much. Surely we weren't *afraid*? Afraid to risk our faith? This was Saturday. If we were brave enough to come, he would pick us up Friday for the meeting that night. Davy and I both felt the presence of evil, though our minds said it was rubbish. Still, after a glance at Davy, I said we'd go. After he'd left, we talked about it—the sense of evil we'd both felt so strongly. And we both felt uneasy.

Next day, Sunday, at Evensong in St Ebbe's, still uneasy, I prayed very hard indeed for protection against evil. And then, as I knelt there beside Davy, it happened. I could only describe it later to Davy as an opening out or a seeing through: what I saw (?) or sensed was immense, infinite, overwhelming, *loving* power—it was, I said, *like* seeing legions upon legions of angels. Whatever it was, I knew from that instant that we were in no danger from those Southampton powers, if there were any. And Davy took assurance from me. I waited for Friday with the quiet confidence of a saint. The denouement was queer. After all his desire for us to come, on Friday the chap never showed, nor did we ever see him again. Did his spirits, if he had any, warn him we might bring danger? At all events, that glimpse of Heaven's immense loving power was never to be forgotten. Under the Mercy.

Now, it seemed to me, I was again—in the nudges, in the recall to the Obedience, and in the vocation—experiencing Heaven's power and love and mercy.

It was plain to me that January that I could not actually begin *A Severe Mercy* until the long vacation of summer when I should be able to immerse myself in it—I assumed that two or three summers would be required. It was also plain that my almost-finished novel must be laid aside for the duration. And what I should do from now till summer was to think about *A Severe Mercy* and the problems I already foresaw. And I should pray.

That spring there came a challenge to my newly redeemed faith—not from an atheistic secularist but from my own bishop of southwestern Virginia. In the Episcopal diocesan newspaper, he devoted the Bishop's Column to "A Letter to a Fundamentalist", real or imaginary: he spoke not only of the Fundamentalist's Biblical literalism but of his *creedal* literalism, saying: "No creed can be final, because inevitably it will be affected by the world view and the psychology and the philosophy of the age." The creeds, that is, are not unchanging truth but are to be modified by the secular Spirit of the Age.

This moved me to bite the bishop; and the editor, with no doubt the bishop's sportsmanlike approval, ran my remarks as a guest column in place of the usual Bishop's Column.

Reply to the Bishop's Fundamentalist Letter

A fundamentalist, someone said, is one who believes that the entire King James Version of the Bible, complete with Preface, was dropped from Heaven. On the other hand there is the sort of modernist who believes that *nothing* came down from Heaven, not even Christ our Lord. The Bishop in his 'Letter to a Fundamentalist' rightly deplores Biblical literalism and rightly applauds, in the name of truth, Biblical scholarship—the genuine scholars, he no doubt means, who bring no unverifiable assumptions (such as the assumption that miracles cannot occur) to their study of the text.

The Bishop also deplores "creedal literalism", which is not quite the same thing, for the creeds are theological statements of minimal and essential belief. One may, indeed, believe *more* than the creeds—for instance, one may believe in angels—but in a church where the creeds are daily recited one may not believe *less*. After all, if we say "I believe" *not* believing, we are a liar. But the Bishop does not speak of disbelieving; indeed, he acknowledges that there are "limits to unbelief", though he does not tell us what they are. He suggests that the baptismal and ordination rites do not spell out the Apostolic Faith with fundamentalist rigour; but then in a church where we say "I believe" to the creeds in the daily offices these rites need not spell it out.

The Bishop rightly points out the impossibility of imprisoning "the whole of God's truth in any formula of words." Of *course* not! Does anyone, even the Fundamentalist, affirm the contrary? The creeds are *minimal* truth. The whole of God's truth is *far more* than the creeds say; it is not *less*. For the *creeds* (not the 242-page book on Anglican doctrine the Bishop speaks of) are "the official statement of our beliefs."

The Bishop holds that if we can say "Jesus Christ is Lord", we can be a Christian and, even, perhaps, an Anglican. He does not say what we, affirming that only, are to do when the great affirmation of belief that is the creed is said in our church. But, quite apart from that question of honesty, I cannot help but feel that the statement "Jesus Christ is Lord" is somewhat inadequate, if not misleading, as a proclamation of the Apostolic Faith. It may mean no more than that we think Jesus was a good man whose moral teachings (the not-too-inconvenient bits) we intend to follow.

The creed says Jesus Christ, in truth, "was made man", but it *also* says He is "very God of very God." God Himself! That is the terrifying assertion of the creeds: that the God who made the far-flung galaxies lived in *this* world and was killed and rose again from death.

There may be phrases in the creeds, such as "begotten, not made," where too much literalism is misleading; after all the Church was trying to express a truth that staggers the mind. But when it comes to "very God of very God", there is no room for talk of "creedal literalism" (or 'creedal illiteralism' either). *It's either true or it isn't.* Either Jesus Christ was literally and uniquely God, or He was not. Jesus said to the woman of Samaria, "Ye worship ye know not what." Jesus was, you see, rather out of touch with the twentieth-century mind, for He was suggesting that it was desirable to know what one believed. The creeds are, quite precisely, what we who hold the Apostolic Faith *believe*. If we say "I believe" and do not believe, we say a lie. "Very God of very God"—nothing less. As long as we say those creeds they represent the faith of the Anglican Church, necessary to be believed. If we stop saying them, the Apostolic Faith will have died in our church, and the faithful will go off and become Roman Catholics. The Bishop might, as Shepherd of the Flock, reflect on the truth that, although fundamentalism is a danger, the watering-down of the Apostolic Faith is a greater one.
(Professor) Sheldon Vanauken, MA; B.Litt. (Oxon); St. Stephen's. Forest, Virginia.

It isn't the enemy lurking outside the cathedral door that the Church needs to fear but the enemy within. If the once-given supernaturalist Faith is true—the Faith the Saints and Martyrs died for—then the essentially secular unbeliever, however kindly and nice, inside the church doors (especially the ones in clerical vestments) are a greater danger than all the atheists and agnostics in 'the world'.

I wrote a limerick, published later in the *New Oxford Review*, that was meant for every dishonest priest or bishop who did not believe what he asserted he believed when he said the creeds.

> There was a young man of divinity
> Who *could* not believe in the Trinity,
>   But he won his degree
>   And episcopal see
> By fixing his eyes upon finity.

During these months I read a good deal of more or less recent theology and had some long talks with the theologians at the college. Gradually I formed some disrespectful ideas about some of the theologians I was reading and their contribution to the Faith.

Not to mention their intellectual arrogance. It seemed to me that the historico-critical method of N. T. criticism, so much vaunted by those who used it, was as unbalanced and as much based on unproved assumptions as the method of the Fundamentalists. The Fundamentalist, seeing with the eye of faith, *assumes* that everything in the Bible, including Jonah in the whale, is literally true. The historical critic, seeing often enough with a secular eye, *assumes* that everything miraculous is untrue. Moreover, I could not see that the historico-critical method had, in fact, established more firmly or finally discredited any of the things that Christians had always believed, only cast doubt upon them by shaky chains of linked hypotheses.

Finally I wrote a little critical-of-the-critics guide for Christians that I circulated among the religion faculty at the college and other friends. It, too, was later published in the *New Oxford Review*; and, like my "Reply to the Bishop", it illustrates my thinking on the eve of writing *A Severe Mercy*.

A General Rule for New Testament Criticism

If the N.T. Critic states or implies

(1) that an accurate prophecy must have been put in after the event (assumption: prophecy cannot occur);
(2) that miracles must be otherwise explained (assumption: miracles cannot occur);
(3) that a miracle like the Ascension contravening modern cosmology, i.e., Heaven can't be "up" or out, can't have happened (assumption: the infinite God can't have had purposes obscure to critics);
(4) that a statement can't have been made when it was recorded as having been made because its theology or ecclesiology is too advanced for its period (assumption: no witness could have been ahead of his fellows);
(5) that something in Matthew, Luke, or John is an intensification or elaboration of Mark and is *therefore* less accurate or reliable (assumption: no witness with greater knowledge could have later told the complete story);
(6) that a N.T. event is a "typical something-myth" or a "fulfillment saga" (fulfilling Old Testament prophecy) and is *therefore* not something that happened (assumption: [see (1)] the

infinite God could not have intended to turn anticipatory myth or prophecy into fact); or

(7) that Jesus' words were misunderstood by His followers and the early Church, but are clear to the Critic (assumption: the mind of the infinite God is not unlike that of the Critic);

then read no further in Critic, use as doorstop or kindling. The criticism is invalid because it is based on invalid assumptions that cannot be proved, *or* derived from the text. Guesswork based on such assumptions is of no value.

One thing more I wrote that spring was precisely for the young men—and young women—"Who *could* not believe in the Trinity", meaning of course that they *would* not, having breathed the not very fresh air of secularism, stale even in the days of Imperial Rome. But the Trinity comes down in the end to the Incarnation: God the Son as well as Son of God, upon whose authority we know of the Holy Spirit. As always, the fundamental question is: "What think ye of Christ?" The playlet that follows (later published in *Eternity*) contains, as nearly everything I write does, my answer— a rather simple answer—to that question.

THE PLAYWRIGHT INCARNATE

A play about a play about a play

One night some of the characters in Smith's play got to talking, right in the middle of Act II. They were all, drinks in hand, in Bob's comfortable rooms at the University. The windows were wide to the spring night, and the chapel bell was striking eight o'clock.

BOB: Look here, have you all heard this crazy story that's going around—a story that this play we're in is being written by somebody named Smith who made us and the whole University? What nonsense! Science says the University has always been here. And Smith—I've never met him. Nobody has. He's not even in the University—I checked.

TOM: Well, he couldn't be if he's outside the play writing it, could he? He's not in our time and space at all, supposedly. But Linda says she can hear his voice inside her somehow.

LIZ: That's why she's rooming with that awful Beth—because Smith wants her to be kind to Beth.

BOB: What's the matter with her? Voices! Where's this crazy stuff coming from?

TOM: Well, there was a fellow named Smithson at the end of Act I. Of course we weren't here then. Anyhow, he started it. All he talked about was Smith and what Smith wanted us to do. But he also said that *he* was Smith, in some way. He said that anyone who had seen him—Smithson—had seen Smith. If Smith exists, Smithson just could be his word to us.

KAY: Wasn't there some kind of trouble? I heard something about it. Didn't he get killed?

JIM: Yes, that's right. It was some sort of demonstration. He was talking to a crowd about Smith, and some minister called the cops. They said he was killed resisting arrest.

BOB: So the great author gets shot in a street brawl! (Laughs) So now who's writing the play? In fact, who was running things when he was alive and asleep? (Laughter) Some Smith!

LIZ: According to Linda, Smith was writing it—and still is.

BOB: Come on, Liz! Either he was in the play or he's 'out there.' He can't be two people!

TOM: He could be. I wrote a story once and put myself in it—but I was outside, too.

JIM: It's too improbable, though. I might buy the idea of Smith the creator, but not one that sticks himself in the play and gets killed. Undignified! Dumb! But a lot of fools do believe it. They've got a sort of club called the Smithsonian, and the Smithsonians say that Smith invented the play and put Smithson in it to tell us about Smith himself.

BOB: A lunatic! Saying he was the author! Megalomania! Getting himself shot proves it.

TOM: I was talking to that Jewish guy, Paul Bishop, the other day. He used to hate the very name of Smithson, but then he had some sort of experience on the way to Danville or somewhere—after Smithson was dead. He said Smithson spoke to him. So now he's a Smithsonian, one of the leaders. He says the play's a great experiment because Smith lets us choose. Smith wants us to help him make the play come out right because we *want* to. Paul says Smith loves us a lot. He put himself in the play to tell us what he wants us to do.

LIZ: And we killed him!

BOB: I'll do what *I* want to do! Dammit, there's no proof at all. Look at the play—each scene grows out of the one before through perfectly natural causes. Listen—*we* invented Smith!

KAY: Of course we did. And Smithson was just a character like us, only with delusions. A nut!

TOM: Still, it's possible, you know. I was outside my story, but there was a Tom that was me in it, too. If there's a Smith outside this University, how else could he speak to us? But there'd be a risk: he'd have to be all character as well as all Smith—so he could be killed, you see. Maybe we ought to look into what Smithson said if he sort of died for us.

LIZ: If we can hear Smith *in* us—as he must be if he made us—Smithson is the only way.

KAY: Oh, Liz! You've been listening to Linda too much. Why don't *I* hear the voice of Smith?

LIZ: Have you ever tried to? Would you want to hear it? Smith's not going to *make* you listen.

TOM: She's right, Kay. Look, do you know what's so impressive about all this? It's the idea of a sort of trinity: Smith outside writing the play; and inside as a character; and with each of us, too. I don't know whether it's true, but it's exactly the way it would be if it were. Like that story I wrote. And, also, you know, it'd be all *NOW* to Smith, sitting there out of our time: this conversation or Smithson living and dying or even the way it all comes out. This thing has the feel of something true. A sort of rightness.

BOB: Tom, for God's sake! You sound like a Smithsonian! It's just a cult, man! There's no Smith. (Shouts) All right, Smith! Show yourself! Speak! (Grins) See? No Smith!

Smith smiled slightly as his eyes ran down the page. Then he looked at the end of Act I, a little sadly. "Yes, that does it," he murmured to himself. "The way." Then he looked at the ending of the play, the last scene; and he smiled again.

CHAPTER VI

Putting God First:
The Obedience

Playlets and attacks on faithless clergymen and satires about theologians were for my idle time, weekends when classes and meetings were not going on. But the truly important activity was neither the writings nor the teaching: it was the thinking and the praying about the vocation God had given me: to write *A Severe Mercy*. I thought about it every day, mulling over the problems I should be confronted with.

There was one problem of form that bothered me more than all the rest. It seemed to me that certain significant events in my boyhood that affected the marriage of Davy and me—my three-part "Code", for instance, or the choice of the heights and the depths over the middle—ought to be in the book before the story of Davy and me began, as should Glenmerle itself; but at the same time it seemed to me that a book about our love should begin with our meeting. I didn't want an early chapter opening with "I was born on a Tuesday evening." I thought and thought about it: there *was* no solution. And then, I saw it. I quote from the Afterword.

But not until the long vacation could I get down to the actual writing, which for me requires long hours of total concentration. Now, though, I could think. And pray, including despite good health the prayer to live to write it. I foresaw huge problems. One was that of reconciling my sense that a book of Davy and me should not begin before we met with my desire to set the Glenmerle scene in advance to avoid digressions in the Shining-Barrier chapter. Thinking about it one night for the manyeth time, I saw no way. Next morning the solution was clear before my eyes were open. I would begin with the night walk into Glenmerle, in actuality late in the story, making it like an overture in music, stating all the themes that would later be developed, distanced a bit by the third person.

The whole book would be a flashback from that moment when Glenmerle was revisited—a Glenmerle haunted by her. Now I knew how the book should begin.

But not quite yet. My plan was that after the early-May Commencement I should go a-travelling to distant friends until early June. Then, home again, after a day or two of rest, I should plunge into my 'vacation vocation'. Instead, I spent the May flat on my back with a virus. If Virginia were Camelot, there would be legal laws against viruses in Maytime. Anyhow, the question now was whether to go ahead with my trip and postpone writing the book until the following summer or give up the trip and get to work. I sacrificed the trip. I would obey God's command.

So on the first of June, 1976, on my bed with the typing desk, I began. I assumed it would take two or even three years. Veiled from me was the fact that as that year, which had begun with the vocation, came to an end, the manuscript would be on its way to its London publishers. Now I was writing the first sentence: "The country road stretched ahead white in the moonlight and deserted." Another paragraph from the Afterword will summarise the next seventy-eight days—all of June, all of July, and seventeen days of August. Long days, every day—about a thousand hours in all.

When I began to type on June 1st, the shape of the book was set. I wrote each chapter thrice before going on to the next; and it was, like that long-ago Illumination of the Past, a reliving with tears and laughter and deeper understanding. It was total absorption: seven days a week up and writing by 3:00 A.M., continuing without pause for meals until about 3:00 in the afternoon. Lots of coffee. Evenings correcting and reading the diaries. Nights dreaming and, somehow, thinking. Often I awoke knowing that some unforeseen thing must be touched upon. I prayed a lot, almost hourly, that Christ would be in me, speak through me. Perhaps because of the prayer, one anticipated problem—where to draw the line between candour and reticence—seemed, along with other problems, to solve itself. Two days past mid-August I stopped; the third draft was done. Another, later.

It looks like work, hard work. So it was, but it was joyous work. Perhaps the most joyous I have ever known. Intense concentration, somehow even when I was asleep. Caring for nothing but the book—and God. It seems to me that I was never in a sustained way closer to Christ. Decisions about what to include or how to include it seemed to make themselves as I got to them, and I believed that the book was under His guidance, to which I strove to be utterly open. I prayed again and again that Christ would think through my mind, love through my heart, and speak through my (two) typing fingers.

It was joyous work, partly because I was close to Christ, doing His will of my own free will and desiring nothing so much, and that is always joyous. But then, too, it was reliving the days of our loving. In the book I describe what I called the Illumination of the Past in the months after her death. That was now twenty years before. And now, studying our journal, writing the book, I was having another such Illumination, this time with more joy than grief—not that there weren't a few tears. The first time there had been music, even scents, to make the past come alive. Now, more than compensating for those aids, there was the intense concentration, the intense *seeing*, of writing.

I sent each chapter—each written three times before moving on to the next—to my dear friend Dom Julian, the Benedictine monk of Portsmouth Abbey on Rhode Island, who had been at Oxford with me. He was so moved and delighted by the Oxford chapters that he wrote a marvellous little poem, "Ah, Studio!" I loved it and was sad that it was the wrong period to be included in *A Severe Mercy*; but then in a last-minute, delighted inspiration, involving urgent cables to London, I included it on the dedication page. But that lay ahead. Now at the time of reading the Oxford chapters he dubbed me knight, later doing the actual accolade with a small sword; and he has never, from that day to this, failed to address letters to "Sir Sheldon". Half a joke, a praising joke—but not without a slender validity, for churchmen as well as knights could create knights.

A few times during the writing I drove out with Nelly to Elk Hill—she was always welcome—to dine with Lady Frances and Barney. Elk Hill on a summer night, starlight on the lawns, and the Glenmerle I was writing about overlaying it in a ghostly way. Lady Frances, too, read the chapters with praise and some good suggestions. I didn't stay late, for three o'clock in the morning comes right early in Virginia.

Late in the summer, friends came back from their summer travels in England or Europe and told me their tales of cathedrals and countryside as well as lost luggage and missed trains. Still, all very colourful. And I had sat here in Vancot, wearing my two fingers down to stubs, having no adventures—or so they commiseratingly thought.

But that was not the way of it. Not at *all*. What I had been doing was not merely plodding, or even trotting, along in the manuscript. I had been cantering along a country road with Davy, well mounted in a summer dawn. The walls of Vancot had dissolved, and Davy and I had wandered about Glenmerle in Maytime and climbed the cloudy green mountains of Hawaii. The rakish schooner *Grey Goose* had met storm and the night of the sea-fire; and the spires of Oxford had reached up into the sky just beyond the book wall. I did, after all, get that grin from Jack Lewis in his rooms in Magdalen. Laughter and tears. Adventure and all the colour and play of life. I had had more in that vivid summer of writing than all my travelled friends put together. And it had all been touched retroactively by the sacred—a sort of golden light.

What a seventy-eight days it had been! But now the summer was ending. The manuscript was laid away with copies off to friends. But the elation continued. My old friend Edmund Dews arrived from Santa Monica, Edmund who played a significant part in the Oxford chapters. He read the whole book one night and had nothing but praise for it. And we had a civilised dinner together.

Some young men from Oxford arrived—it had been arranged that they were to spend a night in my cabin at the Rock—and I took a friend, Pat Kelley, a Bonhoeffer scholar on the theological faculty of the college, with me to the country that evening to help entertain them. Pat also had read my manuscript, and we talked about it as we drove out to Amherst county. Nelly came, too, and was everybody's pet and lover. The log cabin has a stone terrace in front, bounded by a low stone wall, just right for sitting. And there were chairs. It was a late summer night. The stars out there, far from town lights, were bright, and Cedar Mountain rose up blackly against them. Apart from the stars and a lamp in the cabin, there was no light anywhere to be seen. The stream coming down from the waterfall burbled beside us, and crickets chirped, but otherwise a hush lay over the hills; no breeze was blowing. We all talked in low voices so as not to offend the night—talked of Oxford, where Pat, too, had spent a term, and of Virginia, and of Christianity. I include the account simply because it was part of the great happiness of the aftermath of completing my manuscript. I was, as it were, walking on air.

I knew the book was good through friends who confessed their delight and tears in reading it. I felt it was Christ's doing, not mine, and I was grateful. The psychologists say we should love ourselves, and, while I tend to believe it unwise to think too much of self, I must say that in this time of feeling that I had done God's will—fulfilled His command—I was happier about myself than I had been for years. Like Nelly who is so pleased when she obeys.

That late summer and the fall, I went several times to the Rock, just to be alone. (The friend who owned it with me dwelt in Washington and couldn't often be there.) Once I had even tried writing on the terrace, but the writing got slower and slower, stopping when I watched a bird or ducked from a bee, and finally ceased altogether, and summer seeped in. I was probably turning into a frog.

So the fall term began—began with my speaking to a large group of students round the fire at a nearby lakeside lodge on the wholeness of C. S. Lewis as scholar and Christian.

There is no need to recount in detail my dealings with publishers. I asked a lot of them if they wanted to read it as it was—singlespaced, both sides of the page, a smooth third draft but another to be written—pointing out that by reading it now they might influence the final draft. I included a page of comments by friends, some of them, like Clyde Kilby, Tom Howard, and Paul Holmer, writers themselves. Some did want to read it, and I sent it, pointing out that other publishers were reading it, too. Meanwhile I was annotating the master copy with friends' suggestions, along with a hundred afterthoughts of my own. In the end, a London publisher and three U. S. ones wished to publish, giving me the pleasure, rare for unknown authors, of choosing the publisher for English North America.

But, first and most electrifying, came a letter on November 30th from Hodder & Stoughton, London: they would publish for the United Kingdom and the old British Empire (less Canada) if they could have the final draft by January 10th, just about the anniversary of God's command to write it. My plan to write a leisurely final draft the next summer vanished like morning mist. No matter what, I *would* get that draft done and in the mails by the end of the year.

Because of final exams, I couldn't begin until the third of December: then—Battle Stations! It was like the summer, only more so. That is, ten to twelve hours a day typing, and another two hours proof-reading—and drawing the tiny diamond pictures to celebrate each chapter's completion (no thoughts of their being published). I took off Christmas eve for the carols at St Stephen's and dining at Elk Hill with Lady Frances and Barney and others; and Christmas afternoon for dinner with other dear friends; but neither really broke my schedule. And I finished on the 30th, a day before my deadline: two copies of the manuscript went separately off to London by air. Then I took time for several deep breaths, and the joyful year of the *vocatio* ended. I had obeyed.

No word is more precise, more the *mot juste*, for the next year, 1977, than *exaltation*. Far more so than after the book was published and the splendid reviews and awards were pouring in. It was simply exaltation over having written it. It was also the year of the publishing process. I made my editor's life a burden by thinking up changes and additions. And he thought of a few: I learnt with astonishment that the past tense of 'dive' was 'dived', not 'dove' which was a rootless Americanism. The book was, of course, published with English spelling that I mostly used anyway. At the last minute I sent in three new paragraphs, one of which on marriage I thought right important, but it was too late for the First Edition. (That particular paragraph, beginning "One insight from the past..." is in the last few pages of Chapter VIII of the later editions.) There were, naturally, some battles with the publishers, cables flashing back and forth, but I won more than I lost. Still, the publishing, despite long letters and the crisis times of galley proofs and page proofs, occupied for me only a small part of the year. Yet, whatever else was happening, the book was never far from my thoughts, and the exaltation remained.

Early on in the year, while I was so happy, a most unhappy letter came from a friend whose little son was dying and all my friend's hopes as well: he could not understand why God would let it happen. Later, another friend wrote to tell me of a young woman he knew who had gone rushing to the hospital where her husband, struck down by a drunken driver, lay dying. He was dead when she arrived. Then, even as she was turning sadly away, her house—and their two babies in it—was burning to the ground. Almost unhinged, she abjured her Christian faith and cursed God. I wrote to this friend a letter to show her that was almost the same as the letter I had sent to the first friend. Letters on God's will. Those two letters were so long that I decided to write what I'd said—I had a copy of the second one—in an essay that I could then send to other folk who might be facing similar heartbreak. This I did.

The essay, entitled "God's Will", was published in due course by the Episcopalian journal, *The Living Church*; and it has, in fact, been sent to a good many suffering people by me (and perhaps by others). My reflections on the problem of pain follow.

GOD'S WILL

Reflections on the Problem of Pain

"I still can't get over it, Jane, losing my baby. Just before her second birthday. But it was God's will."—"God must be testing Sue by giving her cancer."—"He broke his back when the tractor turned over. It was God's will, of course."—"God took both our children."—"How can a good God let the Cambodians starve? I refuse to believe in a God like that."—"All three of his sons, such fine boys, died when the cruiser was torpedoed. It was God's will."—"How can God make me suffer so? I hate God!"

It was God's will. Or, as Allah wills it. Is this, in truth, the way of it? Does God indeed award a cancer here, a car wreck there, all according to His high and mysterious purpose? Does He punish Mr and Mrs Smith by willing the death of their child when the drunken youth rams their car? Does God will the earth to quake? Did He will the deaths of millions, Christians as well as Jews, in the Nazi death camps, or at the murderous hands of Stalin?

It may be indeed that good men must sometimes suffer to learn that their only lasting joy—their only security—is in God. Some may be called upon individually to bear the weight of the cross for His sake, nor can we always see how their pain shall be to His glory. But in speaking of every disaster as God's will, we forget something essential to the Christian faith: the Fall and its consequences. The story in Genesis may be taken as literal truth or as myth; but *myth* implies an essential truth. Moreover, the Fall is not only affirmed by St Paul, it is affirmed by redemption itself—redemption in Christ—for redemption is *from* sin. The sin that entered the world with the Fall.

Let us consider what the Fall was and is. It is man, a created being—a *creature*—in rebellion against his Creator. It is man in his pride seeking independence—autonomy—by choosing something other than God. By choosing *himself*. Self. Self-centeredness. Selfishness. Self-expression. Self-realization. Self-fulfillment. Some of these sound quite innocent, don't they? But Christ's command was to *die* to self. We are not roused to enthusiasm by the idea.

A question arises: Why did God let the Fall happen? Why didn't He give Eve a frightful slap and say in a voice of thunder: "*Stop* that!"? Why did He *let* us become infected with sin? We are so addicted to self, so infected, that our self-love doesn't even shock us, we hardly notice. But God allows us choice. That is the answer to the question of why He didn't slap Eve. A simple answer—and utterly astonishing. He not only made living, moving creatures. He made creatures capable of saying "No" to Him, of defying Him. Unlike the trees, we have free will. God's great experiment was to create us free to *choose* to love Him (the only love worth having) or to reject Him. We love Him and serve Him, or we love our self and serve that self. We don't admit we're self-serving, but we're often proud to say we're self-sufficient, without need for God.

But if we are fallen—infected with sin and addicted to sin—what hope is there for us? Perhaps God, not caring, has abandoned us? —He cares so much that He allowed us to drive the nails through His hands. My God! He loves us that much! The phrase has become so boring as to lose meaning: Christ came to save sinners. Awesome meaning, in fact.

He came down from heaven—God Himself—and became man and died in agony as man, trusting forsaken (as He had to be to taste the whole of death). When we suffer, let us remember the Son trusting the Father—and the validation of the trust in the Resurrection. Christ was, precisely, God's action to save us from the Fall. On our own we cannot conquer our addiction to self, but with Christ in us we are not on our own.

When the Fall occurred, it was not only man that fell. All creation (at least on earth) somehow fell too. We cannot know how it was before—whether it was only with the Fall that the lion learned to bite man. And we don't know whether there is indeed a Prince of this World, an archangel, himself fallen after "dubious battle on the plains of heaven." But we may remember that that ominous figure, however much not "in" among Christians these days, was spoken of with authority by our Lord. What we cannot know is what that fallen creation—and that prince—may have to do with the cancer that tries our trust.

The finite mind of man cannot comprehend the infinite mind of God. We can know only what God has revealed to us in Christ. We know that we have choice, for He told us. And we know, even with our finite minds, that if men can choose evil, other men will suffer. Three-quarters of the suffering is clearly traceable to man's own cruelty and greed. And we know—it is much—that He loves us and that we can trust Him. We can hold to that.

It is the implications of free will that I wish to explore. That we were given choice is one of the things we know. But it was not Eve only making a choice, and choosing further to tempt Adam: consequently he was faced with *his* choice, and he made it. And we have been making choices ever since: the Nazis were men making choices, so is the fellow who snaps at his wife at breakfast.

But choice has consequences or it wouldn't be choice at all. If we pull the trigger, the bullet strikes, and our victim gasps and dies. If God gives us freedom, freedom to choose, He must allow us to have what we choose—the taste of the apple, the death of the man we shoot, or, if we insist, Hell—or it wouldn't be choice at all. He must allow the consequences. And the consequences of the consequences, going on endlessly, involving the innocent.

If a young man drinks too much (a choice) and pridefully decides to show his girl how fast he can drive (a choice), he may smash hideously into your car, killing his girl and leaving you paralyzed for life. Is this God's will (except in the sense of permitting the choosing)? It cannot be, for that would mean God forced the young man to choose evil (self). He chose; the consequences follow. The girl's family plunged in grief. You unable to send your son to college. The policeman who came to the wreck not being somewhere else to stop a crime.

But there may be good consequences, too—God will bring these about if possible. You and your wife may learn to trust God more deeply; the young man, haunted by grief, may become a Christian. But those would be bringing good out of evil, not bringing about the evil in hopes of the good. The *evil* was the consequences of a choice.

To say that because God is sovereign and all powerful He can simultaneously give us freedom to choose and compel our choice is not to say something profound about omnipotence but to speak nonsense. The glass is either transparent or opaque. The Holy Spirit urges us towards the good, not towards the evil. And, of course, our good choices—our prayer for strength to bear pain or for healing—also have consequences. The consequences of good acts also go on and on.

Millions of people choosing, millions upon millions of choices, choices at every second of the centuries. *One* choice is like a stone chucked into a still pond with the wave spreading out in all directions. But *all* the choices: imagine an ocean with a constant hail of stones plunging into it and a chaotic tumult of boiling waves in a patternless storm. Only God could comprehend it.

The murderer is making a choice. So is the monk praying in the night. The rapist is a monster of self-choosing, as is the woman who feeds on her children to bolster her ego. The man who rushes into a burning house to save a neighbor's child; the businessman who cuts his neighbor's financial throat; the child who tortures the cat. The choices are not in a vacuum: someone else is helped or harmed, including the cat.

Sometimes it is said about monstrous evils like the Nazi death camps that, if there were a God, He would stop them. Why *doesn't* God stop such human suffering? Let us, then, suppose He *does*. Let us imagine God looking down at the Nazi death camps: the squalid misery, the near starvation, the cold, the brutal guards, the firing squads, the skinny children herded into the gas chambers. God sees it all and hears the wailing and the prayers: "Help us, oh God! Let our cry come unto Thee!" —Suddenly the divine fist slams down upon the table, and thunder drowns out the guns below.

"By God!" He says. "It's too much. Eating an apple is one thing—but *this*! I never dreamt that my men could be this wicked. I *will* it to stop."

Well, of course it stops. A Nazi guard turns a handle to start the gas flowing in upon the huddled victims behind the heavy glass. He yawns, he's done this so many times. No thrill left. Then he notices that the people in the chamber are not clawing their throats. Odd. He gives the handle another push, just as the walls of the gas chamber dissolve. He and the other guards snatch out pistols and fire. God catches the bullets in His hand. In time the prisoners shuffle away, finding that the perimeter fences have vanished.

God has acted. Elsewhere, booted feet ascend the stairs, and a door is kicked in. Storm troopers enter, guns leveled, and the man they've come to get cowers. But the blow and the kick do not land; and the storm troopers, bewildered, go away.

Now that God is acting, He will have to act the next time the Russians purge a few million people. In the meantime, there is the Hitler war. Hundreds of Luftwaffe bombers are over London, bombs whistling down. But God's hand is in the way. Londoners go back to bed. The roar of the guns on the Russian front is stilled. A submarine fires a spread of torpedoes. It appears that two at least will strike the cruiser, and 800 men will die, including one family's three fine sons. God reaches into the water and seizes the torpedoes. The proud cruiser steams on.

But agony is not to be measured quantitatively. The 50 people in a gas chamber—a quick death, after all—or one man being hideously tortured, hour after hour, day after day, by the Secret Police. God stops that: no line can be drawn. And the woman in a hospital, her body eaten up with cancer: she is suffering almost as much or perhaps more—who can measure? God, committed now to action, acts. The woman draws a long breath, flinching. It doesn't hurt. She sits up and asks for lunch.

A rapist is leering down at his terrified victim. Then he finds an invisible wall between him and her. In a few moments she pulls her torn frock round her and goes, possibly sticking her tongue out at the shrunken man. A woman watches her husband drink the coffee she has put strychnine in. She turns pale when he gives her a kiss and goes off to work. Another woman screaming at her tired husband, as she has done for years, is suddenly voiceless. A boy's cruel epithet flung at a high school girl who would be scarred by it is heard by no one. The child's hands torturing the cat go limp. The cat goes away, tail in air.

All this—it's right nice, isn't it? This is the God we want, we think. We are ready to re-elect God, God. But let us look further. When all this begins to happen, people will be astonished and unbelieving, victims and predators alike. Of course many of the victims are predators in their own ways: the man in the death camp may be, in what he thinks of as better times, a rapist. People will go on for a while trying to find pistols that will work and have fun again.

But finally it will dawn upon mankind that God has stopped all victimizing. You cannot shoot anybody, but also—since God can't draw lines—you cannot bark at your wife or cheat on your income tax. The fist cannot connect. The cruel word cannot be said. Free will has been repealed. No one now chooses to be good; he *must* be.

Newspapers shrink. No more wars or rumors of war, no more corruption in Washington, no more murder trials, no more juicy scandals. Lions lie down with lambs, and capitalists with workers. Almost every novel ever written will soon come to seem unreal, for they were about a world where good guys strove with bad ones, and courage meant something. And goodness.

The gift God gave to man was the freedom to choose. If God acts to prevent the consequences of choice, the gift is withdrawn. No one will choose to shoot if the bullet cannot strike. No one will accept cancer with fortitude and prayer if there is no cancer. No one will wound with a cruel word if it is unheard. For awhile people will wistfully yearn to hurt somebody, but new generations will have forgotten choice. No longer will it be salvation through the redemptive sacrifice of Christ. Indeed, the Passion itself will seem meaningless to a world that has never known suffering, a world where wickedness is unknown.

But, also, a world where goodness is not chosen and is, therefore, unknown. To finite man, what meaning can *goodness* have if there is no badness? Is this, after all, the world we should like? As it is now, we are moved by valour and goodness because they shine in an evil world as stars shine in darkness.

No stars, so to speak, in our new world. God's grand experiment of creating people free to love and trust Him or to hate Him will be all over. We, compelled to be good without choice, shall sink into apathy. Perhaps our minds will decay. We shall not have achieved autonomy. We shall have become automatons. More and more like vegetables, merely existing. We who were created for the stars.

After all, perhaps it is as well that God is running the universe, not us.

When God became one of us in Christ, He never promised us an easy time or said that Christians would be spared. In fact, the lions in Rome were already looking forward to their first taste of raw Christian. What Jesus said was: "Take up your cross and follow me."

We shall suffer because of evil loosed into the world, most of it men's choices. Despite a shudder for what may lie ahead for me, I say thank God—imagining a world without choice. Pain may seem an unmitigated evil—and, unless it draws us or others to deeper trust in God, it is. But would we escape it by rejecting God's grand gift of freedom? We must indeed use that freedom to lessen the suffering in the world: thus good comes from evil.

And if we must suffer, let us remember Jesus forsaken. And, like Him, trust in agony—remembering that God Himself in awesome compassion is suffering with us. In the end we shall have what we have chosen: we shall have Him: and in the light of His face all the suffering unto death—the bearing of our cross—will then have been less than a half-remembered dream.

There were other writings that year while waiting for the book to appear. In the continuing battle for the soul of the Episcopal Church, torn between secularism and faith—the Spirit of the Age *versus* the Holy Spirit—I wrote, after deep thought, an essay on priestesses. I had been a keen feminist since the '60s, but now, now that God was first, I was asking, not what women's will was but what *His* will was. And I came to believe that the attempt to ordain women was contrary to His will. The editor of the *New Oxford Review* entitled the essay: "Since God Doesn't Make Mistakes, WOMEN'S 'ORDINATION' DENIES THE INCARNATION." But this will come in a later chapter.

The battle between secularism and faith was not, of course, limited to the Episcopal Church. It raged in nearly all the churches, and in some, indeed, humanistic secularism—or neo-Modernism—had virtually won. This was the real struggle of our day, not Anglican v. Puritan or Catholic v. Protestant, but the Christian *faith* v. secular neo-Modernism. But the battle lines cut across every denomination. As I said earlier, the deadliest enemies of the Faith are *within* the churches, and the deadliest of all are the neo-modernist ministers and priests and bishops—and their theologians—who take their lead from the secular world and the Spirit of the Age.

I now wrote a heart-felt poem about these unadmitted apostates *in* the Church, published in *Christianity Today* and elsewhere. The 'Shepherds' are not only bishops but all the ministry. In mediaeval stained glass the blue is technically called 'the light', admitting light, and background for the reds and yellows. Thus in the poem I'm using "Light" with a double meaning.

The Shepherds' Reformation

The new apostates' breath
Shrivels divinity up.
Unproved assumptions gauge
Their scholarship: their lord's
The Spirit of the Age.
They stab with secular swords
    The wounded side
    Of the Crucified,
And holding the holy cup
They urge the ultimate death.

As suavely they speak the Creed,
With every word forsworn,
    From His Father's side
    And His fainting Bride
The Son of God is torn.
The flung´stone´shatters
The blue´stained´glass´:
The Light of Heaven scatters
Upon the pitying grass.
—But what if He's risen indeed?

A great truth had been taught me by a dog: the *meaning* of the words in the Book of Common Prayer: "whose service is perfect freedom" (The Second Collect, for Peace). How can service be freedom, perfect freedom? The dog, decades before, was a wheat-coloured, mostly-collie bitch named Gypsy; and I had included the story of Gypsy, entitled "The Fall", in *A Severe Mercy*. She was in my service—I was her lord—but she had learnt to disobey when she was out of reach. Consequently, though she never understood cause and effect, she, the runaway, lost all the freedom she previously had enjoyed to wander our broad acres and had come to live in a pen. And I, in the '60s, had been a Gypsy, a runaway. I had followed my shining soap bubble, running after it across the sunlit grass, as she had run after her imaginary rabbits. And the result of disobedience, for me as for her, had been a pen of my own making.

In this year of waiting for the Book to be published I thought of the truth—the *deep* truth—that in His service was perfect freedom. Gypsy, despite many opportunities to return to the obedience, had never done so; and she had run away a last time and was lost for ever. My story was happier. God in His mercy, after a good many nudges, had recalled me to the Obedience—and to penitence. I had deeply and painfully repented of my sins, the deepest repentance of my whole life. I hardly knew the *meaning* of real repentance till then. Davy had been convicted of sin before her conversion in Oxford. In these months after the return to the Obedience, *I* was. And I confessed, with pain and joy, to Father Julian, my confessor despite my being Anglican; and he had given me the pure water of God's absolution. But God's mercy was greater still: He had, I believed, entrusted me—me, the disobedient sinner—with a task to do: the vocation He called me to. And I *obeyed*, of my own free will. And thus I came to understanding of the *perfect* freedom of being in His service. The freedom of free-will *choice* of obedience. It was pure delight. And with it the delight of known forgiveness and absolution. Of course the compunction for my sins—what is left after repentance and absolution—remained as it always would (like a healed scar); but it did not diminish the delight. Indeed, perhaps it enhanced it—a sign of forgiveness.

On the deepest level those were my meditations. On another level some lines from Masefield were echoing in my thoughts as a true summation of what he and I and many another man were doing in our writings—*exactly* what I had done in *A Severe Mercy*.

> For all men praise some beauty, tell some tale,
> Vent a high mood that makes the rest seem pale,
> Pour their heart's blood to flourish one green leaf,
> Follow some Helen for her gift of grief...

The days were drawing in. The autumn leaves were blowing in

the wind. At the beginning of November would come the Book. I ached to see it. The publisher for English North America had long since been chosen, Harper & Row; and they, craftily, were simply photographing the English masters and so would have their edition in Confederate grey out within days of the London one.

Then in the post, air mail from London, came the Book, very handsome in a dark forest-green jacket. I held it in my hand. And as I held it, I felt, quite unexpectedly, a powerful sense of something *discharged*, something completed. Perhaps, I later thought, it was the *vocatio*. Or perhaps atonement.

A few days afterwards it occurred to me to burn the old diaries and letters. Davy and I could never read them together in old age. What they had existed for in the master plan was to be the source for *A Severe Mercy*, although they contained a thousand times the material I had used. But, as I said in the Afterword, I knew I should not come this way again. And I did not care to have any possible later scholars scrabbling about in their pages. So one by one I put the journals on the glowing coals of the fire, and the photograph albums (save for a dozen pictures) as well; and I watched the loved pages curl and blacken and for ever perish. I have never regretted the act. Something *was* completed.

A Severe Mercy had a totally unlooked-for effect on my life, although it took me awhile to realise it: it bridged the two halves of my life, the first half with Davy, the second without her. Anyone might have thought in the late '60s—including me—that the second half of my life was altogether divorced from the first half and would continue to diverge. But now *A Severe Mercy*: it was *about* the first half and it was *written in* and *experienced* (as a book) *in* the second half. The two halves had become *one* story. The theme of my life with Davy became the theme of my whole life, known now, not merely to a few friends, but to tens of thousands. (The present book makes it still more one.) This realisation that it was all one story gave me great content.

An old college friend, Paul, read the book about Davy and me and with patient craftsmanship made me a beautiful model of *Grey Goose* under the wind for my mantelpiece. She is a sort of symbol of this unity of my life, belonging to Davy and me yet stemming from the book in the later life.

Now that I had written the book I never expected to write, it seemed almost inevitable that I should have done so. But it wasn't at all. I might have disobeyed. Or been unworthy to be called to write it.

There were copies of the book for the friends who had been kind enough to read it in manuscript. Almost immediately there was a book-party at the college, laid on by the theological faculty and the college bookshop—Pat Kelley, who had bought me lunch on 'Pub Day', now presented me with a copy, from him and his colleagues, of the 1559 Book of Common Prayer in a graceful little speech. A few days later *Time Magazine* spoke of my book, and half the county rang up to tell me I was "in *Time*." Lady Frances and other friends in England and English North America (the book appeared at almost the same moment in England—the first edition—and in the U.S. and Canada) wrote to praise it.

If I am to tell the whole story, I must say something of the reviews and awards. It is not to boast, for I thought constantly that the book's success was indeed Christ speaking through me, and to Him be the honours. But even before the year was out splendid reviews were pouring in from both England and the United States, and bookshops were running out of copies in that Christmas of 1977.

Indeed, if that year prior to publication in November was the year of exaltation of my spirit, the following year, 1978, could only be described as heady. The reviews, almost all of them, were what the trade calls 'rave reviews'; and there were at least a hundred and fifty of them from all over the world—the book was translated into several other languages. My London editor, Tony Collins, said of the British reviews, "In our experience only a very few authors get the sort of applause you are getting." And, along with the reviews, a stunning and wholly unexpected flood tide of moving letters from readers everywhere, letters and phone calls and visitors. (I answered them all, a couple of thousand of them.) To Christ be the credit, but it was I being praised. Most men manage to bear up under that, and I did. Then there were the awards, seven in all, beginning with *The National Religious Book Award* in 1978 and ending with *The American Book Award* (TABA) in 1980.

It is, beyond doubt, far more important what a book does in the hearts of men, and still more important how it serves the Kingdom; but except for glimpses and surmises, these things cannot be known except to God. And the tangible evidence of success that no writer really despises—the reviews, bookclubs, awards, reprintings, and royalties—are unquestionably a bit heady. Especially if totally unexpected: I had thought *A Severe Mercy* would be for the few. I remember thinking that some day, maybe after years, I might get one letter about it, from perhaps a New Zealand sheep farmer—though why a NZ sheep farmer I can't think. I was not prepared for hundreds and hundreds and the phone ringing night and day. So the outward and visible signs of impact are exciting; and if, underlying all that, there is a sense of gladness and accomplishment about the work itself, that is better still.

The book, in my fancy, was the child we never had. I thought of that round the time of the completion of the manuscript, and the thought continued. It was a son perhaps, going forth into the world now with vivid memories of his mummy and daddy, making friends out there, not writing home but occasionally sending home the odd cheque. But I did hear from those who invited him into their homes, so I didn't lack for news of him. The labour—the labour unto death—had been the mother's, but he couldn't have existed without both of us. And the shaping of our son had, with her death, been up to me. But that was all done now: he was out of my hands, on his own. But not, of course, out of my mind. Indeed, as parents often do, I felt, with some truth, that Davy and I lived on in our child. A curiously pleasing little fancy.

The great fact of my life was not the success but the closeness to God. I may not have been on speaking terms with Him in the later '60s, but I assuredly was now. I saw the sacred everywhere. A little poem I wrote one morning after a look out of the window suggests this. (It was published in *Eternity*.)

Cardinal

> This is no chance,
> This bird of flame
> That grips my glance:
> I see God's Name
> In scarlet flight
> And know that He
> Along the light
> Is hailing me.

Although the reviews were so favourable, I was bothered by the constant misuse of the word *romantic* (so brilliantly treated by C. S. Lewis in the Preface of *Pilgrim's Regress*). To these reviewers moonlight (however actual) was romantic, neon lights (however fictional) were not. Finally I wrote a parody (including the little preface) of my own first chapter, which was published in *The Wittenburg Door*.

Some have criticized A SEVERE MERCY for being romantic and Sheldon Vanauken for being a romanticist. Mr Vanauken replies: "In the popular mind, apart from the vulgar use of 'romance' to mean two people in love, moonlight and roses are held to be romantic where neon lights and city streets are realistic; and in that same mind romanticism and realism are thought to be opposed, which they are not. In a true account of what really happened, including moonlight, there is nothing that can be called 'romantic'." For all those who are pleased to think themselves anti-romantic realists, we offer a parody by Mr Vanauken himself of his own moonlit first chapter, "Glenmerle Revisited".

Jake's Place Revisited

The city street stretched ahead, white under the street lights, except for the dark oil patches, and deserted. A single car, a battered old Chevy with a broken back window, was creeping along, its driver looking intently at the numbers on the tall dingy tenement houses that lined the street. The night was hot, and the air that came in the window was laden with the mingled scents of exhaust fumes, urine, and hot asphalt with perhaps a hint of garbage.

The car crept into the curb. The driver uncoiled his long frame and, taking a last gulp from the pint bottle of whisky on the seat, got out, belching as he did so. The night was comparatively still, apart from his belch, though he could hear the roar of trucks from the Interstate not far away and somewhere a tomcat was yowling in frustrated passion.

The driver, a tall unshaven man in his late thirties, walked along the sidewalk, circling to avoid an overturned garbage can and the spilled garbage. Out of the corner of his eye he was aware of an orange glow a third of the way up the sky, and he turned to look across the street at it. It was not the moon but an open window through which he could see a somewhat billowy woman unhooking a bra. At the same instant, from the open door of the tenement that was his destination, there came a smell of garlic and spaghetti, and he was irresistibly reminded of Dolly, his wife who had died a year ago. He could almost hear her screaming at him. He wondered whether he was always going to be reminded of her by the smell of garlic. He hoped not, for he liked garlic.

He entered the narrow hall of the tenement, noticing a headless doll on the floor. Everything was just the same as it had been in his boyhood. He began to ascend the stairs, stepping over a broken tread;

his parents had lived on the fifth floor. As he reached the second floor, there was a squeak and a scrabbling and a big rat scurried down the hall. He remembered all the rats that had infested the place in his childhood. He and his brother had even had names for them, particularly Polly, the brown rat.

On the next landing a door was open on the right, and—yes, there it was: the toilet in its small cubicle: but dry now and cracked, brown inside. He looked at it, and suddenly there was water in the bottom of it again, and children stood around it in the light of the dim bulb overhead. His brother, he remembered, had been trying to push the cat head-first into the water, and he had gone in to help. He looked again, and the toilet was dry and brown, though, by the smell, someone had used it recently.

He continued to climb for another half flight and then sat down on the steps. What was the use of going further? One floor was like another, and he knew no one in the place now. His father, Jake, had another year in prison for slashing that cop, and his mother was dead.

His mother—he could picture her now as she had been the last time he had climbed these stairs. He had pushed open the door, with the screech of hinges as always, and she hadn't even looked up. She had just sat there on the broken chair—the back was gone, smashed by Jake in one of his drunken rages—sat there, mumbling, with the half-empty gin bottle on the table in front of her, and her straggly grey hair partially obscuring her face.

He became aware of a rhythmic gasping sound, and, after a moment, identified it as snoring coming from the apartment a few steps above him. Off in the night somewhere he could hear a siren howling.

He thought of his childhood in this place. He and the boy downstairs had both been members of the Switchback Gang. What times they had had! He remembered the night they had broken the church windows and knocked down the old Father. Those were the days, all right. He thought of his parents, that night when his father had dragged his mother across the room by the hair, threatening to throw her out of the window. How she had screeched! Not unlike that siren, in fact; that must have reminded him. Once again, way up here, he caught that whiff of garlic and heard steps somewhere below. For an instant he fancied that it was Dolly's heavy tread. He shuddered. Thank God he was rid of her! What was he doing here, he wondered.

Then he stood up and walked down the stairs, past the dry toilet bowl, and went out of the house into the street.

The true opposite of the romantic is not the realistic but the classical—the average, the ordinary, not the extraordinary. But the Romantic Vision is as true as the Classical. And it seems to me that my writing displays both.

Of all the seven score and ten reviews, there were only two, both round the end of 1978, that seemed to me, although not unfavourable, wrong-headed enough to reply to—in both cases at the urging of the editors of other Christian publications. I shall give my two replies, in part, not only as what I wrote at the time but as what amounts to a commentary on the book of my own. The first was in *Reformed Journal*.

In reviewing, it is considered rather unsporting, however common, to set up a straw man (or straw book) to knock down. What is it when the reviewer sets up a straw god to knock about? That is what Mr. Anker does in his review of my *A Severe Mercy* (RJ, Nov.).

He quotes a paragraph where I list certain results of my wife's death, and he says I believe (or C. S. Lewis believed) that God killed her or allowed her to die to bring them about. But, on the *same page* (not quoted), I say: "I must not presume to answer [as to what God did], for God may have had purposes beyond my imagining." Is that precisely "a disposition to contain the ways of God within the limits of human understanding"? Nowhere do I suggest that God intended her death. Nowhere do I (or C. S. Lewis) suggest a "punitive schema" nor a "wrathful" or "mean" God, nor is there a word of truth in his charge that the God I set before people is "fussy, unforgiving, and given to making his points with a scalpel." I *can't* think how Mr. Anker could think so. *He* may be haunted by a wrathful Calvinistic God, not I. *My* God is a God of incredible love and mercy.

As is C. S. Lewis's God. Lewis needs no defense by me. Still, since Mr. Anker refers to Lewis's *romantic* Christianity, I shall suggest that he read the Introduction to *Pilgrim's Regress* and be informed by a great scholar of the meaning of one of the most abused words in the language.

I appreciate the good words Mr. Anker had for the book.

The second review I replied to appeared in *Sojourners*, the magazine of the Christian left. It sometimes seems to me that it and other consciously left-wing Christian journals fall into the same trap that politically right-wing journals fall into of a divided allegiance: not mere Christianity or Christianity whole but whatever in Christianity suits their political outlook.

The *Sojourners* review of my book was by Michael Foley, who described himself as a 'house-husband', not knowing apparently that the 'hus' of 'husband' (or of 'hussy') *means* 'house'—'housewife' is parallel to 'housebond' or 'husband'. Like Mr Anker of the *Reformed Journal*, Mr Foley misuses the word 'romantic', both as *True Romances* uses it and in the rather remarkable phrase (my emphasis) about the "*classical* Romantic dilemma". I pointed these things out. But Mr Foley was disturbed about other matters, basically, I think—he being a good *Sojourners* man—that we could go to Oxford or go sailing in a yacht (however hard we had to scrape to do so) when there were hungry mouths in the slums. He has a point—but if no one sought knowledge or beauty, it might be a dreary world. Certainly there would have been no *A Severe Mercy*. At all events, here is part of my reply, published in December, 1978.

Mr. Foley misses the point that two people who subordinate *self* to the love of each other cannot precisely be called *self*ish. Moreover, Mr. Foley fails to distinguish between the Vanauken who was the young lover and the Vanauken who many years later is telling the story with a measure of objectivity and insight. . . .

Mr. Foley's remarks about the "classical Romantic dilemma," my wish "to retain the 'eternal moments' of [my] life forever" and my "wish to recapture a beautiful past" constitute a profound misreading of the book. If he sees in the discussion of eternity only the "quest for stasis," I can only suggest another and deeper reading of the book.

Finally, Mr. Foley says that for those who will never "taste the freedom of the salt spray, never know the wonders of Oxford or the friendship of a C. S. Lewis, Vanauken's re-creation is a snare and a delusion." This is, in effect, to say that unless one has had a yacht, my reflections on coping with loss and grief are without value. This is to say that unless one is at Oxford, my wrestling with the intellectual problems of faith are without value. This is to say that unless one knows a C. S. Lewis, the letters of *the* C. S. Lewis to me are without value. This argument will not commend itself to everyone. Does Mr. Foley, I wonder, refuse to read Lewis's *Surprised By Joy* and consider it "a snare and a delusion" for those that are not Oxford dons? Is Winston Churchill's mighty history of World War II valueless to those who are not prime ministers? And St. John "a snare and a delusion" to those who did not have the dangerous privilege of walking with Jesus? I can only call Mr. Foley's position uniquely dangerous to readers who have been wont to see and find value in other and different lives in books.

At nearly the same time as that review, *Eternity Magazine* told me that my book would win the 1978 *Eternity Book-of-the-Year Award*, and shouldn't I like to write an article for the December issue in which the Award would be announced? Accordingly, I did write one, linked to Christmas Eve, on a theme that had been touched on, not only in an Oxford conversation at the Studio, recorded in *A Severe Mercy*, but in my playlet, "The Playwright Incarnate". In fact, *Eternity* ran the playlet as well as the new article, "Christmas Eve: That Difficult Birth". I had attempted long before to explain one of the great doctrines of the Faith in what was really a parable (although entirely true): "The Fall" (in *Mercy*). Then, after my moment of inspiration in that Studio conversation, the playlet had been a modern parable to illuminate the great but difficult doctrine of the Incarnation. But the Incarnation is the heart of the great doctrine of the Trinity that puzzles so many Christians even though they accept it. And the new article was another interpretation along the same lines—that of the author incarnating himself in his novel along with his created characters. But, since the author is always, to some extent, in all of his created characters, even as there is something of the Creator—the Holy Spirit moving us, if we will hear—in us, the analogy is an interpretation of the Trinity as well as the Incarnation.

C. S. Lewis somewhere says that one who can't explain a doctrine in simple terms to the uneducated doesn't understand it himself. Anyway, the following is my attempt at explaining in simple terms these difficult but central doctrines.

Christmas Eve: That Difficult Birth

Christmas Eve. Images of the Magi and the blazing star over Bethlehem. The lovely old carols and candlelight. After all, perhaps, the oxen kneeling devoutly in their stalls on the holy midnight, if only we were there to see. The Christmas tree with its angel and the yule log burning. O holy night.

Even today, despite the blare of commercialism, some sense of hope remains, even for unbelievers. For a little while the world is a better place. Underneath the gaiety there is still a sense of a world surcharged with mystery on that holy night. The frosty stars glimpsed between the car and the house are more awesome than on other nights, almost frighteningly so: We are glad when the front door opens to the cozy warmth within.

To say that Christmas is more than presents and tinsel and cards on the mantelpiece is, for Christian readers, to say the obvious. Even unbelievers, I think, often sense that it is something more—more than a season of goodwill; more even than the image of holy Mary smiling gravely down at the pretty babe while three camels lope through the night towards the village that has become the centre of the world. Here for a moment, here in the manger, is the still point of the turning world.

> The safety of the world was lying there,
> And the world's danger.

One may reflect upon those lines by Mary Coleridge, comparing them perhaps with Charles Williams' haunting lines on the Annunciation that strike the same note:

> [Gabriel] with veiled eyes and proud head bent
> Received the holy-syllabled assent,
> Whereon the loves of all the nations hung.

The central event of earth's history. Everything that was, everything that had ever been or would ever be, brought to a focus there in Bethlehem. Not Jerusalem or Rome or London or New York but Bethlehem. The God of all the universe, the Power that shaped the suns, lying in a stable. God become man. God accepting the way that would lead Him, in a few short years, to brutal execution, nails through His hands, pain tearing along the nerves, flies buzzing round the blood and sweat. But here in Bethlehem at the beginning of the road the supreme miracle has occurred. "He came down from Heaven and was made Man." Credo. This we believe. The most awe-inspiring, awe-requiring moment of all history.

If we say in the creed that we believe and do not believe, we say a lie. If we say that we are Christians, we are saying, according to the definition at Antioch, that we believe in God become Man at Bethlehem. This is the meaning of Christmas—O holy night!—that He came down from Heaven and took upon Himself the pains and danger of our flesh: God Himself. God Himself one of us. O holy night in very truth.

We accept it, but it is not easy to believe. That is why it is belief, not knowing. It is the Christian *faith*, not certainty. Even so, it takes some believing: this difficult birth. A lion is not a lamb. How could God be a man? How could a man be God? How could He be God and man at once? If He was God, then, when Jesus was a baby or asleep, who was running the universe? Well, God the Father was. But, then, two Gods—one "up there" and one in Bethlehem? No, one God. God the Father running the universe and God the Son at Bethlehem—but only one God. "He who has seen me has seen the Father... and I and my Father are one," Jesus said. But... well, how could it be? It's so—so incredible. Must we shut our reason down at midnight on Christmas Eve?

It is very hard—a difficult birth, if we have to accept all that. There's no trouble about Him being a man, a very, very good man. That's easy enough. And some who call themselves Christians, hopefully, content themselves with believing merely that—a good man.

"Content themselves," did I say? I'm not so sure that they *are* contented. After all, they are in a sort of limbo between the Christian faith and outright disbelief. If they go to church and the creeds are said, they cannot in honesty say, "I believe." And the carols on Christmas Eve remind them of what other men have believed. O holy night: But what's so holy about the birth of one who is merely a man? But of course those old carol writers, like the creed writers, didn't have the advantages of our superior knowledge of things, did they? We know He couldn't have been more than a man, don't we? Do we?

Those who *call* themselves Christians but know better than Christians do and reject the meaning of the holy night have to face an uncomfortable question: Why should they pay the slightest attention to anything this man who was only a man had to say, unless they happen to agree with it anyway? We can all agree that we ought to love our neighbors, except of course the awful ones we happen to have. But what does the 'Christian' who doesn't believe that Christ spoke as God do with the harder sayings? The hard sayings on divorce, for instance. Or that most terrible verse in the Bible: "Inasmuch as ye have not done it unto the least of these, ye have not done it unto me." Or the possibility of the dread voice at the end saying, "I never knew you; depart from me." The Christianity-and-water people have their own dangers and difficulties. One either accepts Christ as God or rejects Him; there isn't really any halfway house.

Our concern here is not with the unbelievers who consider Jesus to have been merely a good man—they are not apt to be reading this anyhow—but with the Christians who *believe* in the Incarnation but find it difficult, almost a stumbling block. There is no manner of doubt but that the doctrine of the Incarnation—God made man—is the central doctrine of the Church through the ages. Hard though it is, there is one comforting thing about it: If you can believe *that*, you can believe anything. That is, if you can believe that God lay in a manger, you aren't going to balk at the well-attested resurrection or even at the virgin birth. A God who would accept the manger—and the cross—is a God who can do anything. The problem, then, is to see whether we can find a way to look at the Incarnation that appeals to our reason so that we can be comfortable with the birth of God on that holy night.

Now, I am a writer, not a theologian. And writers deal with words—and even with incarnations. Thus when I think of the Incarnation—the Word of God made flesh—I think of it in terms of the writer's craft, especially the writer of stories. But we've all read stories, and most of us are planning to write one when we get around to it. To talk about the Incarnation, then, in terms of story-writing is to talk about it in a way that will be easy to understand for all of us.

Suppose, then, I write a long story—a novel. I invent or create an imaginary town with invented streets and houses and other structures. Perhaps a college if I want to or an industrial plant. And of course people. I invent or create as many people as I need. To be sure, these people (since I am not God creating out of nothing) may slightly resemble people I have known. Anyway, I create a young man, teaching in my invented college, covered with the ivy I've caused to grow on its walls; and I create a young girl for him to fall in love with. Perhaps I create the young man's stern father, too, and the girl's annoying brother. And so on.

Now, suppose I decide to put myself in my story, under a different name, of course, to be the hero's friend. Behold! There I am, walking upon the college campus I have built, wearing my familiar tweeds, smoking my pipe. Perhaps I make myself a bit younger in the story so as to be about the same age as my friend—almost, as you might say, my son.

So I am in the novel, having long talks with my friend, saying always my own words to fit those circumstances. Thus I am not only in my study writing the story but I am *in* the story, interacting with the characters I have created. *They* are created, but the I in the story is not a created being. He is I. In fact, I am *incarnate* in my created world. And the I-in-the-book speaks for me, the writer-in-the-study: he speaks my words. It all makes a sort of sense, doesn't it? There aren't two me's: I-in-the-book and I-in-the-study are *one*—just as Jesus said that He and the Father were one.

And while the I-in-the-book is living in the book, I-the-writer am outside of it, outside the invented town, sitting in my study, working the whole thing out. I am, therefore, like God-the-Father as I plot my story and write it; and the I-in-the-book is like God-the-Son, being me, yet doing my will. We may also note that since I invented all the other characters they all have something of me in them, though they are not me. Still, the fact that I created them and something of me is in each one, even the bad ones, is a little like God-the-Holy-Spirit with us all. Thus we have the whole Trinitarian God, who is yet *one* God, not three. I-writing-the-book and I-the-character-in-the-book and the I that am with all my created characters are *one* I, not three.

Now, here's another thing. My novel has a time pattern of its own, not the same as mine outside. I may write a week in one sitting—or years. Moreover, I-the-writer (or 'father') know how the whole thing is going to come out, since I of course have a plot. But the characters in the book wouldn't know. The book's time is a created thing, just as the time we live in is (like space) a created thing.

For God, out of time, all our yesterdays and all our tomorrows are in His Now. Just as every page of my book is in *my* now. Jesus, we may suppose, did not know the future, for instance when the Second Coming would be. That's why one of the most important things that Jesus said was that He did *perfectly* the will of the Father. Thus if Jesus spoke of the sanctity of marriage, it was because the Father, knowing what we call past and future, willed Him to do so. Or if Jesus chose only men for His apostles, thus creating a two-thousand-year tradition of a male ministry, He was doing perfectly the will of the Father. The I-in-my-book does perfectly what the I-in-the-study wills him to do—for the I-in-the-study knows how the whole novel is to come out.

One more point. Since my novel has some 'bad guys' in it, it may be necessary for me, the writer, to allow me, the character, to get shot and killed. Or if my novel is set in Roman times, crucified. Of course the characters of the book are not really independent or conscious—that's where the analogy differs from the enormous mystery of God. And yet, as every writer knows, the characters do sometimes 'run away with the story.' Because of some character's developing personality, one has to write the scene differently to what one intended.

At all events, the writer writing his book and putting himself incarnate in the book is a way of looking at the awesome miracle of that holy night that makes sense. All man and all God, the doctrine says. And the I-in-the-book is all me (the writer) and all character.

Thus the star blazed over Bethlehem because God Himself lay helpless in the manger. O holy night, indeed.

I have not said much of 1978, the heady year of the reviews, except a bit about the reviews themselves and the awards, and my writings. But it was also a year of travel.

There was a splendid trip to England, a coming home—for me, whichever way I go, to England or to Virginia, it is coming home. There were interviews in London with magazines and the BBC; and I saw old friends in various parts of the country. One old friend David Griffiths, a Royal Chaplain at Windsor, took me to a Sunday lunch in the officers' mess of the Life Guards that I enjoyed a lot. At Oxford I visited another old friend Peter Crane, and lunched in my college. Going round to the Studio, I saw that the always-sagging roof had finally caved in, and the Studio was marked for demolition, so I went off and bought a spanner to take off the door knocker that so often had summoned Davy and me, and carried it off to Virginia for the Vancot door. My Virginian friend Belle Hill, who had been at a Wordsworth Conference in the Lake Country, was collected by me; and we explored beautiful Dorsetshire before flying home.

In the autumn I went north to visit old Oxford friends Lewis and MaryAnn Salter and to be present at his inauguration as President of Wabash College. I marched, gowned, with the faculty—curiously appropriate, I thought, since I had once been briefly a member of that faculty before Davy's illness had led to my resignation before I ever got there. I went on to Wheaton College to receive an award and see friends there, particularly Clyde Kilby.

Curiously enough the Christmas vacation that year was like the one two years before when I was doing the final draft of *Mercy*. This time I was going flat out on a final draft of my neglected '60s novel *Gateway to Heaven*, the completion of which was celebrated by Belle's inviting me to dine on meatloaf and her putting on a long gown for the occasion. But after dining and drinking a glass or two of claret, I suddenly collapsed with tiredness and had to go home to bed at nine.

To glance ahead, *Gateway* was published by Harper & Row in 1980, after their senior novel editor had pleased me by reporting that my novelistic instincts were sound as a bell, and after I had travelled to Frisco for a bit of wining and dining and talks.

But back to Christmastide of 1978, I paused in my whirlwind of writing, as I had done in 1976, for the carol service at St Stephen's and dinner at Elk Hill with Barney and Lady Frances; and on Christmas Day, again as always, a Christmas dinner with my English friend Jim Cocking and his wife Margery, who had been one of the nudges. And with my godson, John Cocking.

A year later when I dined at Elk Hill on Christmas Eve, Lady Frances lay in the churchyard at St Stephen's. And when after dinner, as always, the candles were lit on the tall tree in the drawing-room for the singing of carols, Lady Frances's granddaughter Ann, looking, I thought, like Lady Frances might have looked as a girl, lifted up her pure and lovely voice in the hushed candlelit room and sang "O Holy Night", whilst Nelly beside me nuzzled my hand.

The four years, 1975-1978—the Year of the Nudges, the Year of the Vocation, the Year of Exaltation, and what may be called the Year of the Reviews—have been described rather fully, for they were of immense significance in my Christian pilgrimage. Also, those years, I think, will be of interest to other Christians who like to see how God acts in different lives. It will not be necessary to describe all of the later years in the same narrative fashion—indeed, the next chapter will not be narrative at all but simply a discussion of the loves.

No years since Davy's death twenty years before had been so happy as these four, nor so intense. And they were years in which, by the very nature of the book I contemplated and then wrote, Davy seemed very close to me. There was hardly a line of *A Severe Mercy* that I didn't, so to speak, submit to her, imagining, that is, what she would say of it. Once, at least, I rewrote a section because of measuring it against what she would have thought—or did think.

The power and drama of these years were mostly within me (though there was the public acclaim in the last one). I do not know whether I have shown that inner drama to the reader; but, for me who lived it, the drama was as powerful as that of any period in my whole life: the drama of God's action, loving and merciful, in that life. The readers of *Mercy* who wondered if I could ever be happy again after Davy's death should find an answer in the account of these years. We are, I think, so made that our greatest happiness is in doing God's will. If I am right, those who rebel against God do not find either joy or happiness, except momentarily, for they are rebelling against happiness itself. There is only one fountain of joy.

In the '60s I pursued the shining soap bubble of earthly joys and freedom from God, and the bubble broke as all illusions must do. And then in the '70s I found real joy and real freedom—perfect freedom—in His service. I was happier sitting at my little bed-desk typing away than I ever had been running after the bubble. The happiness was in Him.

And yet I should not have found that happiness, that exaltation, had God cast me off as the disobedient sinner I was. Instead, in His mercy, He patiently drew me back to Him.

Thus it is that I *know* that my life, and all lives, are under the Mercy.

CHAPTER VII

The Loves

It was the vanishing of one I loved—and still love—that left the hollow in the centre. Putting the neighbour first is, at best, love for known men and women. Putting God first is loving God incarnate in Jesus Christ, both in His intolerable sternness and His heartbreaking tenderness—loving an altogether human man who was at the same time altogether God.

We are always feeling love, or longing for love, or thinking about love—and, if we are not, we are dying inside. Love is the one thing we can give away endlessly—be spendthrifts with—and yet have ever more of. God is the sole fountain of love, but He pours it into us, Christian and unbeliever. If we, in turn, pour it out upon others, God pours fresh love into us. But, I think, love must be fresh and sparkling. If a man does not love, perhaps because he's been hurt or because, like a terrorist, he has put hate first, then I think the love in him dries up, hardens, yet leaves no room for fresh love. Only by pouring out our love day in and day out can God top us up daily with His outpouring of endless fresh love, like the endless outpouring of light and warmth from the sun. Even at night that light is reflected by the moon, our lady of the night, and the evening star. So *we* must reflect—reflect by loving—God's love, possibly melting the hardened love, like sludge, in the soul of the loveless. It is, quite simply, all our duty and all our joy: to love. To love God (God in Jesus); to love neighbour, to love all our loves.

But, though we feel love and think about love and talk awkwardly about love, we are extraordinarily confused about love—the many faces of love. I know this by the questions asked me by readers of *A Severe Mercy*, moved by the love of Davy and me. (As I have been moved by their love and warmth and gratitude.) Does inloveness (*Eros*) come twice? they ask. Are lovers also friends? Can the 'one flesh' of marriage—true union—happen a second time? How does affection—affection for one's father or sister—relate to the other loves? Is it a lesser, almost negligible thing? And charity (*agape*)—how does it fit in? How is friendship for your friend to be balanced with inloveness for your beloved? Is friendship lesser?

All these questions and more have been put to me by readers, for Davy and I did have an extraordinary love to which we devoted all our minds as well as all our hearts. And I had—we had—deep and dear friendships. And in the end we had to face the intrusion of God into our love, which led to thinking then and long meditation later. In other words, I have thought about the loves more than most people—thought about them all my life. Perhaps, then, I do have something to say. Indeed, ever since *A Severe Mercy* and the questions from its readers, I have thought that, if ever I wrote another book, I should write something about the loves. And this is another book.

Indeed, this whole book has been about the loves, my lost love (though not really lost, only temporarily—in time), and love for the neighbour (and the peril of putting him first), and love of God (and the happy joy of so doing). This is, then, the moment to discuss the loves. The four loves—affection (*storge*), friendship (*philia*), inloveness (*Eros*), and charity (*caritas* or *agape*)—in the great clarification of Lewis's book of that name. In all I shall say, I am indebted to him.

Let us notice first of all the inadequacy, the paucity, of the English language for talk of the loves. There isn't even an English word for the state of being in love, except the word I invented in *Mercy*: inloveness. Yet it's the love we talk about most.

And only two of the loves possess a verb—and they are inadequate. One can say, "I befriend you," or "Didn't I befriend you when I saved your life?" but it has come to mean, in most contexts, aiding someone, not having friendship with someone. Although one can say "I venerate you" or "I hate you", one cannot say "I affectionate you." And no verb for charity: "I caress you" has lost all connection with charity; and "I cherish you", though closer, doesn't really mean "I have charity or *agape* for you." It would be splendid if 'cherish' were to come to be associated with charitable love. Anyhow, "I love you" must serve for all the loves with its ever-present danger of confusion, for, unless it is said just right or to the right person—one's mother, say—"I love you" means "I'm in love with you." Or even, merely, "I want your body!" One might say to a friend, "Although I haven't written, I still love you", but mostly "I love you" to a friend is liable, we feel, to be dangerously misunderstood.

Similarly, while we have 'friend' and 'beloved' (and 'lover'), we have no words for the object of affection or the object of charity. The Polynesians who live by the sea have twenty or thirty words to describe the ocean, off soundings or in lagoons, in storm and tranquillity; and the Eskimos probably twenty for snow. I shouldn't be surprised to learn that the Chinese have hundreds to describe the subtleties of taste. But the subtleties of love cannot be expressed in English, and I doubt that they can be in any language. It is strange, for we live with the loves and by them, yet the paucity of the language makes it impossible to express simply fine shades of meaning, the infinite textures and mixtures of love.

The most celebrated of the loves in modern literature, the love most people think of when they hear the word 'love', is inloveness, the most dramatic and intense of the loves. Often the most fickle, also. The love of lovers. Some readers perhaps, in seeing the title of this chapter "The Loves", thought, more or less hopefully, that I was about to confess the many fair ladies who had shared my bed. Certainly a book entitled *The Loves of My Life* would suggest a series of beloveds, not friends, not one's dozen children, and not those cherished in charity. There is no doubt that in millions of minds inloveness is held to be the most important of the loves—almost the only love worth mentioning, especially in this erotic and sex-centred civilisation of ours.

On that love, then, I should like to introduce the only essay I have ever written specifically on inloveness. It was written and published in *Fidelity* in 1983; and for our discussion it may clear the air a bit.

The (False) Sanction of Eros

"I don't even know how it happened," said John. "The kiss, I mean. But when it did...Well, perhaps you won't believe this—I was just amazed!—it simply seemed so *good*, so *right*, that I *knew* we had to go on together. Betty felt the same way. It was what love and marriage are all about." We were discussing, or rather John was, his pending divorce from Sue, who had now left town with the children, and his intention of marrying Betty. Knowing my fondness for Sue,

John had drawn me into a deserted corner of the smoking room at the club to say how sorry he was about her and to explain. Now he looked at me earnestly and, with a light punch on the arm of his chair, he said, "It's the one thing I'd like you to understand: that it seemed so good and right. That's when we both knew we'd have to get the divorces. We belonged together."

I don't recall what I said. I suppose I said that I quite understood. And in a way I did, or at least I was beginning to glimpse something. I was remembering some almost identical words a few months before. A former student of mine, Diana, had come to see me. She had read a book I'd written about my own marriage, and she was, I think, troubled at what I might be thinking of her divorcing Paul. He was a rather gentle lad who had been quite shattered by the sudden loss of his wife and little girl. I heard later that he had quit his job and joined the navy. "It wasn't Paul's fault," Diana said. "It was just that it felt *so good and right* with Roger that I knew it would be wrong to go on with Paul when I love Roger. You can tell when something is right."

That *feeling* of goodness and rightness: both Diana, Paul's wife, and John at the club had invoked it; and because of it they believed themselves justified in breaking up the marriages they had vowed to be faithful to. On the other hand, John's wife, Sue, and Diana's husband, Paul, both of whom perhaps had trusted their mates' promises, almost certainly felt no goodness and rightness at all in what had happened, though of course they were not in a position to judge their spouses' feelings. Yet Diana at my house and John at the club had both urged that *goodness and rightness* with evident sincerity. And they were decent people, not at all the sort who understand only farmyard relations. They wanted me to understand that they wouldn't have done it—broken their vows and brought pain to their spouses and children—if something (they didn't ask what) were not telling them it was meet and right so to do. They were, in fact, invoking a higher law: the *feeling* of goodness and rightness. A feeling so powerful that it swept away—swept away in an instant, according to John—whatever guilt they would otherwise have felt at being commitment-breakers and whatever uneasiness they felt about the children. And it was something they didn't expect—a feeling that *surprised* them. A feeling so powerful and unexpected deserves examination.

Divorce, to speak moderately, is not uncommon in Western society, even among Christians. But how should it be otherwise in a society dedicated, not to duty or reason or God but, increasingly, to pleasure and above all to sexual pleasure? A spouse's falling in love with somebody else is, to be sure, not the only cause of divorce, but it is certainly one of the great causes and has been all through history. The marital vows, even when they are not regarded as a meaningless form of words, are taken lightly, not because of an intention of breaking them but because lovers are so sure they will never wish to break them. So unhesitatingly they speak the strong words of their promise—"forsaking all others...for better, for worse...till death do us part..."—and they know in their hearts that of course it will be so. Nevertheless, unconsciously there is a reservation: if they could conceive that love might die, their reservation might be expressed "till failing love do us part." But the vow is, "not till love dies but till *we* die": that is the promise. Indeed, what the lovers are saying is: "As long as I feel towards you what I now feel, this high and holy thing, which of course I always *shall* feel, I will keep this vow."

Yet John had ceased to feel that "high and holy thing" for Sue, Diana for Paul; and each had come to feel it for another. That is, it wasn't a person *qua* person they had been in love with but a person as evoker of a feeling, a thrill. Their true vows had been to the feeling. Presumably they didn't think of it so, but they had, in effect, merely *transferred* their vows to others. And why not, if vows are but feelings?

At all events, as I reflected upon the identical words they both had spoken, I began to think that I was onto something—something I straightaway dubbed "The Sanction of *Eros*." To sanction something is to make it sacred; it is, as it were, a sacred approval, a divine okay. And John and Diana in speaking of the goodness and rightness were clearly not referring to any thoughtful and considered judgement of good and bad, right and wrong; they were appealing to something higher than judgement, higher even than their own desires. But, equally clearly, the sacred approval they felt could not possibly have come from the Father of Jesus Christ whose disapproval of divorce is explicit. It is *Eros*, the ancient pagan god of lovers, who confers this sanction upon the worshippers at his altar. It is a false sanction that deceives his votaries into calling the bad good and the wrong right. Inloveness may indeed be an innocent and lovely gift to those heart-free, but it is not innocent—it is, in fact, sin—when it leads to betrayal of spouse or friend or child. The pronouncement of *Eros* that *this* love is so good and so right that all betrayals are justified is simply a lie, as is his specious promise that this new love will go on for ever. Indeed, *Eros*, may descend upon John or Diana yet again, and again, with the same pronouncement and the same promise. And they will again believe it: "This time it's for keeps." About this 'serial polygamy' so characteristic of our age, C. S. Lewis in *The Four Loves* says:

> [T]he grim joke is that this *Eros* whose voice seems to speak from the eternal realm is not himself necessarily even permanent....The world rings with complaints of his fickleness.

What is baffling is the combination of this fickleness with his protestations of permanency. To be in love is both to intend and to promise lifelong fidelity. Love makes vows unasked; can't be deterred from making them....

Diana's vows to Paul, John's to Sue, had undoubtedly been utterly sincere. I remember Paul and Diana then: their faces had been alight with love, and they couldn't take their eyes off each other. They had *meant* "forsaking all others" and "till death do us part." What, then, had gone wrong? What brought them, all the loveliness broken, to the divorce courts?

There were, I think, two things they didn't know and one deep misunderstanding. Three matters that no one had ever taught them.

The misunderstanding was of what vows are. They thought the vows perhaps an expression of their feelings: a confident *prediction*, as it were, of what they would feel—this high and holy ecstasy—for ever. So of *course* "till death do us part"—nothing else could possibly part us. Of *course* "forsaking all others"—have we not found, each in the other, incomparable perfection? They were utterly sincere. They believed their prediction. As Lewis said, "Love makes vows unasked; can't be deterred from making them." But it is the promise of *Eros* of eternal inloveness that makes the vows no more than a prediction. They do not understand that the vows are *their* promise—to God as well as each other—for the times when they are not feeling the ecstasy of inloveness. No vows are necessary for those in love; nothing can separate *them* but force. The vows are a gift from one to the other; not a protestation of love. That's what they don't understand. Here and now they are saying, each to the other: "This is my *promise*. This you can trust. This you can lean on in the bad times and as long as life shall last: whatever I may *feel* at any given moment, I *will* be faithful. Never fear. You have my word."

The shattering loveliness of being in love will not—*cannot*—despite the radiant promises of the deceiving god go on at every moment for ever: this is one of the things they didn't know. Some ministers do warn of this, but the lovers, hugging their secret assurance, often will not believe. They expect "the high mood that makes the rest seem pale" to go on for ever: "the thing which lovers...with such worship wooe." But inloveness, though it is *like* Heaven in that it is truly loving another as oneself, is not Heaven. Heaven is not won so easily. Inloveness is only a foretaste of bliss, and we cannot live permanently in those bright highlands yet. We are human (that is, fallen), and we cannot yet bear, it seems, to look at even one person—let alone everyone—with such intensity of love permanently. Self (what *I* want) re-asserts itself. The beloved, shockingly, is perceived to have faults, and lover snaps at lover. This may, the first time, seem like the end of the world, but it is not. With wisdom (a little) and charity (a lot), love deepens and becomes whole, including the humanness and faults. It is charity (*agape*) that sustains love; inloveness cannot do it alone. But if inloveness is, so to speak, taken up into charity, then—only then—inloveness returns as a frequent sudden joy through all the years. This is what hadn't happened with John and Sue, Diana and Paul. The deep charity—wanting nothing so much as the good of the *other*—had not redeemed their loves. Perhaps it was beginning to—John spoke tenderly of Sue—but they didn't know that inloveness must sometimes sleep with the daffodils under the snow.

And, far worse, they were not prepared (almost no one ever is) for the amazing Sanction of *Eros*. When the voice of the god, like a high, clear bugle, pronounced their new loves, not ordinary infidelity but extraordinarily, *uniquely*, right and good, they were bewildered and awed but accepting. Whatever it might appear to the world, *they* knew that these loves were different, sacred. *They did not dream that every other lover has the same assurance*. The deception of *Eros* that comes as a sacred sanction to this particular love lifts it out of the rut of ordinary betrayals. Perhaps John had intended to be faithful to Sue and Diana to Paul. No doubt Diana had more than once rejected the advances of frisky males at parties and John ignored, with a thought of Sue, many a bright-eyed flirtatious glance. They were perhaps confident in their strength to resist temptation. Too confident as it turned out. One moment they were merely playing, a little more gaily than usual, because they really liked the playmate. Perhaps at one point little alarm bells sounded; I'm convinced there's always an instant, fleeting it may be, when one knows he is playing with fire and senses he should draw back. But confident in their strength, they ignored the warning; and then, suddenly, *Eros* had overshadowed them. They looked at each other with shocked and adoring eyes, and then bewilderingly, not to be resisted, came the Sanction of *Eros*— *this* love, unlike all others, is good and right and for ever—and they were undone.

We all know that countless marriages are wrecked by one of the spouses falling in love with what used to be called the Other Woman or her male counterpart. And, since art follows life, the modern novels and films are full of triangles and betrayals. But let us notice how often the storyteller sets it up so that the betrayed spouse more or less deserves it as being unkind, unloving, or a bit of a bore. Scarlet letters are no longer in fashion. Our sympathies are with the lovers, not with the betrayed spouse. Or the betrayed Church in the case of a nun or priest breaking vows. And never—never once in any novel or film I can think of—does the betraying spouse seriously think of the meaning of broken promises. Both duty and the given word are, like

honour, merely wretched remnants of the 'middle ages.' The Spirit of
the Age proclaims sexual love to be the greatest good. In the books
and the films we share the happiness of the happy lovers: love itself is
lovable. The lovers may experience difficulties—uncooperative
spouses and superiors—so that we may share their anguish; but the
lovers must never face up to the real meaning of betrayal of their
vows, for that would mar their happy love. I knew of a monk and a
nun, both under lifetime vows, who fell in love and sought dispensa-
tions, sincerely believing that God wanted them to do so. A few years
ago a married Episcopal clergyman fell in love with the wife of the
Senior Warden; after divorces and remarriage the happy couple departed, not for darkest Africa in disgrace but for Texas and a bigger
church for him. No one minded except perhaps the betrayed spouses.
The Spirit of the Age—not the Holy Spirit—ceaselessly proclaims
erotic love (or even barnyard sex) to be the ultimate good; and, therefore, anything that stands in its way, solemn vows, duty, loyalty, the
words of Our Lord, is seen as chains upon the soaring human spirit.

All thoughtful observers of our society see it to be sex-saturated,
and Christians, at least, lament the erosion (or *Eros*ion) of marriage
and the family. But almost no one—neither clergymen nor novelists—
really understands this deadly Sanction of *Eros*: the overwhelming
feeling that *this* particular love, unlike all others, is right and good
and blessed. Young lovers of course feel it, which is why parental opposition to their offspring's choice is rarely successful. And the married man or woman who falls in love with another feels that same
Sanction, invariably forgetting that it is exactly what he once felt for
his spouse, invariably feeling that this new love is "the real thing at
last." And so, because of the Sanction, the seeming blessing from on
high, he becomes ruthlessly determined on divorce and re-marriage.
The Sanction 'proves' to him that he is right to break his vows.

If my friends, John and Sue, or my former pupil Diana and her
Paul, had been carefully and explicitly warned that if they ever *did*
fall in love with another (however unthinkable) they would *certainly*
feel what would seem a sacred approval granted to that new love
alone, they would, at least, have been less likely to be taken in by it.
It was clear that the most amazing thing to them was the almost-mir-
aculous feeling of goodness and rightness—the Sanction. If they had
known long before it happened that it was to be expected, that it
would not be unique to them, surely they would have at least enter-
tained some serious doubts as to whether the feeling of goodness and
rightness was to be trusted. John's conscience had troubled him a bit
about "poor Sue," and perhaps Diana's about Paul, but the Sanction—the seemingly divine approval—had overridden conscience:
they *knew* what they were doing was good and right. But if they had
had serious doubts about that goodness and rightness, they might
have heeded conscience.

It is incredible to me that with the evidence plain before us the world is not echoing with warnings about this Sanction, but I've never heard of anyone who understood it. "Great is Diana of the Ephesians," the ancients used to say; today we must say "Great is *Eros* of the Hellenes," and only by understanding the lie the god proclaims in the accents of truth can the marriages of people like John and Sue, Diana and Paul, be saved. Saved through knowledge of the (false) Sanction of *Eros*.

My chief concern in that essay was the falseness of the seeming sanction of *Eros* as a sanction for the violation of marriage vows. It is, of course, equally false as a sanction for the violation of priestly vows of celibacy. Moreover, though I find it hard to believe, I have heard of priests and ministers who manage to believe that it sanctions homo-*sex* as an activity that violates neither vows of celibacy nor of marriage (on the grounds that homo-sex is an aspect of friendship, which it certainly is not). The false 'sanction' cannot convert sin into virtue.

There can be no doubt that the radiant god *Eros* can overwhelm us mortals again and again, though never again with quite the fresh loveliness of first love. Still, we are in love, more or less denying previous loves, crying, "The real thing at last!" and "This time it's for keeps." The false promise of *Eros*. And that is the answer to one of the questions put to me by readers, whether inloveness can come twice.

Eros promises for ever. The promise is not in itself to be relied on. But if inloveness, especially first love, is taken up into charity, infiltrated by charity—if, that is, the couple add to inloveness what they may call 'just plain love', cherishing, wanting each other's best good (we are up against that inadequacy of language here)—then the love may indeed be for life. I think that real 'one-flesh' union may come but once, though I am not certain. It lasts until death takes one of the pair—true union—and, I believe, beyond death, through all eternity. There may be no marrying in Heaven, but I believe, as C. S. Lewis believed, that the one-flesh union endures there.

Indeed, it is in eternity that all the loves shall become all they are meant to be. Inloveness—putting another at the centre of one's being—is a foretaste of Heaven. But so is friendship—a man laying down his life for his friend. And affection: think of mother love at its purest or of a father running into a blazing house to save his little lad.

Some readers may have experienced the seeming sanction of *Eros*. Reading "The (False) Sanction of *Eros*", they may have felt that turning away from a new love is more than flesh (or will) is capable of. And, indeed, that is precisely the implication of ten thousand love stories—that *Eros* is not to be resisted, that faithfulness to one's spouse is impossible once one has fallen in love with another.

But let us consider faithfulness in other contexts. A man might 'fall in love', so to speak, with China or Italy or France—their cultures, their wines, their manners—but if he, being in fact an American or Englishman, transferred his *allegiance* and betrayed his native land, he would not be respected by either the people of his native land or the adopted one. Or, again, a young man might meet an older woman who was more sympathetic and understanding than his own mother; but if he, then, failed in his duty to his own mother, she being perhaps in need, that, too, would be equivalent to divorcing the spouse one has sworn to cherish for another. We have ceased to see unfaithfulness to marriage vows for what it is. The naval officer betraying his country. The trusted friend betraying friendship. The Nazi or Communist youth turning in his father. All betrayers are kindred, whether for advancement or *Eros* or money: thirty pieces of silver.

Apart from the non-human loves (or likes) for strawberries or nature, poetry or painting, horses or boats, there are, according to C. S. Lewis, three natural loves—affection, friendship, inloveness. And one supernatural love—charity, sometimes called 'Christian love', which is the same as *agape*. Any of the three natural loves may be a great love. Inloveness doesn't deserve to be automatically at the top of the hierarchy. It may be the most intense, but either of the others may be more constant and long-lasting. What is certain about all the natural loves is that they will perish, be poisoned by selfishness, unless there is a large admixture of charity, that is, selflessness.

Charity is generous love, selfless love, *giving* love: generous and giving, careless of return. It is the love of Christ for us. It is self-sacrificing love. A mother's love for her babe is an image of self-sacrificing charity, although there is a certain amount of instinct in it. Charitable love, which is forgiving love, wants the best good of the beloved at whatever cost to the lover. A wife who urges her husband to do what will take him away from her because she knows it is truly best for him is also an image of charity. Without charity, inloveness will surely die, all the more swiftly because of its intimacy and intensity, and often turn to hate; and without charity towards one's spouse, betrayal is easy. And friendship without charity will fail every real test of friendship, for the generous self-lessness is not there, though friendship may die more slowly through not being put to the test. Affection, too, must inevitably be poisoned and turn into the hell of domestic hate unless there is that generous, selfless, giving and forgiving charity. The Holy Spirit at our side, Christian and unbeliever, is always urging us towards charity. We don't always listen. Self asserts its importance. "What has she ever done for me?"—"He doesn't care about me." Me-ism. The death of charity. And thus the death of all the loves.

Affection, for most of us, is the first love we know. For us, it is need-love: our loving parents answer all our needs. They may have need of their children, too, but ideally, their love is essentially giving-love. At all events, affection is first of all *familial* love: the love of parents for their children, and the children's love for their parents and for each other. In literature it is portrayed above all as mother love, self-sacrificing and generous—yet sometimes demanding and selfish under the guise of sacrificial love. Father love, too, is celebrated, as is the love of two sisters or two brothers. Affection, unlike friendship and inloveness, is not based on natural affinity (save that of blood) nor upon shared interests. Our affections are given to those who are *there*; we do not choose them. And not only *there*, but *always* having been there: we have never known a time when our parents were not there, and even younger siblings soon seem to have been since the beginning.

Similarly, affection is extended to others who have been around for a long time, not only uncles and aunts but the old gardener or the old schoolmate or the old dog. Indeed, affection is often expressed by the word 'old'—old friend, old chap, old thing, old girl, old dear. There is something of permanence and stability in this love. Since most of our loves are a mixture, affection in due course is added to friendship and inloveness. Sometimes, indeed, it precedes inloveness, as when we suddenly fall in love with an old schoolmate or playmate. In the long years of youth a schoolmate or university acquaintance may begin to seem an 'old pal' after only a year or two. And a girl and boy, without much in common except attending the same classes and cheering for the same side in games, may jump from affection to inloveness overnight—or may believe that a mixture of affection and sexual attraction *is* inloveness, and so enter into marriage.

A special sort of affection is that between man and beast. Many a horse has been loved and has returned that affection. Even more so, a dog—such as Flurry or Nelly—whose affection for the master, adoring affection, seems mixed with forgiving charity. As pure a love as I've ever known. And then there are cats.

We have considered charity, necessary to all the loves, and looked at the simplest and sometimes the dearest of the *natural* loves, affection. The other two natural loves—inloveness, which certainly causes us the most heartaches, and friendship, the least understood in the modern world—need more extended consideration.

First, though, another essay about the modern world contrasted with a slightly older world. It is important at this point, for, despite its title "The Bachelor", it suggests, I think what is happening to marriage in our time and some of the reasons why friendship is not well understood. The essay, written in 1980, was published in *The Hillsdale Review* in 1982.

The Bachelor

A knight bachelor was literally a free lance who used that lance under the flags of others, as opposed to a knight banneret who led his retainers under his own flag. Certainly the bachelor today in a world of couples, married or common-law married, is tempted to feel, somewhat uneasily, that he is indeed following a different flag from most people and marching to a different drum.

Let us define 'bachelor' for our purposes as a man of any age, whether previously married or not, who is now single and *intends* for the foreseeable future to remain so. Marriage depends on intention, as expressed in the vows; and we shall predicate a less-binding intention in the state of bachelorhood. A man who has lost his wife through death or divorce may emerge from his shock and grief determined to re-enter the marital state as rapidly as possible: he is not properly a bachelor, merely a transient in singleness. But if he emerges with a feeling of 'never again', we shall call him a bachelor. Of course that intention (like the different sworn intention of a husband) may be undermined in a minute by a pair of melting blue eyes, whereupon he forsakes the order of knights bachelor. But, whatever the future, the bachelor is a man who *now* intends to remain single.

The word 'bachelor' is not only opposed to 'banneret' but, much more commonly, to 'spinster'—also, by the bye, a word of upperclass origins, the daughters of the gentry. She, too, is in a single state, and much that may be said about the bachelor may apply equally to her. But there is one profound difference: her intentions are often not the decisive factor in her state. Despite the shrill battlecries of the feminists, it is still the man who has the option (that abominable advantage) of proposing. The spinster may be very wishful indeed of ending her single state; but she may be brought, perforce, to accept her spinsterhood by the dearth of bachelors not only eligible but *willing*. Then, too, though feminists insist that women have a right to both a career and a husband, many a bachelor who may be thinking wistfully that it would be right nice to have someone to get his dinner and keep his shirts—and children—in order tends to shy rapidly away from majors in the army, however petite.

Most all bachelors, on the other hand, can find a wife quite readily if they want to. So why does a man *choose* to be a bachelor? If any reader at this point feels himself coming all over Freudian with 'knowing' thoughts about how all bachelors are homosexual or 'something' (sexual), he should wash his mind out with the strong soap of genuine thinking. There are, to be sure, homosexual bachelors (and homosexual husbands, too), both those who indulge their inclinations and those who for Christ walk the rocky road of celibacy. But there are other reasons—many of them—for bachelorhood. Some men, quite simply, do not like the look of marriage. Others are having too much fun playing the field—what used to be called 'gay bachelors' before the lovely and useful word 'gay' was perverted from its true meaning. There are men who are bachelors, like Dobbin in *Vanity Fair*, because the 'one woman' is unresponsive to them or is faithfully married to another. Others are bachelors because death has taken the wife with whom there was a deep and lasting union. Then there are men who are so wrapped up in some mighty ambition that they don't have time or freedom for marriage. A monk or a priest in the service of God. A scientist or poet reaching for the stars. A naval officer for whom the Fleet comes first. An explorer or adventurer. Some of these may vaguely intend eventual marriage, which may or may not occur. Finally there are the men, young men, in increasing numbers I think, who are rejecting the responsibilities that go with marriage. Whether this is lack of maturity or an accurate perception that in *modern* marriage the discomforts outweigh the comforts, we shall consider later. These days, certainly, no young man (or older one) is impelled through the doors of matrimony in order to 'have sex' with what used to be called 'nice girls'. In that way it is far more of a man's world than ever before, and there is reason to suppose that the tribe of bachelors may increase. At all events, there are, in fact, a great many reasons for bachelorhood, and perhaps fewer reasons for marriage than there used to be.

Still, there are lots of couples, whether married or near-married (today the precise arrangements of 'Bob and Linda' may be obscure). Not only are there lots of couples but readers of books about past ages may have the vague impression that couples today are more *obtrusively* couples than in the past. But why not? This is an age of freedom. We are indeed the freest age that ever was, aren't we? Homosexuals are coming out of closets, people are living together without wedlock, and pornography is assuredly not under the counter. Brave new world. Anyway, it shows that we're the freest, doesn't it? And the wisest—look at science. If we know all that, we *must* be wise. So we are a great age, apart from taxation and inflation and pollution and missiles and monster government and noise and millions of people blocking the view. And a slight uneasy feeling that things are getting out of control. Still, we are not here concerned with the possible decline and fall of everything but only with the state of being a bachelor in this best and freest of all possible worlds.

Before we consider what it is to be a bachelor in this best and freest, &c., it might be well, for comparison, to have a look at what it has been to be a bachelor in most past ages, though we shall take the late nineteenth century as both typical and closest to our own—the age of Sherlock Holmes and Dr Watson, bachelors (at least until Watson fell by the wayside). What was it like to be a bachelor in that London of hansom cabs and gentlemen's clubs? First of all, the choice of bachelorhood was a wholly reputable one. Some men preferred to marry, others preferred to be clubmen and men-about-town—why not? Although Freud was at work in Vienna, his theories were little known. The late Victorian Englishman (or American) did not at all suppose the world to revolve about a sexual axis and was disinclined to suspect homosexuality without proof. If an empire builder, an Oxford don, a Royal Navy officer, or a clubman chose to be a bachelor, nobody thought it in the least odd. Indeed, husbands not infrequently felt spasms of envy of their bachelor friends' freedom. If two young bachelors and men-about-town shared a flat and a close friendship, no suspicion rested upon them. There are, one perceives, other kinds of freedom. Moreover, the gentlemanly bachelor of 1880 was socially in great demand; he was thought of among hostesses almost always as an *eligible* bachelor. There were innumerable dinner parties and country houseparties in that happy day of lots of servants; and an extra man was always needed to take the spinster aunt or dowager in to dinner—and, even more, to be exposed to the sparkling glance and discreetly hinted charms of the daughters of the house. The great hostess game of the century was the snaring of the eligible bachelor—as he was well aware.

In the nineteenth century and *all* previous centuries there were two distinct though naturally overlapping worlds, the world of men and the world of women. Women were not in politics or industry or the armed forces, nor did they, for the most part, concern themselves with such matters any more than men concerned themselves with domestic affairs. There were exceptions, especially in the higher ranks of society where great ladies were both knowledgeable and powerful, sometimes manipulating the hands that steered the ship of state. Still, by and large, men ran the Empire and business, and women ran the household and Society.

In most households, both middle and upper class, there were, in addition to servants and nannies and lots of children, mothers or mothers-in-law and often unmarried aunts and cousins. Among these, with the addition of bosom friends, a complex, interesting, female society existed, which the husband, about whom theoretically the whole thing revolved, came home to and departed from. After dinner, whether a dinner party or just the household, the wife gathered up the ladies and led them off to the (with)drawing-room for female chat and intrigue, leaving her lord and sons and male guests to their port or claret. In the morning the gentleman departed for Whitehall or the City, feeling in Browning's phrase, "the need of a world of men for me." He lunched with other men at his club, as well as working with other men, and often, no doubt, remained in town to dine and spend the evening in talk round the club fire. In the world of sport, although ladies were taking up lawn tennis and croquet, it was still mostly the men who followed the hounds or shot pheasants or went off to a lodge by a trout stream. The point is that, since husbands left their wives at home, bachelors and married men were on the same easy footing in the world of men.

Before we leave this nineteenth-century world, a very comfortable one for bachelors, let us notice the premise upon which that society and *all* earlier ones firmly rested, a very basic premise indeed. C. S. Lewis has used the term, "the common judgement of mankind", to refer to deep-rooted beliefs about the nature of things held by all men and women of all times and in all places—*not* something to be lightly tossed aside. And that basic premise of nineteenth-century and all earlier societies was the common judgement of mankind that men and women are *different*—a deeper difference by far than merely the plumbing arrangements. Different in tastes, aptitudes, capacities, natural interests, and in quality of being. Different through and through—which difference is what makes for the delight of each in the other.

Long ago Aristotle laid down for guidance in virtue his principle of the Golden Mean—for instance, the virtue of courage is the Golden Mean between an excess that is foolhardiness and a deficiency that is cowardice. A judgement about the truth of things is not of course in the same class, but, by stretching a point, we could say that the *excess* of the judgement of men and women being different is the belief that men (or women) are superior. And the *deficiency* perhaps may be the feminist notion—the unproved theory—that there is no difference at all except the anatomical.

The bachelor in 1980, in spite of this being the best and freest of all possible worlds, is in many ways in a less happy position than the bachelor in 1880. Why has this melancholy decline come about? The first reason—one of the greatest—is the decline of the separate worlds of men and women that have existed in all previous centuries. We need to examine what has happened. The complex world of the household and Society is almost gone. The work of that world, the cooking, the sewing, the candlestick making, has yielded to ready-made clothes, factory-made food, and gadgets. There are fewer children—one or two. Mothers-in-law and spinster aunts can't be coped with in small-box houses or flats and are shunted sadly off to what are ironically called 'homes'. Servants and nannies (regrettably) are becoming but a memory. Consequently civilized dining, not to mention dinner parties, is a fading custom: the world of Society is going. The big household is a thing of the past, and the wife is no longer part of a lively world of women. Talking to the fridge is not the same. What, it may be asked, has this to do with the bachelor? It has this to do with him: he is no longer in demand for country weekends or for dinner parties or for exposure to the bright eyes of the daughter of the house. She, if she can be found at all, is acquiring men on different terms and exposing more than eyes and ankles.

As a direct result of the decline of the world of women, women have come forth into the world of men. Even back in the nineteenth century there were stirrings of feminism, and now in the last third of the twentieth century it has become a force to be reckoned with. If women are to be in the work place, they are, very naturally, not going to be content with only the second-rate jobs. The once-sacrosanct men's preserves of business and banking, law and medicine, and even (rather excessively) the armed forces, are being invaded. Even the still-more-sacrosanct gentlemen's clubs and fraternal lodges are beginning to open their doors. This is revolution, greater than any political one; but whether this unisexist homogenisation of men and women is wise remains to be seen. It is *happening*, and there is a higher-pitched note in almost every place where people gather. If that common judgement of mankind is true, the consequences may be disastrous. At all events, for the time being, at least, the values that were thought to inhere in men and women forgathering with their own sex will be diminished. Again, though, the question arises how the decline of the world of men affects the bachelor in particular? It affects him in this way: where once, in the world of men, it made little difference whether a man were a bachelor or a husband with a wife at home, except that a bachelor was freer, now the husband is likely to be lunching with his wife and perhaps working with her too, as with a husband-and-wife team of doctors. And playing golf with her later.

I remarked earlier that readers of older books might have the impression that couples are more *obtrusively* couples now than in the past. So they are. The wife is no longer tied to her home; and husband and wife, man and woman, are doing far more together than ever before. As a result the bachelor, once an equal citizen of the world of men, finds himself far more isolated than he used to be. Whether it be in club or pub, watching ball games or horse races, sailing or golfing, men are with women. It really is a world of couples. The bachelor, therefore, feels a sort of pressure to become part of a couple.

Another reason for the less comfortable state of the bachelor lies in the way our age sees itself. The ancient Greeks saw the Egyptians as religion-saturated men. In the Age of the Enlightenment man was seen as essentially a rational creature. The Marxist, if there are any genuine Marxists left apart from a few radical Jesuits, sees man as nothing but an economic animal. And *we* see him as a sexual one. If ancient Egypt was religion-saturated, we are sex-saturated. It is, very likely, the swing of the pendulum from Victorian restraint or prudishness. That was an extreme, compared to the eighteenth century or the sixteenth. But when the pendulum swings from an extreme, it goes to the other extreme—and we are it. I fancy that later, more balanced ages will look back upon us with considerable astonishment and distaste. Not only are we deluged with every sensual urging that cynical intelligence can dream up, but our minds are jungles of half-baked psychological theory about sex, including of course the intensely sex-focussed Freudian one. The truth is, surely, that man is a reasoning being and a spiritual being as well as a physical being. Just as it is a lie that everything in the end comes down to Marxian materialism, so is it a lie that everything comes down to the quest for the ultimate orgasm.

The sexual obsession of our society inevitably affects the bachelor. If sex is what man's all about, then what is that man doing single?

"Listen, Bud, don't tell me that those guys are monks for the glory of God: there's something behind it, see?"—"Of course that chap's not a bachelor because he cares only for his work—there's something wrong with him." —And so on. We are obsessed with sexual explanations. The very word 'bachelor,' which had a certain dignity and assurance, implying a rational choice of one of many goods, is in decline. There is, almost, only one good—sex. Today the bachelor is likely to be called a 'single' or, worse, an unmarried man, both suggesting an unnatural or incomplete state. A state to be remedied as soon as possible. Hence the pressure that the bachelor feels to get himself coupled.

Worse, there is that suspicion: if a man is unmarried, there must be 'something wrong' with him. Something wrong does not mean, as in another age it might have done, that the man is a robber or a spy; it means something sexual. Despite the well-publicized fact that marriages are breaking up at the rate of ten a minute, hinting rather that they can't have been notably cheerful, we still feel, with complete irrationality, that there must be 'something wrong' with the man who deliberately refrains from entering into one (or six or seven). The idea that a man can have no other spring of action than the sexual is genuinely absurd; but the absurdity is in the very air of this best of all ages.

Thus the bachelor, who in the nineteenth century felt himself envied, now feels the pressure of the 'something wrong' suspicion. And two bachelors living together, since they couldn't possibly be motivated by friendship or some great shared interest, are put to the necessity of proving themselves continually by the conspicuous consumption of women, unless they want to be looked at with a more specific suspicion—homosexuality. It is strange and sad: the friendship that the ancients held to be the highest of human loves, precisely because it was *not* clouded by passion, is not even believed in by a society so 'knowing' that it sees only the gutter and looks for an orgasm in every woodpile. Thus the bachelor is on the defensive. Not only does he seem to be surrounded by couples, but he feels that he must show his couple-potential by being seen with a woman, even if he'd rather stay home and read a book. Well-meaning people, inspired by the couples mind-set, form 'singles' groups so that he can meet more women. He's a bit uneasy at being seen often with another man, however comfortable and easy the friendship. Where in the past neither he nor anyone else would have thought it odd to enjoy friendship, today there is the suspicion. What is worse is his *feeling* that people may be wondering about him. And worst of all is when the bachelor, breathing the somewhat sordid air of this society, is led to wonder about himself. Why *doesn't* he want to live in a suburban box with a wife and one and a half kiddies? Is there—*is* there 'something wrong' with him?

Being a bachelor, then, in this 'freest of all societies' is not easy. The boasted freedom is, in fact, the freedom to flaunt the *old* conformities while being locked rigidly into *new* ones. Women don't have to be housewives—but they're given a hard time by the feminists if they *want* to be. Girls are free to sleep around—but they are not free to say no without risking isolation. Men can take girls to bed without scandal—but they can't form close friendships with other men without risking suspicion. After all, we are not so free. And bachelors, beyond a doubt, have suffered a loss of dignity and respect and a limitation of choices.

Just as the world of 1880, so comfortable for bachelors, changed into the brave new world of 1980, so we are on the way to a still-newer world. It might be worth while to speculate about it, extrapolating from what can be seen now. Here is a story of now. A handsome young couple in their late twenties: they lived together for a while and then married. Three months later the man wanted a divorce—not because there was anything wrong; he wanted to go on living with her, but he felt stifled by *marriage*. He got his divorce though *she* didn't like it and parted from him. As we have seen, the state of marriage affects the bachelor. Where is it going?

Marriage, traditionally, exists for women. Men, to be sure, have wanted a son to leave the name and estate to; but, apart from legitimacy, have frequently shown contentment with an unofficial harem. Augustus the Strong of Poland sired three hundred children before he lost count. But in women—all female mammals—the 'nest-building' instinct and the mother instinct appear to be powerful, despite some wishful feminist denial. If the instincts are there, denial won't alter them. For the woman, then, marriage offered 'the nest' and food and protection so that she could get on with the babies. So women have sought matrimony. But what was in it for men? Men, traditionally, have sought to bed women without having to marry them. That was made as difficult as possible by the 'virtue' of all 'nice girls'—and the danger. In earlier centuries, as we have seen, the great game, good humoured but real, was to trap the eligible bachelor. And the bait in the trap, no doubt about it, was the bright eyes and the suggested-but-not-revealed physical charms, the nicely calculated glimpse of a slender ankle. Charms that could only be got by holy wedlock—for life. But marriage offered the man more—a clean and comfortable home, full of flowers from the garden, for him to come back to from the world of men, an adoring wife to listen to him and soothe him and wait upon him and see that his dinner was the way he liked it. He might sometimes envy bachelor freedom, but the bachelor sometimes envied him. If the husband spent a good deal of time at his club, if he went off to some shooting lodge, if he, even, had a mistress in due course, these things were more or less to be expected. 'Togetherness' in today's sense was not insisted upon. So when a man found himself saying, "I do," and a little later stepped across his own threshold with his arms full of fragrant (and of course virginal) womanhood, he perhaps did not greatly regret having been caught. —All this does, indeed, sound like a different world, but it is the pattern of all the centuries. And it is worth noticing what each of them got from the marriage.

Today, although women seem as anxious as ever to be married or re-married, all is changed. The man is less concerned about a son to leave the ranch-house to, and, with over-population, there is less sense of a duty to have children. No man need marry to discover a girl's hidden charms; they are flaunted in public in the scruffiest way possible, becoming markedly less alluring. And the old scheme of persuading men to accept marital responsibilities by making sex with 'nice girls' unavailable except on the bed of matrimony has altogether collapsed. The sexual revolution, quite simply, is a male dream come true. Women and marriage are the losers.

But what of the 'something more' that marriage has traditionally offered? Working women have little time for home-making. Pervasive feminism is modifying wifeliness—the adoring wife. She is demanding that her husband share the housework. Perfectly fair, but he may reflect that as a bachelor he let the dust get an inch thick and now he's made to dust daily—and where's that at? What compensates? Well, pals and all that. But he just might think that another man (who also doesn't mind an inch of dust) might be a better *pal*, and as for sex, who needs marriage? And he just might conclude that a liberated woman with all her rights (however just) is not what he wants to be married to. Or, like that young man, stay married to. Easy divorce has taken the door off the trap.

So it is a day when the traditional inducements to marriage are either free or disappearing, when marriage offers few comforts yet the same responsibility, and when statistically it has a good chance of ending in the divorce court—which only begins the tangle of child-support payments and custody wrangles. The sexual revolution and feminism are rather a deadly combination against the venerable institution of matrimony; and the day may be coming when the question, "Do you take this woman to be your wedded wife?" will be answered by the man, "No fear! Not on your life!"

Is this where we are going? The stage beyond the nuclear family? The day when marriage dies (except, one may hope, among Christians)? Women of course would continue to have children. Perhaps they may draw together in vast complexes for mutual support, men and boys prowling the perimeter like wolves, discovering anew the old comradeship of the hunt—and *all* bachelors. Once again the separate worlds of men and women, far more separate: but hardly an improvement on the nineteenth century. It may not happen of course. Society may take some other turn, restoring marriage.

Conspicuous by its absence so far (especially in an essay by me) is the relationship of love to marriage. But if there is genuine inloveness and if it leads to deep, true union (which it does not always do), then it is, of course, the *vital* factor that can make any sort of marriage—past, present, and future—a happiness and a frequent, sudden joy. When such union exists, hardships can be gaily borne and divorce is unthinkable. But the bachelor, by definition, is on another road.

The bachelor, if he is to understand himself and his position, must comprehend the forces that bear upon bachelorhood, which is why we have looked at the past and possible future as well as the present. Does anything emerge from the examination that can guide the bachelor in today's world? Of course, understanding is itself the best guide. But perhaps a bit more may be said.

The most important thing of all is this: the bachelor should hold up his head. Merely seeing that this is a day of distortion of all things sexual ought to give him confidence in himself. And there is much to be said for the damn-the-torpedoes-go-ahead attitude with respect to what 'they' are possibly thinking. The bachelor's own inner confidence (like the lack of it) about himself and the validity of his choice is something that can be sensed by others. And it *is* a valid choice and has been all through the centuries.

It is worthwhile considering what bachelorhood has going for it. First of all, it makes possible single-minded commitment to some great goal without neglect of a wife and children: many a book has never been written because of duty to a family. Then, too, bachelorhood is in many ways comfortable. One eats when and what one pleases. Reads all night if he chooses. Works without interruption for as many hours as necessary. Goes to see whomever he pleases without explanations. He has more time for friendship, both with other men and with women. If he is childless, he may be able to appreciate and love his friends' children the more. A bachelor becomes so used to freedom that he finds it difficult to give up if he does marry.

There is a great deal to be said for calling oneself boldly a *bachelor*. It is a strong, independent-sounding word and suggests a deliberate choice. A way of life. 'Unmarried' is a bit like 'unemployed' or 'unfed'—negative and crippled. 'Single' ('one-legged') isn't much better. But *bachelor* makes a statement, and it conjures up a tradition as well as images of jolly bachelors in literature. (Women would do well to reconsider the case for 'spinster', also a word of strength.)

What of the Christian bachelor? Is his position different? He believes that God created man and woman to cleave together into one flesh, not till love dies but till they die. He has more reason, then, to be cautious instead of rushing into a marriage. And he knows from St Paul, who was a fellow bachelor, that a Christian can remain single and still do God's work. Only—the Christian bachelor knows that he must remain celibate. In that way he must be different. No flesh pots. In this sex-saturated age celibacy is regarded as next-to-impossible, but Christians—monks—have proved in all ages that it is not impossible.

For bachelors in general, it is time to assert that the single state is an 'alternative life-style' with its own rewards and dignity. The word *bachelor* itself makes that statement. If a bachelor wants to share a flat with another bachelor, he should do it and damn-the-torpedoes. If he is lonely, he should endeavor to find other bachelors: undemanding friendship is one of the great things. And above all the bachelor should *hold up his head*.

Marriage is clearly threatened. And yet marriage (the one-flesh union) is what inloveness—*Eros* with his promise of eternal love—points to. The alternative, common in our day, is serial polygamy: a series of husbands, a series of wives, or a series of concubines—no real union, of course, with any. Curiously enough, this sort of thing was common once before in history, in Imperial Rome. According to Juvenal, Roman women often named their years for the husband of that year—the Year of Gaius, the Year of Marcus. But Jesus forbade divorce, showing Himself out of touch with the modern mind. Of course that could be put another way.

But marriage, however hard beset, will continue to be entered into, with the hope or, among Christians, the firm intention of its enduring. And marriage, at least in the modern world, begins with inloveness, the most mysterious of the natural loves. No one can say why these two people fall in love or what precisely inloveness is. One thing it is *not*: it is not simply sexual desire—indeed, sexual desire is often in abeyance, or felt to be an intrusion, when a couple is first in love: the wonder and the marvelling are enough. And inloveness is always or nearly always mutual. No sound of one hand clapping here. The lover may wonder with anguish whether the delightful other could possibly love him, but the other is probably wondering the same thing. I have likened falling in love to a spark leaping back and forth from one to the other, inloveness building up and up like the voltage in a coil. If it is not mutual, it is either infatuation, like that of girls for film stars; or, just possibly, in the case of a man falling in love with his friend's wife, it is encountering the faithfulness of that wife who has recognised and fought down and extinguished the same first spark in herself.

Inloveness is the only one of the loves that can be easily expressed—and must be. "I love you!" in the right circumstances says it all—although, in response to a question from one spouse to the other, the answer, "Of *course* I love you," is not always reliable. But, in truth, people really in love know it, and so does everyone else: they can't keep their eyes off each other, they lean towards each other. While friends stand shoulder to shoulder looking at what absorbs and fascinates them both, lovers look at each other, each absorbed and fascinated by the wonder of the other.

People in love or falling in love may talk animatedly about everything and may, therefore, think that they are discovering a rare and beautiful friendship—indeed, this belief may for a time disguise from them that they are in love—but it is not friendship: what they are doing, in fact, is exploring the marvellous beloved. The criterion is where their gaze is really directed—towards each other or away from themselves. Of course lovers delight in discovering common tastes, likes and dislikes. Let them but find they both love strawberries, collie dogs, a certain musical group, and a particular book, while both hate a certain actor, caged canaries, and detective stories, and they will be halfway to the altar, feeling themselves to be soulmates. But what they are doing is assuming, on the basis of a handful of not-uncommon shared tastes (practically everybody loves strawberries and, today, denounces caged birdies, and most young folk dislike detective stories), an identity of taste that will run through all the thousands of not-explored attitudes.

In this exploring it is each other they are fascinated by; they desire above all things to find these common tastes—often swallowing small reservations that may later bulk large—in order to prove to themselves that they were made for each other. They are overwhelmed by the god; *Eros*, needless to say, is the most overwhelming of the loves, possibly excepting the fire of the saints' love of God. But, although *Eros* is promising for ever, and their *Eros*-blinded eyes see only perfection in each other, it will not be happily-ever-after if they feel, once they've got to the altar, that they need now do nothing further but exist in bliss. The very perfection they see in each other makes it certain that the human faults in each, which their friends can readily perceive, will be to them shocking discoveries, almost betrayals. Unless their love is already beginning to be pervaded by charity, it will begin to die as the blindness of *Eros* wears off. Its very intensity and intimacy as well as its high expectations make the need for charity the greater. Without it, they will join the long queues at the divorce courts.

In my own marriage, the central story of *A Severe Mercy*, Davy and I had an initial advantage. Although we were in love and had heard the forever promise of *Eros*, we had noticed that our friends who had seemed so ecstatically in love last year were not so now—or were ecstatically in love with someone else. Of course our love was different. Wasn't it? But what, we said, if it weren't? We talked about it. We looked more closely and saw failed loves everywhere. This was serious.

Then, with a modicum of wisdom, we decided that, if this marvellous and joyful love were to last, we must *make* it last: we must protect it not only from the outside world but from ourselves, the selfishness in each of us. And so we raised the Shining Barrier—all that complex of rules and principles and frequent talks on the state of the union I told about in *Mercy*. But what of charity? We were not Christians, and 'charity' to us meant baskets to the poor. Still, even if 'charity' meant nothing to us, the word 'love' meant a lot; and we perceived that it meant more than ecstasy. It meant, we said, fetching for each other "a cup of water in the night" and also being willing to ask for it. That, surely, was not too bad a definition. A cup of charity.

Moreover, 'love' meant, we said, subordinating self to our love. Even then we saw, without Christianity, that self was deadly; and I wrote in my early poem, "The Shining Barrier":

> For self's a killer, reckless of the cost,
> And loves of lilactime unloved are lost.

We may have thought we were subordinating self to inloveness—in a sense we were—but it was in truth to God Himself, however unknown to us.

We decided, too, that the anger of one of us towards the other was a greater sin against love than whatever provoked the anger. And we were resolute that our love should not fail: we should get to the root of every difficulty and, by talking it out, overcome it.

Thus, even if we didn't understand the word, charity was no small part of what we meant by love. The charity was not perfect, but it was there from the first; and, more important, it grew *within* in-loveness.

I have touched upon my own love in order to illuminate the discussion of inloveness in general. That mysterious love, that high and lovely love, can only endure, as every lover wants it to do, if it is infused by charity. Then while inloveness sleeps, as it must sometimes do, the lovers can be content with 'just plain loving'—affection and charity—and, sooner or later, inloveness, soaring on bright wings, will come again. And again.

Before we turn to the third of the great natural loves, friendship, I must say what I should not have to say but for our present society's need to see a sexual meaning in everything. Friendship is not a homosexual relationship any more than mother love is an incestuous one. We must not take the perverse form of anything as the normal or basic one. A homosexual relationship is, in fact, closer to *Eros* than to *philia*. Homosexuals, either men or women, fall in love with each other, after all. It is the realm of *Eros*.

But the homosexual pair cannot go on to marriage. They may *say* they are married and even get some trendy clergyman to pronounce them wed, but it is no more than empty words. Seeds sown in the Sahara. A mad bishop might 'ordain' a horse, but it wouldn't be a priest.

In the '60s, when my faith was weakened anyway, I became very sympathetic with homosexuals I knew in the Movement, some of whom seemed truly in love with each other; and I decided the Church was wrong to condemn homo-sex. It was, I fear, a case of loving the sinner and so loving the sin, too. I still feel the deepest sympathy with the pain of the homosexual (I cannot use the lovely and irreplaceable word 'gay' for him), but, while his *love* is not wrong, he must, I believe, face the fact, if he's a Christian, that homo-*sex* is sin. I should like to think otherwise but I cannot. But it is not for me to judge or reject a homo. who does think otherwise. *Eros* is powerful, and celibacy is scarcely a twentieth-century ideal; the homosexual's choice can only be filled with pain. A fifty-year-old homosexual told me once he had never known a happy homosexual. But I have wondered whether a homosexual couple, in love but celibate, sublimating physical desire for the love of Christ, might not be astonishingly happy, even as a celibate monk can be radiantly happy. But I've never known a homosexual pair who have chosen that austere way.

Friendship is the least understood and, perhaps for that reason, the least valued of all the loves by modern society. This was not always the way of it. Not only was it highly valued in the nineteenth century, but it was hailed as the *highest* of the loves by the ancient civilisation precisely *because* it wasn't clouded by passion and emotion, and because it was deliberately chosen. But today, in our sex-obsessed society, there are unread people who deny that friendship even exists; it is, they say, only disguised homosexual desire; of course they are the same people who deny that inloveness really exists: *it* is only disguised lust. As C. S. Lewis says, these people merely "betray the fact that they have never had a friend." And never known inloveness. In both cases, one can see why. When a society is sick enough to reduce everything to sex, such stupidities are bound to arise. The loves of Paris and Helen, Lancelot and Guenevere, Heathcliffe and Cathy, become no more than lust; and Roland and Oliver, Damon and Pythias, David and Jonathan, become secret homosexuals. If we deny the existence of beauty, we don't disprove the dawn and lilacs; we disprove our ability to see.

It is because friendship is so little understood and even denied that I must say more of it than of the loves we celebrate.

But what *is* friendship? To turn again to Lewis, friendship begins when one man says to another: "What! You, too? I thought I was the only one." The only one with this particular vision of poetry or Northern mythology or God or sailing to the far islands. The only one in the town or the college or the office that loves fly fishing or chess or model-ship building or gourmet dining. Friendship is always *about* something—something outside the two men that both of them love (anything, that is, but a woman). Or both hate, as men in the Resistance hated the Nazis, or Southerners in the 1860s hated the Yankee invaders and carpet-baggers. As I put it earlier, friends are not fascinated by each other; they are standing shoulder to shoulder gazing at what absorbs them both. And talking about it endlessly. Moreover, unlike lovers, friends are always delighted to welcome a third with the same love into their company. The same compelling interest. Although friendship begins with, and is sustained by, that mutual 'what-you-too' discovery, the friends, as they together pursue their absorbing interest, find deep brotherly affection growing in them to enhance their friendship. When a man lays down his life for his friend, as Damon pledged his for Pythias, it is a mixture of friendship and affection—and of course charity—that impels him to do so. Indeed, that mixture is friendship at its highest.

If this is friendship, then it is plain that we today misuse the word. I would offer the world my 'law' (Vanlaw): If a word can be corrupted, it will be. We refer to 'our friends' when we mean, in fact, our acquaintances, pleasant folk we feel affection for but share no great interest with. The word 'friendship' still has meaning, but 'friends' as in 'our friends' usually doesn't. Two men who work together on something they are both passionately interested in may be indeed friends; but, if they bring their families together and mutual affection binds them all, the only genuine *friendship* may still be that of the men. The lonely woman who longs for 'a friend' is almost a stock figure of pathos; but what she is really longing for, in the absence of inloveness, is affection. (How we need parallel words to 'friend' and 'friendship' for affection!) If that lonely woman had any great and absorbing interest in something outside herself and her cat, anything from stamp-collecting to Wordsworth, she could probably find friends, and affection to boot. Young men, reluctant to call their girl anything so final as their beloved, call her their "girl-friend" or just "friend"; but friend is just what she is not. All of these misuses or extensions of 'friend' blur and debase its meaning with no real gain. The young people could as well stick to 'my girl' and 'my boy'—or 'my young man' or even the old 'beau'.

Friendship has so far been portrayed as mainly a love between man and man, and so it is often thought of. Women, not without hostility, have often professed themselves unable to understand the power of men's friendship, and have indeed resented it. One angry woman said, "There's a solidarity among men that no woman can beat." My father told me once that he had five friends, any one of whom would drop everything and travel halfway round the world if he telegraphed, "Come, I need you." My mother played bridge and went shopping with other ladies, but I can't imagine her saying or even thinking of anything like my father's remark.

Still, is there such a thing as female friendship? Girls have 'bosom friends' (as they used to be called), but one gets the impression of highly emotional relationships, even 'crushes', close and confiding but likely to end in slaps and tears if one of them walks with some other girl. These would scarcely be friendships. On the other hand, the great ladies who once ran Society undoubtedly had trusted friends among the ladies, all being interested in the proper management of affairs. The key, as always, is the shared interest in something outside the friends. Women who are good wives and mothers, although they may compare notes on husband handling and exchange recipes, find their absorbing interest in their own homes—an unshareable interest. The old saying that "love (inloveness and family love) is to man a thing apart but 'tis woman's whole existence" contains a truth that is relevant to women's friendship. I have heard girls moan about 'the dearest friend' who got married and no longer writes or rings up. But now that women are leaving home for offices, it is probable that some of them are developing interests they can share in friendship. By and large, I think that women's friendships are rarer and probably less steadfast then men's.

Also, it may be that the 'couples mindset' mentioned in "The Bachelor" is tending to inhibit friendships even among men. Women are coming out into the world, but it is not a world of women as it used to be a world of men.

What, then, of friendship between a man and a woman? I've already suggested that the animated exploration of each other—in conversation, that is—by young couples, or indeed older ones, is not friendship, despite "What! You, too?" exclamations, since the absorbing interest of each is in the other. I think, therefore, that genuine friendship between a man and a woman is uncommon, just as it would be uncommon between homosexuals or lesbians. After all, if, as the ancients said, the mark of friendship is that it is *not* clouded by emotion or passion, the relationship between the sexes is not usually described in quite those words. A real friendship between a man and a woman with a deep common interest in, say, the theatre or music, might begin; but the very closeness engendered by the shared interest might easily lead to their being, all in an instant, overwhelmed by *Eros*. Even if that did not happen, sexual awareness would tend to prevent the easy, *unselfconscious* relaxation of friendship.

Gender antagonisms may also—even an edge of them—make friendship difficult. The masculine attitude expressed in the often-repeated saying about women—"You can't live with them and you can't live without them"—strongly suggests that long-term, undemanding friendship between a man and a woman is difficult. America's greatest fictional detective, Nero Wolfe, once remarked of a female suspect: "Except for the innate and universal flaws of her sex, there may be nothing wrong with her." Most male readers, I expect, gave that a wry smile. No doubt women have similar words for men.

I do not say that friendship between a man and a woman is impossible. In fact, I know it isn't; I have dear women friends and I value them. Moreover, a husband and wife, after they've become easy in steadfast matrimony and the fires have died a bit, may develop a lively shared interest in something outside themselves—in nature and the environmental movement, for instance. As may older people in general. But male-female friendships, while not impossible, are, I think, rather uncommon.

The friendship of man and man is unquestionably one of the great loves: all of history and literature attest to it. The modern world, though, is hostile to it. Not only does our obsession with sex make it vaguely suspect in shallow minds, not only does the couples mindset inhibit its development, but women, whether the wives of the married or the office mates of the unmarried, feel that a man's attention might more properly be directed elsewhere than to his friend. To themselves, that is. Moreover, the feminists beating at every door—boys' schools, men's colleges (even West Point), men's lodges, and gentlemen's clubs—turn every place where masculine friendships were fostered into breeding grounds, marriage marts, or at least social groups.

It is ironical that the feminists should at once insist on the vital importance of all-female consciousness-raising groups—'sisterhood' groups—*and* clamour for admission to every masculine sanctum. It suggests that old female fear of men's friendship.

And men, the oppressors, amiably yield at every barricade. They seem not to realise that, if something is gained, something is lost. And certainly they fail to understand the truth that the presence of even one woman in a group of five or ten men changes the group's character: *even one woman*, young or old, for the men cannot help speaking to impress her. The male, boy and man, shows off for the female. This change in the group's character may be a good thing or a bad thing, but it *is* a change: something easy and relaxed has become something livelier and more self-conscious.

Champagne has replaced claret. Is it to be champagne always and everywhere?

Allow me to stress what I have just said, for it is a remarkable yet little-known truth. A truth that may easily be experimentally veri-fied. Even one woman added to a men's group (and, I am told, even one man added to a women's group, e.g., a sisterhood group) ineluctably alters the character of that group. A degree of self-con-sciousness, a faint tension, takes the place of relaxed unselfcon-sciousness. It may become a better thing or a worse: but it is never the *same* thing. Both are needed.

At all events, as long as men hunt and shoot and fish together, as long as women can't make (play on) the football team, and as long as men go off to the wars together, men's friendship will go on. In-deed, women's being into everything, backed by the manipulating hand of government, may eventually tighten the bonding of man to man. And the excesses of our excessive age are likely to be bal-anced by the inevitable swing of the pendulum towards the next age.

One of the questions put to me by readers was how should a man balance his love (friendship) for his friend with his love (inlove-ness) for his wife. I might be thought to be the last one to ask since I put one of them, the latter, so far first; and, anyway, do not know. But I have meditated on the question over the years; and, at least, I do not put either love to one side as a lesser thing.

I grew up before mid-century, and I grew up reading the books of still-earlier times. My father gave me *Treasure Island* on my tenth birthday: a grand adventure tale of a lad going to sea with a shipload of men to find a lost treasure. A girl along would have seemed to me absolute heresy, and I probably shouldn't have read the book. (If I had a small son today, I'd not buy him the modern, feminist-inspired stories in which—unlike the Narnia tales—boys are not boyish nor girls, girlish.) As it was, I read all of Stevenson. And my father and I both loved the grand tales of Rider Haggard about mysterious Africa. And of course I read the stories of the knights of the Round Table. And, partly because of the books I read, I grew up putting a high valuation on friendship. One of the three rules in my boyish Code (along with not betraying beauty or the sword) was "Never betray a friend." I had a real horror of be-traying a friend, but never so much as thought of a rule about not betraying one's lady. (Of course I rapidly developed one when

Davy and I fell in love.) So 'friendship' was a word of power in my boyhood, and still is.

But even then I was aware of conflict. Knights were held back from the Quest by ladies. Officers in Kipling had to choose between the brave life of the regiment, where their friends were, and their wives who feared and resented the regiment. This, indeed, was the conflict I expressed in my long-perished essay on "Squadron *versus* Apron Strings". Kipling's officers' wives usually won, and so did Davy.

In an earlier chapter of this book I told of my school friendship with Johnny, "the laughing fellow rover," who met his death soon after our abortive adventure; and of my college friendship with my flying comrade, Bob, of Squadron 13—not only the adventures we actually had but the great adventures we planned once we took the "long trail". Our plans of course collapsed when Davy and inloveness intervened.

It is utterly clear that those friendships met the essential criterion of friendship: they were *about* something. We gazed, not at each other but at adventure and the long trail. If I had forsaken inloveness for the long trail, I should have felt a bit guilty about it as well as wondering what might have been. As it was, I felt a bit guilty at abandoning the adventure road with Bob—not so much at abandoning Bob himself but at abandoning what our friendship was about, the thing itself: the long trail with a laughing fellow rover, the *way* of that particular friendship. I was not, of course, renouncing friendships, only putting them in a lesser place.

I had other college friendships that still endure, one of them 'about' poetry and a vision of life that stemmed from it. Readers of *Mercy* will recall the Christ-centred friendships that revolved about the Studio in Oxford. They have all endured, but one of the most alive friendships over the years has been that with Dom Julian, which was based on poetry as well as Christ, as I say in my introduction to the book of his poetry, *There Shines Forth Christ*. But there were other friendships that were not Christian, one of them with Edmund Dews being based essentially on a shared appreciation of that which is civilised. One almost life-long friendship will be touched on in a later essay in this book, "The Knight's Move"

And yet, during the years with Davy, I thought from time to time, somewhat uneasily, about the friendship—the active comradeship—of men. Davy and I had put our love first, so far first that there was, so to speak, no second. We sailed together, studied together, did everything together. There was no women's circle for her, no men's club or lodge for me. We had friends, but we had them together—an aspect of sharing. After all, we were 'one flesh', and we *would* be taken together. I was determined to include her.

But friendship develops on a man-to-man basis, and if it comes to include two or three others, there ought not to be an 'inner circle' (Davy and me) of two of them. I really knew this, I think, but wouldn't admit it to myself. Perhaps fortunately, circumstances beyond our control excluded Davy from some places I had to be: ships of the Navy, seminars at Yale, my dining club and the common rooms at Oxford, and luncheons and other meetings with C. S. Lewis. I accepted this as the way of the world, wishing it were otherwise; but now that it *is* otherwise, now that the feminists are breaking down the doors, I have come to understand that there was good in that old way. For friendships grew and developed, notably that with Lewis, as they otherwise *could not* have done.

But, then, I sometimes felt I ought voluntarily to spend more time with the lads. Or a choice would present itself—an evening with a friend or with Davy. Almost always I chose the time with Davy, for our love was first. Yet the other was a tug. Davy, I'm almost certain, did not feel any parallel urges to spend more time with other women. I ought to add, though, that we both recognised the obligation, together or separately, to spend time with anyone in grief or trouble.

If I had spent a couple of evenings a week with men friends, or spent more time at the college hanging about the office as most men did, or gone off with other chaps to a hunting lodge every year, that would have deepened and created friendships—but Davy and I would have been less close: no doubt of that at all. Some would say—some have said—that what Davy and I had was excessive, not balanced. One man even called our marriage uxorious; but that it was not, for 'uxorious' means submissive to a wife or doting, and I was certainly neither. Nor was our way the result of any demand, however veiled, of hers: it was, rather, an ideal of love and union. But *was* it excessive? unbalanced? I should agree that it was unbalanced—that is, it didn't strike a balance between love and friendship. Whether it was excessive depends on whether people can be *too* close or love each other *too* much. Rather like being kinder than necessary.

More given to friendship would have lessened our closeness: we never felt we had enough time alone together anyhow. The nineteenth century with its separate worlds of men and women (much the same in the first half of the twentieth) achieved a sort of balance. The husband, apart from occasional evenings round the club fire, came home to his wife at night. And then in the morning felt, as Browning said, "the need of a world of men for me." I'm not sure that it is permitted to mention such a need these days, and certainly the "world of men" that has existed in *every* other age since the world began has now become hard to find. Perhaps men should ponder the question of whether there is such a need.

But I'm not holding the nineteenth century up as an ideal—*nor*, heaven knows, the twentieth. The nineteenth-century balance undoubtedly enhanced friendship but may not have made for close marital unions. Now that the latter twentieth century is doing so much to destroy friendship, surely we must see its fruit in universally close, happy, faithful marriages and the disappearance of divorce. No? What, then? The English have a nice descriptive phrase: falling between two stools. Our age destroys the world of men where friendship flourished in order to promote 'togetherness' of men and women—and seems to be destroying marriage at the same time. A classic illustration of falling between two stools.

Davy and I had what I can only believe in retrospect to have been a love of great beauty and closeness, remarkable in any age. As C. S. Lewis once said, the 'one flesh' of marriage was "most admirably realised" in it. And it didn't just happen: we quite deliberately chose the way we followed, subordinating everything else to it. If there had been a juster balance between the marriage and man-to-man friendships, the love and marriage would have been less beautiful and more ordinary. At the same time, the friendships would scarcely have been of the David and Jonathan sort, for the great friendships are usually between men who either have no wives, or almost totally neglect them, or are remote from them. In other words, the world of men.

The simple truth is that inloveness and friendship (like freedom and equality) limit each other. Neither can be had in its fullness without drastically reducing the other. (The unique achievement of our age is to reduce both.) The wives who through the centuries have resented and feared men's friendship were right from their point of view that put marriage first. But wives who enjoyed the world of women, shown to us so clearly in Jane Austen, were not displeased when their husband lingered in the world of men. At all events, there is in most marriages a balance, meaning neither in its fullness. Almost a definition of compromise.

With my philosophy of choosing the heights and depths over the middle, it was perhaps inevitable that I should choose to have one or the other in its fullness. And perhaps it was inevitable that it should have been inloveness: surely *it* has higher heights and deeper depths (Davy's death and the grief). But I cannot certainly know, having had but the one in fullness.

There may be glorious heights when two friends ride together into the charge—that "high hour in which he lived and died," as some poet has it; and Housman, too, speaks of battle, when he lost his heart to "a soldier and a foeman / A chap that did not kill me, but he tried / That took the sabre straight and took it striking, / And laughed and kissed his hand to me and died." Or in "Ulysses" where he says he has "drunk delight of battle with my peers, / Far on the ringing plains of windy Troy." These lines, speaking of the "delight of battle" and the "high hour" in which a man fully lived for the first time in his life—and died, are almost inconceivable to modern man facing the nuclear and nerve-gas horrors of our day. And they don't speak directly of friendship. But it is in battle and storm at sea, in hardship and danger, that friendships have found their heights and depths. Or in a great vision or discovery arrived at together.

If, instead of choosing Davy, I had gone off in a rakish schooner with a "laughing fellow rover" or two to look for adventure, it would have been, *par excellence*, the world of men's friendship, friendships deepening in danger and hardship over the years. But I did choose Davy, and we with our Shining Barrier had, *par excellence*, the world of deep, 'one-flesh' union. My youthful "Squadron *versus* Apron Strings" recognised that there was a choice: and I made it.

I do not, of *course*, regret choosing as I did. How could I? But I regret not having had the other in *its* fullness also. If that is possible.

It looks as though it is not possible to have both in their fullness at the same time, but it also looks as though it may be possible to have them both *seriatim*. The young man who doesn't bound straightaway into marriage may find a job that takes him to far places—for instance, as a newspaperman. Or of course a turn in the army or navy. A student of mine has hitchhiked twice across Asia with a comrade and wandered the length of Africa, working only briefly at temporary jobs. And I know of two young men who have sailed about the world—long stays in Tahiti and the Tuamotu—for the past half-dozen years. It's still possible. But if these wanderers later marry, as most do, I don't know how their time of adventure and comradeship affects their subsequent marriages: will they have union in its fullness with that unshareable experience in memory?

Still, from the days of knighthood, adventure with other men first and marriage later has been almost the traditional pattern. We may suppose that young Jim Hawkins came home from Treasure Island to find him a wife in due course. But the traditional pattern might, sometimes, be reversed. After the grief for Davy, I could have taken *Grey Goose* to sea, outward bound. As I so nearly did.

I have said all I can say about friendship in relation to inloveness and marriage. And I maintain that friendship is *not* a lesser thing, only different. It is as deep a love, as noble a love, as inloveness. And Christianly, it is as valid a choice. It is less demonstrative in its expression—a handclasp or a comradely grin—but it can go very deep. Both at their best and fullest are great loves, just as affection is.

Despite putting inloveness first, I have never for a second not valued friendship; and I have had some splendid friendships—some of which have deepened since Davy's death, or only arisen since then. But, fine though the friendships are, I have not had one of the great friendships, tested and tempered by danger and years of comradeship. Not only did I have Davy but my friends had their wives. And I regret that I could not have had, also, friendship at its fullest. It may be that no one can have both at their highest. And I expect that a man who has had either one completely wishes he might also have had the other. I know I do.

In fact, I should like to know *all* the loves in their fullness, including the fire of the love of God that the great saints have known. One life is not enough. But Heaven is wide and deep, and eternity is for ever.

CHAPTER VIII

Women and Men—and Neuterists

This book and *A Severe Mercy* before it are the story of a pilgrimage towards Heaven, unique as everyone's pilgrimage is but similar to thousands of other stories, told or untold. One point of similarity, as most readers will, with perhaps a wry smile, recognise, is the wrong turnings. Few of us avoid them. And then, not without difficulty, we must scramble back to the main road.

If the wrong turnings and recoveries involve ideas, we are apt to explain the process as change and development. But there is a curious aspect of change and development: what appears as logical development to him who undergoes it, looks to the outside observer like change.

I was a radical feminist in the late '60s and the early '70s—and now I'm not. Surely that is *change*—an about-face, in fact—not development? Not to me it isn't. The wrong turning was the embracing of feminism in a rush in the Angry Years of the '60s without any real thought. But, having done so, I went a long way on that path before I began uneasily to suspect and then to be sure that the direction was wrong. The process of discovery and recovery seems to me to be logical development, given the original mistake of not thinking. Development not change. But the open-minded reader must judge.

Even as I write that phrase, "open-minded", I wonder how many people really are open-minded on the subject of feminism. How many people in the 1860s were open-minded on the quite reasonable question of whether a state that had voluntarily joined the Union might later withdraw? How many were precisely open-minded on what we should do about Vietnam? How many liberals will even read a conservative argument—or conservatives, a liberal one? We are not distinguished by our open-mindedness. The feminists are always appealing for open-mindedness to their arguments (which I certainly gave them). I wonder whether a feminist reading this book will open-mindedly consider this chapter.

I do not, I must hasten to say, reject all of feminism. Women should certainly receive equal pay for equal work—*and* equal commitment. Moreover, I distinguish between women who merely want fair play and the feminist organisations and leaders who are far more extreme. The essential feminist argument that I reject is that equality means identicalness, like two ten-penny nails. The essential position *I* maintain is that equality means equal in value, equal in importance. Not like two identical nails but like a nut and a bolt that are of absolutely equal importance in holding something together but are different and complementary.

Those who deny the deep and innate difference of men and women (apart from trifling differences important only in the bedroom) are the 'Neuterists' of the title—the Unisexists. They go against the deep wisdom of all races and all history. They also go against the Bible.

One of their arguments is that the people of past ages, including Jesus and St Paul, were conditioned by the culture of their time. Leaving apart the fact that Jesus, Son of God, did perfectly the will of the Father in eternity (not culture-conditioned), the feminists neglect one point: that *they* themselves are totally surrendered to late twentieth-century 'culture', as culture-conditioned as the young Nazis in the '30s or the Victorians of the 1880s. *Every* age has its characteristic illusions (Nordic supremacy or witchcraft). The feminist vision of woman—of equality as sameness—may be the great illusion of *our* age.

A friend of mine who, as a student, was jailed for a sit-in supporting the blacks—Jim Hunter, whom I spoke of in the chapters on the '60s—has written a splendidly ironical little poem (*New Oxford Review*) called "Do You Remember Women?" Do you remember them, that is, before unisexism, "When difference was a source of life?" And he ends by saying he feels "Much like a lion without a den / Now that all of us are men." If difference is a source of life—and I may add, of delight—it is that difference that the neuterists seem bent on eliminating.

I have sometimes dared to wonder whether the neuterists might possibly be suffering from arrested development: an inability to accept *fully* their own womanhood.

The feminism of the 1920s was too early for Davy and me to be aware of. It had perished in the rigours of the Great Depression, just as it will perish again if there's another rock-bottom depression or a devastating defeat in war, and we again go back to basics. At all events, when Davy and I were married feminism was simply not on. Women, despite some doctors and editors, were mostly housewives, but they seemed happy as well as a good deal freer than men. Nevertheless, as I have told in *A Severe Mercy*, I was determined to renounce husbandly authority: we should discuss everything, and we should not act until we both agreed; and we should share housework and cooking. Davy did not demand this in the name of women's rights: it was my initiative, though she was pleased as well as astonished. In that day it was astonishing. But it was done in the name of love. Not 'rights'.

But there is a certain irony here, not apparent to us then. The male headship that St Paul lays down means, not bossing, but *leading* or *initiating*. That is why God the Father, while He created and certainly comprehends both genders, is masculine: He initiates. And it is why Jesus, one with the Father, *had* to be born a man: He is head of the Church: it is the *Church* that is *she*: the Bride of Christ. And the irony in what Davy and I did was that *I* initiated our feminist arrangements, though I didn't appreciate that irony until after her death. And I concluded then that male leadership was inbuilt in the Creation and could only be denied at heavy cost to love. But we didn't suspect it during her life—unless *she* did.

For in the last year of our years together, reading deeply in St Paul, she began to desire to be, not a 'comrade-lover' but a *wife*. I'll say more of this later in the chapter. After her death and after the '60s had reached the Angry Years, I picked up on the first hints of the new feminism, as I said earlier, and wrote my angry feminist tract—and also wrote, under a pseudonym, a spirited article demanding the 'ordination' of women to the priesthood, in which I made much of Galatians 3:28. The article was secular to the core—this was at the lowest ebb of my faith—but was couched in Christian terms. Disguising secularism in Christian language is quite easy—not a few of our theologians and preachers do it all the time.

At the end of the '60s, when everyone, including me, was seeking the country, there came the first hint of my being on the wrong road. Only a disquieting hint; I remained a strong feminist after it. I had gone out to the Rock—the hundred-and-fifty acres I owned with an absent friend—and I decided to climb Cedar Mountain. With me, much enjoying the expedition, was Nelly, my light-hearted border-collie. As I climbed up through the trees, I thought about the wood at Glenmerle, and thought, too, of shooting with my father and of sitting on a log with him, listening to his wise and amusing observations on life. Spotting a log that commanded a bit of a view, I sat down with Nelly at my feet and listened to the silence. I suddenly thought of what Dad would have said about the feminists. And then of what C. S. Lewis would have said. I didn't, in my imagination, care to mention my own feminism to either of them. And being there in the deep country, Glenmerle in my mind, I thought of the realities of nature, where cows are not bulls nor mares stallions. Nelly nuzzled my hand, and I thought how feminine—how ladylike—she was. And there on the sunny slopes of Cedar Mountain, with the *real* world—as the country always seems to me to be—all round me, I suddenly and treasonably felt, not that feminism was wrong but that it was—silly.

It was not in harmony with the real world. I commanded this thought to be banished, but it never quite was. I couldn't forget it. Someone once suggested that all important decisions be made, not in chambers but out among the trees. Interesting to imagine the Supreme Court sitting about on logs, deciding.

Then came the Year of the Nudges and the return to the Obedience—though it was not immediately apparent that feminism was in any way disobedient. Still, I was not willing to have the Prayerbook changed even along feminist lines. And I thought I'd not mention feminism to Lady Frances. And thinking deeply about Davy, I perceived that with her love of St Paul she would not be sympathetic with Women's Lib.

One day I picked up that article of mine urging female 'ordination'. Reading it, I was shocked, first by its angry tone, and then by its secularism. And I saw that, like most feminist articles, it was begging the question—assuming the truth of what was to be proved—whether God Himself wanted priestesses. That was the *only* question that mattered, not what women wanted or thought were their rights. Unless of course they wished to return to the ancient Minoan religion of the mother goddess, calling it 'Christianity'. Some do aim at that, I think.

Anyway, *no one*, male or female, has a 'right' to ordination, nor are women 'oppressed' if ordination is not what God wills for them. It's like saying that homosexuals are 'oppressed' if they can't marry other men. Behind all such thinking is a denial of differences. But what if God *does* want priestesses? Is it, as many have said, the Holy Spirit leading us into new truth? What *is* God's will—can it be discerned? I was now asking the question that mattered: "What is *God's* will?" And I studied and thought.

Then I wrote a new essay, though I didn't know who would publish it. In 1978 the *New Oxford Review* did. The essay follows, showing in its first paragraph how well I knew the feminist arguments. Indeed I was still a feminist in all but this one matter.

Since God Doesn't Make Mistakes:
WOMEN'S 'ORDINATION' DENIES THE INCARNATION

The case for the 'ordination' of women to the sacramental priesthood is very appealing. It appeals to our sense of fair play, of simple justice. Women have, in fact, suffered grave injustice: why is their being denied the priesthood not an aspect of that injustice? But the case rests not only upon justice but upon the equally appealing proposition that Our Lord the Holy Spirit is leading the Church of Christ into a new understanding of the roles of women—and who are we to argue with the Holy Spirit? It is perfectly clear that women have the brains to be priestesses or even learned theologians; and no less clear that they have qualities of sympathy and understanding that would enhance their ministry. And, after all, neither Christ nor even the alleged misogynist, St. Paul, ever laid it down that women cannot be priestesses, and St. Paul, indeed, can be held to have implied that they could be in his great statement that there is neither male nor female in Christ Jesus. The fact that Jesus, so sympathetic to women, still did not, in that patriarchal Jewish world, make some woman, say, Mary Magdalen, an apostle was perfectly appropriate to His time and place. He also did not make a Gentile an apostle. Therefore, just as the Church made Titus and other Gentiles bishops (or apostles) when the time was right, so now we should not be restrained by Jesus's not appointing a woman nor by the resulting tradition from following the leading of Our Lord the Spirit into new truth.

It is all most appealing and compelling. It was all so appealing and compelling to me in the late sixties—I being a strong advocate of women's liberation from the first—that, brooding upon injustice to my sisters and engaging in what I was pleased to call thinking upon theology, I was moved to write a spirited article urging the instant 'ordination' of women. One uncomfortable question that I did not ask was: How do we know that men and women are, apart from the plumbing, the same, spiritually the same? We do not, in fact, know that. Another question, even more uncomfortable, is assumed by the proponents of women's 'ordination' to be raised only by die-hard, male-supremacist opponents; but it is a real question all the same: How do we know that it is Our Lord the Spirit that is compelling us and not the Spirit of the Age? Those who find that question meaningless have perhaps answered it, at least for themselves.

Being myself unable to answer either question with assurance, I finally raised the question: What, if anything, is the bearing of the Incarnation upon the priesting of women?

The Incarnation is surely the central doctrine of our faith. If we are of those who speak contemptuously of "creedal literalism" (which appears to be shorthand for the assertion that we can say the Creeds without believing them and still, somehow, not be liars) we perhaps brush aside "He came down from heaven and was made man" and "very God of very God." But there are many in the Church—who may be called Christians—who do *not* brush these statements aside, who *do* believe the Creeds, and who hold the Incarnation to be of the essence of the Christian faith. I for one. And I speak to others of like belief.

Still, what bearing does the believed-in Incarnation have upon the priesting of women?

I am a writer, not a trained theologian. Let me, therefore, begin with an analogy that may make a certain amount of sense to those who write or read stories. Suppose, then, I write a novel and put myself in it (perhaps under a different name), as writers often do. I am the author, not the Author of All Things but the inventor (creator) of this particular story. For my novel I invent (create) an imagined city in an imagined time and place full of imagined characters. But I, too—*not* imagined or created—am in the (invented) city, talking to and interacting with the invented characters. I-the-character, wearing my familiar tweeds, smoking my pipe, speak to the invented characters, but I-the-character speak the words that I-the-writer give me to speak—the words that I-the-writer would speak in those circumstances. I-the-character do the will of my "father in the study," that is, the writer. I am, in short, incarnate in my book. All man and all God, that is the doctrine. And in the analogy, all character and all author. The analogy is not perfect. For one thing the characters don't have free will. And yet, as many novelists have said, sometimes the characters do "run away" with the story. The logic of the situation in my novel might compel me-the-writer to allow me-the-character to be shot or, if it were set in Roman times, crucified.

One more point about the analogy: I-the-writer know how the novel will end. The characters move in their invented time, and if they were truly sentient, the future to them would be veiled. I-the-writer am not in the book's invented time but in what to the characters would be eternity, even as God the Father is in eternity, though Jesus, God the Son become man, was in created time.

Argument-by-analogy is always dangerous, and any argument based on an analogy with the Trinitarian God would be incredibly dangerous. But I have *not* based an argument upon my analogy and do not propose to. I suggested the analogy only as a possible illumination in our thinking about the relation of the Incarnation to the priesting of women.

Still, the analogy does roughly express what the Church has maintained for some two thousand years of (created) time to be the relationship between God the Father and God the Son when the latter was made man in this (created) world. Jesus, the Church says, was all God and all Man—the body of a man, the mind of a man, the limitations perhaps of a man, yet God in the world. He and the Father were one, He said. And He did the *will* of the Father, He said. Therefore, He knew what the will of the Father was. But, then, to return to the analogy for a moment, I-the-character do the will of the writer as it is given to me to do. *I-the-character can do no other. Jesus, one with the Father, with perfect obedience, chose to do no other than the will of His Father.*

The proponents of the priesting of women point out that Christ, even if He were the incarnation of God, was necessarily of finite mind. He had, they say, the limitations and even the prejudices of the particular (created) time and place of His manhood. Therefore, in choosing apostles, He, a Jew, would of course have chosen only men, even as those apostles, in their turn, in choosing first a new Twelfth and later others, would choose only men. Thus the tradition, unquestioned at the time, became fixed and has endured down the centuries. But we are not first-century Jews, and we should cast aside the tradition that was based upon no more than first-century Jewish prejudice. But this argument neglects one point.

Jesus, indeed, was a Jewish man of His time. *But* Jesus did the will of the Father which He knew, even as (in my analogy) I-the-character do the will of the writer which I know. *Jesus did perfectly the will of the Father.*

Jesus, with the limitations of a first-century Jewish man, did not ever, we may suppose, think of appointing a woman to the apostolate. He did not, we may presume, have the least notion that His not appointing a woman would prevent any woman from being priestess or apostle for nearly two millennia.

But God the Father knew. And Jesus did perfectly the will of the Father.

Just this is central. Before all worlds God the Father in eternity *knew* that on this (created) world *sixty generations of women* would be denied any aspiration to the priesthood because Jesus did not appoint a woman as apostle. Even if we now fling open the barred gates to the priesthood and the episcopate, the wronged generations of women stream back through the centuries.

It may be objected that Jesus did not appoint any Gentiles as apostles either. Perhaps it never occurred to Jesus that either women or Gentiles would be seeking the priesthood. But there were Gentile bishops and priests—Titus, for instance, or Timothy—as soon as the need arose with the expansion of the Church into the Gentile world. Why were there not female priests and bishops? Because of male prejudice in the Gentile world also? That will hardly do. Women were freer in the Greco-Roman world than they have ever been since until this century. They owned property; they were admitted to philosophical schools in Athens; they were often in positions of great influence; and, above all, there were innumerable priestesses of other religions. Christianity itself may have raised some eyebrows but a Christian priestess would not have caused them to be raised a bit higher. Why then, the difference? Why were Gentiles brought into the apostolate even in New Testament times but not women?

The Gospels are very brief; and we know nothing of many things Jesus must have said to the Twelve, except as a surmise from what happened. Thus we may surmise that He must have said that the apostolate was to continue since, after the defection of Judas, the remaining Eleven so quickly chose a new Twelfth. Of course we cannot base an argument upon what Jesus may have said about women. More important perhaps for our purposes is what He did *not* say. Quite certainly He did not tell them that no Gentile could ever be an apostle. The apostles were imbued with His teaching, and the election of the early Gentile bishops must have been in harmony with that teaching. We simply do not know whether He said anything about women as apostles or bishops. We know only that in the Greco-Roman church there were none. Therefore, there is no real parallel between His choosing no Gentiles and His choosing no women.

We come back then to what an incarnational Christian, if I may use what ought to be a redundant modifier, who favors the priesting of women *must* find his way round. Jesus, who did perfectly the will of the Father, did not appoint a woman. Therefore, it was *not* the will of the Father that He should. But, as a matter of historical fact, His not appointing a woman doomed sixty generations of women to be denied priesthood. This denial, known to the Father in eternity, must, then, have been the will of the Father.

And yet, it is said, the Holy Spirit is *now* leading the Church into the new truth that women can, after all, be priestesses and bishops.

But if a woman *now* who is properly ordained by a bishop becomes a real priestess, then a woman properly ordained *a thousand years ago* would have become a real priestess. And, indeed, if women had been priestesses and bishops all along, it can scarcely be supposed that women would have sunk so low in the scheme of things as they did sink after the fall of Rome. Thus women have been gravely deprived and greatly wronged by being excluded from the orders. How do we get around the sixty wronged generations streaming back through the centuries? Did Jesus make an error? But Jesus did *perfectly* the will of the Father. Well, then, did God the Father make an error? Shall we imagine God the Father saying: "By Jove! that was careless. I certainly blew that one! How *could* I have forgotten those sixty wronged generations? Well, I'll make it all right for the next generation, anyhow."

One of two things must be true if women can actually become priestesses: Either God the Father made a mistake and has now changed His mind. Or Jesus who was God incarnate did not do the will of the Father. The first is nonsense. The second amounts to a denial that Jesus was the incarnate God.

Any argument for the priesting of women that is based on the Holy Spirit leading the Church into new truth *must* also account for old error—the sixty wronged generations of women.

I submit that it *cannot* be done without denying the Incarnation.

Galatians 3:28

There was a passing reference in the essay to the famous 'feminist text', Galatians 3:28, which says: "There is neither Jew nor Greek...slave nor free...male nor female, for you are all one in Christ Jesus." Feminists use this to prove that St Paul himself has not only abolished gender roles but proved that females and males are interchangeable in all respects. In the study leading up to the essay, I had considered this passage in particular and decided it meant no such thing, but the argument was irrelevant to my point in the essay. But it needs to be looked at.

The first rule in determining the meaning of any passage, biblical or other, is to look at it *in context*. Here there are two contexts: the particular one of Galatians 3—What is St Paul talking about here?—and the general one of the whole body of St Paul's writing—What are his attitudes elsewhere with respect to male and female roles? or with respect to masters and slaves?

To take the general context first, it is plain that St Paul is not advocating the abolition of slavery (he sends the runaway slave back to his master) but only a new relationship "in Christ" of master and slave. And it is even more clear that he considers role differences of the sexes to be ordained by God. In all his writings, there isn't a hint that he would advocate doing away with separate roles. He strongly supports them. But, then, could Galatians 3:28 be a moment of special and inspired vision?

In Galatians 3 St Paul is talking about *salvation*: how to attain it through being "in Christ". Such salvation is open to Greek as well as Jew; to slave as well as freeman; to woman as well as man. The text is used dishonestly if, torn from context, it is used to 'prove' that women can be priestesses or that Christianity opposes role differences. In Anglo-American law there is neither male nor female in eligibility for free public education, but that particular law says nothing about role differences. Galatians 3:28 says that there is neither Greek nor Jew, neither slave nor freeman, neither male nor female, in eligibility for salvation—but the Greek remains a Greek, the slave remains a slave, and the female remains a female.

Despite denying any validity to the feminist twisting of Galatians 3:28 and to the possibility of the 'ordination' of women—no episcopal ordination ceremony, I believed, could make a horse a priest, as I said earlier, or a woman a priestess—I was still a feminist.

But I was a little troubled by the feminist insistence that wives were slaves. Had Davy been a slave? Well, no; but then we had been early 'feminists'. Was Lady Frances a slave? Assuredly not. Did I, in fact, know any actual woman who appeared to be a slave? I could think of a husband or two who seemed downtrodden but not one wife. Still, there might be one somewhere.

But then I thought that slavery, by definition, is *involuntary* servitude. I knew of a man whose life was saved in war by his officer: he chose to become the servant of that officer for the rest of his life: that was not slavery. No more is it slavery when a woman of her own free will gives herself to her husband. Nor are we slaves to the Lord. In His service is perfect freedom. Egalitarian thinking can be—and is—taken to absurdity. To unreality.

A chapter of NOW was forming in Lynchburg; and, owing to a couple of letters I'd written in behalf of ERA that later seemed to me wrong-headed, I was invited to a meeting. They were having a contest to name their newsletter, and I won it with *NOWadays*. A letter from me printed in it expresses a position I still support.

The Doubled Vision

There is, it appears, a confusion about the ultimate end of feminism. Is it to become man-like? to 'take-over' from men? to replace masculine values with feminine ones? Perhaps the goal should be to *validate*, once and for all, the *other* voice, the feminine one. That voice has never of course been totally unheard, but always as a weaker voice. Easy to ignore.

It takes two eyes working together to achieve binocular vision. Perspective. If one eye is weak, the other does all the work and is strained. If the feminists would give over man-hating and man-copycatting and think in terms of achieving the doubled vision that sees in depth, it would be good for all mankind. To supplant right-eye vision by left-eye vision would be only a variant faulty vision. Only *two* eyes, equally strong, working together can bring about the perfect vision that sees in depth.

Whatever developments are yet to be shown in my view of feminism, I shall continue to hold that the feminine and the masculine are of equal value but deeply different. The two voices, the glory of choral singing, achieving together harmony. The two eyes, differently placed, achieving together (and only together) vision in depth. The nut and bolt, altogether different but equally necessary, holding things together. Davy and I never doubted that we, the feminine and the masculine, were different—hence the effort to see and understand by looking through each other's eyes—and we knew it took both to achieve our oneness.

The question of ordination had seemed the only point of disagreement with feminism; but then a second disagreement began to be apparent: the feminist perversion of the language. My disagreement, given my lifelong love for the splendour of English, was a logical development. Indeed, it was more a development in feminism than in me. But I have never expected perfection in any cause or country or church. Just as well, I think. I did write a mocking limerick for the *New Oxford Review* on the absurdity of feminist language.

> Her unisex temper would worsen
> If as chairman she wasn't 'chair*person*':
>   She required that we ban
>   Those damned suffixes, 'man'—
> So now she's become a wo*person*.

I understood of course why they were thus manhandling (personhandling?) the language; but it simply wasn't the way to do it. The word 'man' (mann) originally meant a person of either sex, and still means that in 'human' or 'mankind'. And 'woman' (wifmann) was a man who was a wife, hence female. ('Dog' is a canine of either sex; *or* 'dog' is male opposed to 'bitch'.) Feminists might change 'chairman' to 'chairperson' or 'milkman' to the silly 'milkperson'; but what are they to do with 'the race of man' or with 'human' and 'woman'?

There was a far simpler and more reasonable solution, as I tried to point out in the feminist press (to no avail). The *right* way to revitalize language is to give old words fresh meanings. 'Chairman', in fact, does not mean a male in the chair; it only seemed to do so because most chairmen were male. What should the feminists have done? Absolutely nothing. As soon as a substantial number of *chairmen* were female, the word would cease to suggest males and mean simply 'the one in the chair'. What monstrosities ('congressperson') we should have been spared!

Continuing to be offended by those monstrosities, I wrote a small satirical story on the degeneration of English, mocking the misuse by showing what tangles it must logically lead to. This in due course was published more or less simultaneously in *The Christian Challenge* and in the Christian humour magazine *The Wittenburg Door*.

The Queen's English

"As long as the iron of English rings from a tongue."—MacLeish

The lamp threw a warm glow over the chesspersons on the board. As the attractive person pondered her next move, the man glanced idly at her books on the end table—a new and adjusted edition of the poems by Walt Whitperson lying on top of PIERS PLOWPERSON. She did love poetry, he thought, noticing, in the bookcase beyond, other new editions of Emily Dickindaughter and Henry Wadsworth Longperson. A novel, then—Jane Austen's PERSONFIELD PARK—followed by A SHROPSHIRE YOUNG PERSON by A. E. Houseperson.

Suddenly the person's hand moved and, as he had foreseen, her queen leaped forward to take his exposed rook.

"Aha!" he murmured, taking the queen with his knight. "Personna from heaven! Checkmate."

"Oh, help!" she exclaimed. "Person the pumps, as that midshipperson from the naval academy always says." She swept the remaining chesspersons into the box and poured more sherry.

"John," she said, "did I tell you the court said okay to my name change? I'm Linda Stevensdaughter now. Bought this outfit to celebrate. Saw it on the personikin in a shop window and nearly fell into an open personhole rushing over to buy it. Had my nails personicured, too."

"Elegant!" said John. "Makes you look to the personorborn. Womanly, too."

"No, no!" she cried. "Wo*personly*. Wo*man* is out. The new thing is woperson."

"Doesn't have quite the same ring," said the man. "Still, far be it from me to fight Woperson's Lib. They're man-eaters who mangle—sorry! I mean person-eaters who personigle anyone who mentions ...er...persontions disagreement. So unisexism forever! To change the subject, I was looking at all your adjusted editions of the poets. What happens inside? In Coleridge is it 'Woperson wailing for her demon lover,' and 'The still sad music of hupersonity' in Wordsworth?"

She nodded.

"Of course," he said. "Sad music. And Donne...'Get with child a persongrove root'! But, Linda, I hate to say it, but have you persons really thought about *person*? It's sexist, you know."

"What on earth do you mean?" said the person crossly. "It's *the* word! Everything is being changed to *person*. Over in London the Mansion House has become Personion House, and we're going to force the Smithsonian in D.C. to become the Smithpersonian."

"That's what I mean," said the man. "Per-*son! Son!* Very male, if you'll forgive me for using the word. You got your name changed from Steven*son*. What about per*son*?"

"Oh, dear!" she moaned. "We'll just have to change per*son* to per*person*. I mean, perper*person*...perperperper..."

"Sounds like a cat," said John. "As the parson said—I mean the parperson—that's not the way. And perdaughter won't do either, will it?"

"You're being sexist somehow," said Linda. "Stop it!"

"Horse personure!" said the man. "I'm unisexist to the bone. We must go forward, men and persons hand in hand, to victory, Lord willing. The last man overboard!"

"*Lord!*" she said. "Now you're saying God is male!"

"Slip of the tongue," he said. "I always call the communion table the High-up Person's Table. And the High-up Person's Prayer: 'Our Parent which art in heaven...thy Monarchdom come...' And I pray 'In the Name of the Parent, and of the Offspring...' That's it! Not per*son*—per*offspring*! There's my contribution to unisexism!"

"I feel a little dizzy," said the peroffspring plaintively. "Maybe I'm getting my period—personstruation affects me like that."

"No, no!" said the man. "It's just the burden of your persondate to win this struggle for unisexist language for wopersons—all hupersonkind, really—even if we have to put gags and personacles on all the poets and lovers of the hupersonities. Right? Out of the ruins of the tongue that Shakespeare spake shall arise the epersoncipated unisexist woperson. And as the iron of English turns into the mush of English, Parent willing, you will be the spokesperson for all wopersonkind, old 'son!"

Author's Note: This personuscript will be published in THE JOURNAL OF PLASTIC ENGLISH for both NAW (the National Association of Wopersons) and RAW (the Royal Association of Wopersons). Anyone who is able to say "chairperson" without wanting to vomit may be an honorary member and will, upon application, receive a handsome tin ear.

The reader became slightly acquainted with Richard and Mary, the hero and heroine of my novel, *Gateway to Heaven*, in an earlier chapter. In the final draft of that work during the Christmas vac of 1978, I expanded a conversation they were having on the differences between men and women. In the extract that follows, the

Agnes referred to is a feminist teacher at Holywell College whose influence on Mary had led to the conversation. The reader may recall my 'country thoughts' about feminism that day I was sitting on a log in the woods with Nelly at my feet. Part of this conversation grew out of those meditations at the Rock. Richard is telling it.

At first Mary was suggesting—and I was sure it came from the embattled Agnes—that, apart from physical differences, men and women were just the same. The apparent differences—men's aggressiveness and women's passivity, or, better, unaggressiveness—were merely the results of conditioning: parental pressure, books, films, society. I laughed aloud at that, I remember, and said she might think otherwise about that if she had grown up at Redrock.

"What do you mean?" she said in an annoyed voice.

"Dogs," I said. "Horses—stallions and mares. Roosters, too. At Redrock we didn't tell our mares and bitches to be a lady—and they didn't read books, although one little bitch puppy ate three chapters of Melville. Seriously, Mary, there's a world of difference. I had a little collie bitch one time, and she was a born lady: gentle, sweet-tempered, and, well—just plain feminine. And the males: full of adventure. They were the ones who were always off to see the world. If they were penned up, they were the ones that leaped the fence or dug under—and went gaily off, ready to fight an elephant if one happened along. And, Mary! you remember my grey stallion, Caesar! Why, Mary, it's ten times as hard to break a stallion. *No one* except someone who grew up in a city could suppose for a minute that there isn't more to male and female than the anatomical. Our ancestors who never doubted down through the centuries that men and women were different—that 'common judgement of mankind'—based their judgement firmly on the observed world of nature. We've got to start with that."

"Yes-s-s," said Mary. "There is a difference, though you must admit it's hard to put your finger on. But that doesn't mean that a woman couldn't be a good doctor or engineer."

"Of course not!" I said. "I've often thought that women, who for millions of years have had to be sensitive to what might be wrong with little inarticulate children—or with husbands!—might be *better* doctors. Better surgeons, too, with their deft little fingers—if they weren't having their periods."

"Well, then, you see?" she said. "The differences don't *affect* anything."

"Oh yes they do!" I said. "You missed my point. I wasn't saying that a woman would be a good doctor in spite of being a woman but *because of it*. Queen Elizabeth was a great *queen:* she used her womanhood, hinting at marriage to keep foreign kings from invading when they might win all by marriage. On the other hand, thinking of Caesar—my stallion—and the male dogs adventuring, I'd a lot rather have my country defended by men."

"Oh, me too!" said Mary. "I admit that. Now that I think about it, I expect there are some jobs that women will probably never be very good at, just because of what a woman's nature is. And some things a man won't be good at."

We talked on for many hours, agreeing more and more deeply that what humanity has always and everywhere believed, that there are deep and innate differences between men and women—however much civilised life tends to hide them—is true. And we agreed that fatherhood and motherhood, while both are good and necessary, are not the same things and not interchangeable.

If any feminist reader supposes that I am advocating that women be doormats or down-trodden females, I urge her to read my novel *Gateway to Heaven* with attention to the character and quality of Mary, my heroine, who tells more than half the story.

A little later in that same conversation, Richard justly remarks: "This world has difficulty in coping with qualitative differences. Thus this—this *unisexism!*" Thus a word was born, based on the common and vulgar 'unisex'. A unisexist is one who denies the deep and innate differences between men and women. Thus no male headship or initiating, no female receptivity or nurturing or intuitive power. Thus the unisexists would neuter the race: hence, 'neuterists'.

As I said in an earlier chapter, modern feminism was born in the Angry Years of the '60s, born out of a false analogy with the blacks. There really isn't any notable difference between a black man and a white, except the skin-deep difference of colour. But the difference between a man and a woman has *always* been held to be soul-deep. It's up to the feminists to prove that it isn't; but they do not do it; they assume it—assume the truth of what is to be proved, which is begging the question. Until it is proved, which I think cannot be done, the analogy is false.

Christianity has always held that the difference is, in fact, soul-deep, that the souls and resurrected bodies of men and women are masculine and feminine through all eternity. Can one imagine meeting the Blessed Virgin Mary (or one's own mother) in Heaven and finding her other than *womanly*? Or St Peter other than manly?

And my own Davy—she wouldn't *be* Davy if she weren't feminine.

Many feminists would reply, "Yes, indeed. But what has that got to do with women being soldiers, radio announcers, or policemen, or with men being nurses or baby-tenders?" The answer is that those jobs were allotted to one sex or the other on the realistic basis of perceived physical and psychological differences of men and women. "But," the feminist would rejoin, "there are *some* women, perhaps only one in a thousand, who would be valuable policemen; should they be denied?" Yes, I think so; for if women are accepted at all, there inevitably follow quotas and sexual-discrimination suits or the fear of them; and far more than the rare 'perfect' coppess would have to be admitted. And protected by the real policemen.

It is *unisexism*—the idea not the name—that is being proclaimed by the Spirit of the Age. And what is proclaimed by the Spirit of the Age or *Zeitgeist* is rarely thought about or questioned. Many Christian women who would deny that they were unisexists are full of unisexism—it's practically in the air they breathe. And they simply haven't thought it through, especially in the light of the Bible and all Christian tradition. The truth is that role-differences are very much of the essence of Christian and Jewish teaching. They need to be re-examined and modified—but not abandoned. Not if we hope to follow the Hellenic ideal of seeing things as they are.

There were great women associated with Jesus, but He, doing perfectly the will of the Father, gave the title of Apostle to none. Yet the Magdalene is a great saint, and Jesus's mother is honoured above all saints and all apostles as the Mother of God and *Theotokos* or God-bearer. The priest and bishop may *lead* the flock, but it is women, responding directly to our Lord, who are so often God-bearers to their men, as Davy was to me. Role-differences. But the feminists cast aside their blessed and sacred role and yearn for men's roles.

It is not Christianity only that affirms the deep difference of the sexes. The affirmation is the common judgement of the human race in *all* time and *all* places. Even today, the middle-class feminists of the big cities are, despite the loudness of their demands, a tiny minority of the living women upon this earth. And throughout the ages the philosophers and the ordinary people have affirmed the deep difference of the masculine and the feminine—the Yang and Yin of China, the Perusha and Prakity of India, the sky god and earth goddess of the Greeks and Romans, the animus and anima of Jung. To Aristotle it was the difference of form and matter, act and potency (intelligibility and potentiality). The masculine has been above all seen as the rational as well as the active and the initiating; and the feminine as receptive, passive, with deep intuitive wisdom.

Dom Bede Griffiths OSB in *The Marriage of East and West* says that the West, especially since the Enlightenment, has been sickening with unbalanced masculine rationality—and that the West is doomed *unless* it rediscovers the feminine intuitive wisdom of the East (the India he knows so well). But to the West rationality is the only desirable quality. And we are blind to the truth that rationality and the knowledge that results from it are dry and arid without intuition and feeling, just as intuition and feeling without rationality become wet and chaotic and 'sticky', even nightmareish.

If indeed the West, as Dom Bede says, is sick with unbalanced masculine rationality, then at first glance the feminist revolution might seem a good thing. But a long, hard look at the unisexist feminists (and many more women are unisexists than know it) discloses the truth that, far from representing feminine intuitive wisdom, they are bent on equalling or outdoing men in rationality and toughness, abandoning the clear springs of their own power in aping something we don't need more of. The more that women forsake deep womanliness the sicker the West becomes. *Feminist* is not feminine.

The androgyny that some unisexists urge would bring about the neutered death of both the masculine and the feminine principles.

What we need is a *feminine* movement, not a feminist or unisexist one.

A beginning point might be found in the wisdom of Confucius whose ethical master principle was for everyone to strive to live up to the Names of their Relationships—the highest connotation of those Names. Thus a woman might do her best to live up to the fullest, deepest meaning of Daughter, Sister, Wife, Maidservant or Mistress, Mother, Friend, and more.

I must at this point tell a story from real life, vouched for by a woman I know. She, an extremely able writer, is a friend of the people concerned, and she told me the story in great detail. Four women, close friends of hers and all in their thirties, had been meeting weekly to study the Bible. One evening they came to St

Paul's statement in I Corinthians 11 about the headship of the husband. The leader for that evening read it aloud, paused, and read it again. Silence round the table except for a mutter from one of the women: "Jim just couldn't do it." Every one of those women— they all knew it—was the head in her marriage. They regarded their husbands as amiable and no doubt lovable blunderers who couldn't be trusted to think of things and run things competently. Someone said weakly, "Does St Paul say anything else about it?" An index was consulted, and the other Pauline statements (Col 3:18; Eph 5:22f; I Tim 2:11f) were read out. There was some discussion. Finally the leader said, "Well, girls—what do we do?" Someone else said, "We've *got* to do it." Another said, "*They*'ve got to—the men." Resolved, they got the husbands together, and explained. The men took it quietly.

Then came the miracle. In less than a year the four women, with amazement and delight, were telling each other and every other woman they knew what had happened. The husbands, all four, had quietly taken over. Every one of them had, so to speak, grown taller in his wife's eyes: bigger, stronger, wiser, more humorous. It was unbelievable, almost a miracle. And, with no exceptions, every one of the women felt her marriage had come to a new depth of happiness—a joy—that it had never had before. A *rightness*.

Seeing this astonishing thing that not one of them had thought possible—not with *their* husbands—the four wives one day realised an astonishing further truth: they realised that their husbands had never demanded and would never have demanded the headship: it could only be a free gift from wife to husband. We are all familiar with the words and concept of a woman's *giving herself to a man*. So familiar that we never ask what it really means. The foregoing story illuminates it. *This is what it means*.

And this is what Davy first intuitively understood and then came in the last years of her life to understand more deeply through her beloved St Paul.

As I said earlier, slavery is *involuntary* servitude.

My thinking, along with that hard look at what feminism really was—and was on the way to—had now led me to the rejection of the unisexist, neuterist Spirit of the Age. Was this change or development? No matter. I had been feminist; I had listened to and indeed applauded all their cause. And now I had come to reject it. The deeper I looked, the more I realised that the heart of feminism was unisexist, and that the liberation they desired was liberation from being a woman. Their unanimous demand for the right of abortion was proof of that. It is often said that Naziism was corrupted at the heart by the death chambers, killing not only the Jews but the old and infirm. If it was so corrupted at the heart, what then of the heart of feminism, poisoned by the deaths of millions of unborn babies, painfully killed in the name of women's rights. The womb, chamber of life, become a death chamber.

The story of the four Christian women—in total opposition to the feminist insistence upon men's oppression of women—taught me that men didn't conquer women but accepted women's voluntary *gift* of themselves, just as men now draw back from headship as women refuse to give themselves.

Now I was ready to write my major essay on Unisexism (Neuterism), the complete story. It was published in December 1981 in the *New Oxford Review*. It is totally opposed to the Spirit of the Age, and I know that it will be largely unheeded. I consider it a grave warning about where we are going. And I dare to hope that *Christian* women—and men (including 'with-it' priests and ministers)—will heed it. I thought as I was writing it that Davy would approve, and that writing it was a kind of faithfulness to her. And to God's plan for mankind.

UNISEXISM

Second Thoughts on Women's 'Liberation'

To challenge the going *certainties* of one's own day—to challenge, that is, the proclamation of the Spirit of the Age or *Zeitgeist*—is to level one's lance at a fire-breathing dragon. A perilous hazard. Consider a challenge in the Germany of the 1930s to the proclamations of the Nazis. Or in the land of the free in the 1950s—when Senator Joseph McCarthy was focusing the anti-Communist fear and hate—consider a loud challenge to the effect that a man is innocent until *proved* guilty. Whatever the proclamation of the Spirit of whatever Age, it is in its own age the voice of absolute, unquestionable truth. To question whatever brave new world is a-borning is to risk destruction by the dragon.

It is a female dragon today, loosely named Women's Liberation. Her proclamation, at first the plaintive cry for fairness of a damsel in distress, calling forth (for perhaps the last time) men's chivalry, has now become very shrill indeed, even strident.

Although the dragon (of any age) has fangs and claws, its most fearsome weapon is the blast of righteous and indignant flame from its nostrils that often ends the challenge and the challenger together. This blast almost always is the accusation in tones of scornful contempt, delivered by the wave-of-the-future folk, especially the slightly ageing, with-it young, that the challenger is an old-fashioned relic, a diehard, a stick-in-the-mud, blind to the glorious new world being born. This devastating attack obviates the necessity of a reasoned reply or, indeed, even hearing the challenge.

But how if the challenger has been to the brave new world—been a citizen, in fact—and is now coming back? The "Second Thoughts" of my subtitle imply *first* ones. This article is indeed a challenge to that female dragon and may well unleash the Erinyes. But that chief dragon-weapon, the withering accusation of being a stick-in-the-mud, cannot be used. I have *been* there, hailing the brave new world. And now I am coming back.

I shall begin by tracing my approach to Women's Liberation in order to establish, so to speak, my credentials. These, then, are the "first thoughts."

Long ago, long before Women's Liberation was ever heard of, I had a marriage that was very unusual for its day, in being based on complete equality. (It is described in my book *A Severe Mercy*.) Husbandly authority was ruled out from the beginning—at, I may say, my insistence, not hers. We shared the housework and the cooking— shocking our friends—and the sailing and boatwork as well. Moreover, we made a great effort, for the sake of understanding and closeness, to learn from one another what it was to be of the opposite sex in the world. In short, it was a marriage that could not be faulted by a modern feminist, unless she discredited it on the grounds that we did what we did in the name of love instead of the name of female rights. After all, the militant feminists almost have to see men as oppressors and marriage as a loveless battleground to stay in business.

In the years after my wife's death, I did not change my ideas about fair play for women. As a professor of history and poetry, I made every effort (before Women's Lib) to emphasize the relatively few notable women in history and the few poetesses; and I urged that there should be more women on the faculty.

Then in the earliest 1960s I became at once involved in the Civil Rights or Black Freedom Movement and, later, in the Anti-War Movement. There is no doubt that I was hearing the Spirit of the Age loud and clear. Nor do I remember questioning it much until the late 1960s turn towards violence and the rip-off. Always in the Anti-War Movement days, I was glad the girls were marching too, though sad that in the meetings the girls, most of them, sat silently. And I was angry that during the inner councils of the Movement the girls were relegated to making brownies. At all events, it may be noted that now, before Women's Lib, it was precisely male and female roles I was wrathful about.

In 1968, with the first whispers of what would become Women's Lib even clearer in my ears, I wrote a more or less flaming tract entitled "Freedom for Movement Girls—NOW!!" (It was not yet *de rigueur* to call college girls "women.") In this pamphlet I spoke very angrily about unfairness to our sisters and about men who were radical in everything but the freedom of their women. I took it for granted that if the doctrine of separate but equal was demeaning to blacks (as it was), the somewhat similar though far more ancient order of role differences of the sexes was necessarily equally demeaning to women. I was assuming that the (literally) skin-deep differences between blacks and whites were paralleled by no less superficial differences between the sexes. But what if *they* are soul-deep?

I knew quite well that there was an immense body of judgements all through the centuries that men and women are deeply and essentially different; but I said away with them; I *knew*. (That is *exactly* how the Spirit of the Age works.) What is so astonishing in retrospect is that I didn't *think* at all—or, rather, I thought but only on the basis of an accepted but unproved, unquestioned fundamental assumption. I did *not* ask whether those past judgements might be true, whether just possibly the whole might be benefited by the men planning the campaign and the women making the brownies, whether there might be value in role differences. The Spirit of the Age speaks in tones of *final* truth.

So I wrote my booklet about Queen Elizabeth I and Sappho and Jane Austen as being great because they weren't oppressed by men (having no husbands), assuming that the only greatness is the sort that makes the history books. And I wrote about the "myth" of separate roles, using 'myth' inaccurately to mean a fiction or lie. And, to replace the cumbersome and imprecise 'male-chauvinist,' on the model of 'racist,' I invented and defined two new words, 'sexist' and 'sexism.' This pamphlet was published in the [antiwar] Movement in December of 1968: and in February 1969, the second issue of the Boston *No More Fun and Games: A Journal of Female Liberation* thanked me for giving the women's movement these "important new words." At the close of the pamphlet I said:

This is Female Freedom, the new radical idea blowing in the wind. Blowing down the illusions of the sexist myth...

The booklet, as I said, was 1968, well before most of today's feminists had even heard of the as-yet-unnamed Women's Lib, and before the wearisome word 'sexist' had yet been heard in the land. I do, therefore, quite certainly qualify as of the vanguard in hearing and supporting the new proclamation of the Spirit of the Age. The dragon was purring (if they do) about me. Later in the first half of the 1970s, when Lib was really rolling, I remained a strong advocate, writing letters to newspapers in behalf of the perennial ERA and writing articles demanding instant 'ordination' of women to the sacramental priesthood and instant appointment of women to everything. Fortunately, I wrote many of these under a pseudonym and so shan't have to eat my words in public; for I now think myself to have been wrong, a not unusual state for me. But I do know every feminist argument, having receptively read them all.

But, surely—some thoughtful reader may be thinking—all this about the Spirit of the Age doesn't affect *Christians*, does it? Christians attend to *eternal* things like the *Holy* Spirit and the Church and the Bible. I might reply that *I* was a Christian in the 1960s, but that would only establish, correctly, that I wasn't attending. But, indeed, have we not heard, to the point of wearisomeness, how the *Holy* Spirit is leading us into new truths? New truths about how, after all, women can be priestesses; and how homosex if loving is, after all, quite virtuous (or, at least, not sin); and how divorce (Jesus just didn't understand) is, after all, not really sinful? New truths that just happen to be contradictory to the New Testament or to what the Church has always believed? New truths that—by the most remarkable coincidence—just happen to be identical to what the *other* Spirit, the Spirit of the Age, is telling the secular folk? Christians, I fear, hear the Spirit of the Age as others do. And, often, their priests and ministers even more so.

Let me offer one specific example. The great advantage of an unchanging prayer book, like the centuries-old Book of Common Prayer, is, according to C. S. Lewis, that the very thing that the people of any period would most like to change is probably the very thing they most need to hear. In our day Episcopalians heartily disliked having to say in the General Confession that we are "miserable offenders [with] no health in us." Surely we weren't *that* bad. A bit thoughtless perhaps but pretty good chaps. The prayer book was revised: out went the uncomfortable words. The joker (the devil is a joker) is that, according to some of the deepest Christian thinkers, the sense of sin has never in the twenty centuries of Christendom been at such a low ebb, partly because of psychiatric 'explaining away.' We simply do not feel ourselves to be sinners and miserable offenders because of a few unfaithfulnesses to our spouse, a few thousand cheated from somebody, or a few divorces: everyone does it. I heard of a married Episcopal rector who ran off with the wife of the senior warden. A bit funny, isn't it? And, anyway, that sort of thing has always happened, towering passion and all. Yes, but in other centuries the guilty couple have at least buried themselves in darkest Africa, and the clergyman has ceased to practice. But this couple simply went off together to another city, where he became rector of a bigger church. Nobody minds. At least, not Episcopalians.

The Spirit of the Age, then, is heard by Christian and non-Christian alike. And one of the things it is telling Christians is to measure the Bible by secular values; for we today are "Humanity come of age" and we know far more than Jesus and St. Paul, creatures of their time. (But Jesus said He did perfectly the will of the Father in eternity.) Moreover, we have so happily absorbed the truth that God is love that we interpret it to mean that He wants us to have any little thing that will make us happy, including apples.

But—what have I said. *He?* A snarl from the feminist dragon. God is not He? God who created male and female must comprehend both (as of course He does): this suggestion of God's masculinity—words like *He* and *Father* and even *Son*—must be eradicated. (Our *Parent* who art in Heaven!) No matter that Jesus thought He had a Father; we know better. No matter that the masculine principle has always been held to be that which *initiates*, so that the soul, whether of man or woman, has always been *she* in her response to the immense masculinity of God. No matter anything, including truth. It must stop. There is now actually a Feminist Bible, dishonestly translated, in which "the only-begotten Son" (can't have that awful male "begotten"!) becomes "the beloved *Child*," who, instead of crying, "Abba, Father!" mumbles improbably, "My loving parent! Source of my being!" —Is there here just a hint as to why Eve was the first to hear her 'Spirit of the Age'?

There is only one wisdom for Christians: to look with a cool and very skeptical eye at all the things their own age is, precisely, *most certain* of. Especially is this true of the certainties that contradict what has been believed by wise Christians down the centuries.

Unfortunately, Christian or no, I did not have that cool and skeptical eye in writing my Lib booklet. But, as a strong feminist in the 1970s, I gradually became aware of a few flaws—oh, very minor—in the vision of the brave new world. It may be useful to show how these developed. Sometimes little, half-admitted uneasinesses may presage the crumbling of a whole position.

I am a writer, a poet, in love with the English language; and I shall be so (in MacLeish's words) "as long as the iron of English rings from a tongue." I objected to the feminist insistence on calling girls 'women' from the first (for the language needs words for people of, roughly, courting age—girls and guys, in America). But the feminist assault on language was just beginning. I understood why they did it, but it was still unforgivable (especially from the half of mankind said to be sensitive to the verbal arts). First came that clumsy three-legged mare, 'chairperson' and its sisters, false to the natural rhythms of English—and completely unnecessary since 'man' as suffix (as in 'wo-man') means simply a human; and the more 'chairman' were used for both sexes, the more it would have resumed its old meaning. As it is, the over-used 'person' both as suffix and alone is becoming obnoxious. Then came the ugly, unpronounceable growl, 'Ms' for any woman who didn't specify otherwise.* And I must not forget the abominable usage, "he or she," like falling over a hurdle in mid-sentence, the death of style. This tin-eared abuse of English was a flaw in feminism from the beginning, although at first sadly tolerated.

Some years ago there was a TV program, "The Ascent of Man", in which a fleet-footed lad running was a symbol of man's race to civilization. There were bitter feminist complaints. Why not a female runner? they said. Sympathetic to 'Lib' as I was, I felt that the absurd had just raised its head. It was a male runner because running is something that narrow-hipped males do far better than broad-hipped females. That is why we have separate races and sports for women. The program might well have chosen a female scientist to represent biology—but a *runner*? A small, insane absurdity, but a flaw. A straw in the wind.

Then one night, reading something about the possible aftermath of nuclear holocaust, it suddenly struck me that the feminist ideal of society is *artificial*. Not the natural order. It could not survive a minute in nature, by which I mean primitive or survival conditions. A hothouse plant. It could not survive the collapse of mechanical society and the protecting law. If our civilization collapsed, as in Rome's fall, leaving a remnant of us, some turned savage, feminism would disappear overnight, gone like an unreal dream. Once again women would seek the protection of men and go back to keeping the hut and—no more pill—the children: Women's Lib not blowing in the wind but gone with the wind. I had wanted feminism to be the true natural order between man and woman, the true relationship. I reluctantly saw that it wasn't (and was hardly a relationship at all). This too, though only a hypothetical situation (at the moment), was more than a flaw: it was a fissure.

---

*Banned now in the '80s by *The Times* (London) as "artificial, ugly, silly...and rotten English...a faddish, middle-class plaything..."

But this hypothetical situation not unnaturally led my mind back to the one other time in history when feminism flourished among the sophisticated classes of great cities—in the Rome of the Antonines, on the eve, according to Gibbon, of the decline and fall. The greatest of Roman satirists, Juvenal, in his sixth satire, gives us a series of portraits of the "modern woman" who has abandoned her traditional duties and pleasures in order to compete with men, not only in literature and law, including giving unasked and unwanted advice to the generals of the legions, but in joining men barebreasted in the hunting field, learning swordplay as if intending to take to the arena, and swaggering about in men's clothes. With the cry, "I am a human being after all! [*Homo sum!*]" they endeavored, not only to out-think and out-fight the men but, according to Juvenal, to out-drink and out-eat them as well. Needless to add perhaps, sexual lib, then as now, was the order of the day. But Rome fell—and feminism can *only* flourish in a sophisticated society with strong protective laws and weak moral standards. Roman feminism perished with the imperial civilisation that protected it.

C. S. Lewis says somewhere that the sound he loves best is the sound of male laughter. I had never particularly thought about it: why not? But then, recently, a man, clearly in the grip of the Spirit of the Age, mentioned Lewis's remark condemningly, adding with the air of one administering the *coup de grâce*, "And what, pray tell, is wrong with *female* laughter?" What Lewis would have replied was instantly so clear in my mind that I simply relayed it to the man: "Female laughter may be an excellent thing. But [with a blow on the table] it is not the *same* thing." It is possible that Lewis then muttered (I couldn't *quite* hear): "Logic—what *do* these schools teach?" Anyhow, absurdity, unreason, had once again touched the feminist cause. Another straw in the wind, flaw in the wind.

Now I began to notice how difficult it was becoming to *find* the laughter of a group of men only. The pubs and clubs invaded. Was there, after all, something to be said for the Long House, at least now and then?

One crisp fall day as I was walking towards the college, the sudden flight of a bird reminded me of boyhood and being, with my father and another man, out with the guns on a frosty morning. And for some reason it occurred to me that I should not have liked to have my mother or my girl cousin along, even supposing they could shoot. This was men hunting as men have always hunted back to the dawn ages. I had been given to thinking that women should be in every scene, like the obligatory black in clothing advertisements. Now I found my feeling about men and guns faintly shocking.

In my youth I was for a couple of years a radio announcer, reading among other things the news-on-the-hour. Showing a bit of incipient feminism, I asked why the women, who did certain sorts of female programs in cooing voices, never got to read the news. The program director pointed out that women's voices were different. And higher, tending to make the needles jump. I went along with these undeniable facts. He then pointed out that when hearing loss occurs as one grows older, the high notes are the first to be lost; and therefore men's voices were more comfortable for the population as a whole. Of course that was back in the days when we could not only admit differences like broad shoulders and broad hips, high-pitched voices and low-pitched ones, but could make decisions as to suitability because of them. But now, in the 1970s, as female announcers did begin to read the news, I noticed that in *that* sort of brisk, authoritative reading they were, in fact, usually shrill on their high notes. And then and later I asked a great many people with hearing loss: and to a woman, as well as to a man, they preferred male newscasters.

In *nothing* is the difference between men and women more immediately obvious than voice. The difference in the voices is the glory of choral singing: the light and soaring purity of the women's voices ascending on the powerful shoulders, as it were, of men's voices. But many feminists were demanding an end to separate parts for the voices. The feminist or unisexist need to deny reality was a deep flaw. Another straw in the wind.

I read a book about the sinking, back in 1912, of the *Titanic*. Everyone knows the story of the gallant gentlemen who stepped back from the lifeboats so that the weaker women and children could be saved. Of course the protection of the female is rooted in our nature: the stags and stallions and other mammals do the same. But this particular writer, mainly concerned with the impact of the sinking on America, had unearthed a new fact. When American women, imagining themselves aboard the doomed liner, read the accounts of her final hours and those chivalrous gentlemen, a good many of the ones who were early feminists abruptly left the movement. They had seen a small floating world in survival conditions. That made me thoughtful.

The foregoing insights—as they seem to me in retrospect to have been—were merely scattered straws in the wind, not all put together as here. They were flaws in a position I strongly supported, so I tried to ignore them—somewhat uneasily. Still I had no thought of re-examining the basic feminist position (or maybe, really, examining it for the first time). As I have said, the roots of my feminist ideals stretched back, before my Christianity, into my early life. And I was not, in the 1960s and early 1970s, inclined to ask what God's will was with respect to Movement goals. Like many others in that troubled time, I was not putting Christ first—and He *must* be first or nowhere. But then in the mid-1970s I was recalled to the Obedience: He *was* first. It was not immediately clear that Christ's being first had anything to do with my practically lifelong feminism, although in reading over my 'girls'-lib' booklet I saw little indication that it had been written by a Christian. Still, it didn't seem wrong.

But then, later, I reread my pseudonymous article urging the 'ordination' of women; and I saw that my arguments on this *totally* Christian matter, though couched in Christian terms, were, in fact, secular and feminist—and wrong. Very wrong. I saw that I hadn't even genuinely considered what God's will might be but had *assumed* (that fatal assumption) that anything that seemed so right to me *must* be God's will. Penitently, leaving apart all *I* thought to be fair and right, I set myself the question: Can God's intention, expressed in Christ, concerning priestesses be discerned? After much thought, I was ready to write a new article: "Women's 'Ordination' Denies the Incarnation" [see page 181]. The result of writing it on me was, at first, to see the feminist demand for that one unique office as merely another flaw, albeit an important one, in the still-accepted feminist position.

But in the course of the article I had asked—and answered—a question: "How do we know that men and women are, apart from the plumbing, the same, spiritually the same? We do not, in fact, know that." We simply *do not know*. We are to be raised from the dead, after the Second Coming, in the body, incorruptible. The Church has always held that we shall be masculine and feminine through all eternity. Not vague 'neuts' drifting about. And if indeed, as I had concluded, God wills that *men* shall form His priesthood, not women—men who would *because of their maleness* represent Christ, *be* Christ, *in persona Christi*, in the sacrament—then, beyond all doubt, there is an *essential* difference, in their very being, between men and women. Without at first realizing it, I had with my spiritual difference question probed to the very heart of the feminist position which is that there is absolutely *no* substantial difference.

In *A Severe Mercy* I described, half-humorously, how my wife, between whom and me there had been such equality and comradeship, began near the end of her life to change. Reading deeply in the Bible, especially her beloved St Paul, she began to *want* to be wifely and obedient to her husband. As I said in the book, I was afraid she would actually obey me if I were to issue a command. She was very humble. I truly believe that she was finding it *liberation* to be a traditional (Christian) wife. Not a comrade, not a partner, but a *wife*. Years after her death, in writing the book, I wrote (a month too late for the first edition) a paragraph (Chapter VIII) on the implications of her turn to a Christian wifehood that was not feminist but was liberating. In her mind of course were St Paul's words on the hierarchical order: that the husband is head of the wife *as* Christ is head of the

Church. During the grief following her death, I had realized that, although we both should have fiercely denied it, "I *had* exercised a sort of headship—in the sense of the initiatory or leadership role—that was accepted, even *desired*, by [her] without either of us being aware of it." Such headship is of course not being a boss (which is the debasing of headship, as 'clinging-vine-ism' is the debasing of wifely response); but it *is* initiating and leading. I wrote in this same paragraph that I had strong reason for being unable to believe that my subtle headship and her acceptance of it could possibly be any sort of conditioning. And I concluded that its existence left me

> wondering without decision whether, despite all feminist denial, such a relationship were not inbuilt in the creation and *effectively* denied—which, after all, we, loving so deeply, had not been able to do—only at heavy cost to love.

If indeed that relationship or order *is* inbuilt in what God has created, then the acceptance of it *would* be liberation. For woman, for man. For Christian and non-Christian alike. Christians, if they are to remain in the Obedience, must accept the New Testament teaching on male and female nature and roles. But that teaching is in harmony with the vision of other, non-Christian peoples on masculine and feminine human nature. The subtle Chinese with their Yang and Yin. Animus and anima. The deep difference. We deny it at our peril. We cannot make a world that is all warp and no woof without disaster. In the quotation from my book I said that I was "wondering without decision." In the years since, I have come to decision on the plain authority of the New Testament, as well as my own careful observation and deep thought, that male initiation (headship) and female response is the natural order and *is* inbuilt in the structure of Creation.

It was at this point in my thinking that I wrote a poem.

Pussycat

Once I saw a wildcat, newly caged,
A-snarl with savage longing to be free,
Small but unappeasably enraged,
The needle teeth all bared at tyranny.

I thought: Could women once have been
    like that?

> Before the building of the cages,
> Before the bars made home a trap,

Before the breaking of the ages,
Before the bowl of milk and slap?

It took awhile to make a pussycat.

The haunted hills and open starry sky—
Do they really linger in your dreams?
    Was there once a savage growl,
Before contented purring on a thigh,
Before the catnip mouse and bowl of cream,
    The pitiful miaul?

But now perhaps the genes are pussycat.

These days, indeed, in talk you greatly dare,
    And after all the law is kind,
And even for the fair what's fair is fair—
    Still, questions linger in my mind.

The difference: whether God intended that?

The lion roars his splendour on the hills:
He *will* be free and if he must he kills.
Small pussy—you have fangs and claws in fact,
But dare you with pawsful of daggers *act*?

Renounce the deference due to ladyhood,
As in your wildcat talk you say you would—
Be *sure*, though, in your blood you hear the call,
Dream still a dream of freedom on the hills.
For it, pussy, will you hazard *all*?

Thus only claim the deference due to lords:
    The ancient courtesy of swords.

The case against Women's "Liberation" is not a case against all
that feminists, including me, have ever said. Of *course* a woman
should get equal pay for equal work (*with* equal commitment). Of
course a woman should be a doctor or chemist if she wants to—and is
willing to pay the price. Feminists, including Christian ones, who
stand for little more than this sort of fair play are not the hard-core
feminists I am writing about: namely, the unisexists. The neuterists.
    Unisexism is a *fundamental assumption*, that is, one of the deep,
unexamined, unproved assumptions that people 'just know' must be
true (though they often are not). An Oxford don once said that Oxford exists to bring out (in the tutorial) the student's fundamental assumptions (HOW DO YOU *KNOW* THAT?), to be proved or

abandoned. Unisexism, then, is the unproved fundamental assumption that men and women are (except for a few trifling external differences that don't *affect* anything, except in bed) the same, psychologically the same; identical; interchangeable. What appear to be deep psychological differences, so deep indeed as to seem to constitute distinct masculine human nature and feminine human nature, are the result of conditioning through the ages by society. (But HOW DO YOU *KNOW* THAT?) Thus there can be no authentic male headship, no authentic masculinity or femininity, no authentic male and female roles in the family or in society. Interchangeable cogs. The androgynous ideal: boys and girls re-conditioned so that they will become, respectively, unmasculine (womanish, effeminate) men and unfeminine (mannish) women. Apart from graver objections, mightn't a homogenized humanity be a little bit *dull*?

The unisexist assumption is, in fact, not proved. Moreover, it rests on the further unproved fundamental assumption that the masculine human nature and the feminine human nature that we all observe—and experimental psychology confirms—to be different is the result of conditioning. This is not only unproved but it isn't even very plausible. It is just as likely—far *more* likely—that conditioning *follows* nature: that is, instead of conditioning (training little boys to be manly, little girls to be womanly) creating the masculinity and femininity, our *innate* masculinity and femininity create or cause the training. Moreover, I believe that body and psyche are a whole, each acting on the other; and no one, even a unisexist feminist, can be a woman in body without her psyche being shaped by that—without, so to speak, thinking like a woman. Apart from these reasoned disagreements with unisexism, the authority of the Bible makes unisexism quite impossible for Christians. As one disgruntled unisexist says, "The Bible is sexist through and through." It is assuredly not *unisexist*.

The unisexist, though, operates on her unproved fundamental assumption, citing only marginal "evidence"—such as boys and girls making equal marks on tests—that, in fact, proves nothing about the central assumption of identity: after all, the marks say nothing about how the learned facts are assimilated into masculine and feminine minds—what they *do* with them. Indeed, the truth is that the unisexist assumption *cannot* be proved—or disastrously disproved—without massive social engineering along counter-conditioning lines. This is already being subtly attempted in day-care centres, schools, textbooks, social work, and children's stories.

See the recent child-care *Growing up Free* by the would-be 'Spockess,' Letty Pogrebin, who says: "Masculinity and femininity do not

exist for me. They are fictions invented to coerce us into sex roles."
(How does she *know* that?) She teaches mothers how to do away with
every hint of gender including the Fatherhood of God. (Not much
femininity in feminists: 'unisexist' is better—or 'neuterist.') Many
kindergarten and other teachers will read this book. Some little children will be brought up by it.

A firm grip on reality is said to be the mark of a healthy mind.
Starting as they do from an unproved fundamental assumption and
treating it as revealed truth, bending everything to fit, the unisexists
are in many ways out of touch with the real world. They wave away
the plain differences between the masculine and the feminine on the
grounds of a hypothetical identity of hypothetical unconditioned men
and women: and they deny unmistakably real, demonstrably real
physical differences as being of any importance. A female runner is
as good as a male runner—except in a *real* race. A female newscaster
is as good as a male one—except to *real* listeners. A female cop is as
good as a male cop—except in subduing a *real* ex-marine crook. A
female fireman is as good as a male one—except in carrying a *real*
victim out of the flames or lifting a *real* beam. *The denial of reality is
perhaps the chief mark of the unisexists.*

But, amusingly, they are not totally divorced from reality. They
may scream for a female runner on TV, but their cries are oddly muted when it comes to *real* sports. Why no demands for an end to separate female events? Why not *one* race and let the best man (pardon
the expression) win?

But perhaps unisexism is right, after all, and all my arguments are
wrong? Then the Bible, including the New Testament, is wrong. And
there are, I think, some other standards to measure unisexism
against. One of these is the common judgement of mankind. This is a
phrase used by C. S. Lewis to mean that which throughout the history of the world has been believed at *all* times and in *all* places. Of
course the Spirit of the Age contemptuously dismisses the past, for
we are, at last, "humanity come of age," and what *we* think is right.
But *every* period thinks that. Antonine Rome thought it. The nineteenth century *knew* from its Spirit of the Age that *it* was humanity
come of age, and now wars were a thing of the barbaric past (but just
over the horizon the guns of August and the trenches). The young
Nazis *knew* they had the secret at last—Nordic racial purity and the
rest of it. Had we not, in view of the noticeable wrong-headedness of
these past Spirits of the Age, best be cautious about our own? Especially when it flatly contradicts the common judgement of mankind?
There is no doubt what *that* is: it is that men and women are *deeply*
different, that there is a deep and fundamental difference between

masculine human nature and feminine human nature. Our science has no evidence to the contrary; and this had been believed in all times and in all places. All the feminists can do is mutter about a great male conspiracy and hint at great pre-conspiracy civilizations where women ruled. Unfortunately for this fond dream, anthropology tells us flatly that no known society anywhere has ever been ruled by females or has not had role differences. (The Amazons are only a myth and, anyhow, had no men to rule.) And the great male conspiracy—well, if one can believe that, she can believe anything. Fairies at the bottom of the garden. But indeed that common judgement of mankind is rooted in all we know of the early history of the race.

Our forerunners back in the dawn age—not screened from nature by a (perhaps temporary) air-conditioned, central-heated, machine-assisted, insulated culture—had to come to terms with reality or not survive. One of the realities was that, although skins might be light or dark and heads long or round, the huge immutable difference in mankind was male and female. Specialization—lawyers, sailors, merchants—lay far in the future; but here specialization was inbuilt. Women had the babies which needed care and women were inclined to give it; and women were smaller and weaker, not fighters, not as good at running after something or away from it. They were valuable, not only because of their ability to make babies, yet they needed protection. (Rome began, we may recall, with the rape of the Sabine women: Romans carrying off armfuls of them, since the Romans had none. It was not felt to be necessary to ask them, only to get them, after which Rome was a going concern.) Men *of course* did the hunting and fishing (for the women and children) and so very naturally ruled. Equally naturally, the stay-at-home women tended the kids and cooked the bear steaks—and, also naturally, "While you're at it, just sweep out the cave, dear." Despite feminist cursing of role difference, we may doubt that their foremothers objected; for, being close to reality, they knew they needed a hunter to kill the bear and bring home the meat—and to protect them. This natural order endured for *millions* of years: the masculine and the feminine, however denied by unisexists, are rooted in the race. If men taught their sons to be warriors and made them toy spears, it was because their survival depended on it. And if some kindly caveman made a doll for his little cavegirl, it was probably because he saw her cuddling a stick or a bit of dry bone. This is our heritage.

Another standard, besides the common judgement of mankind, by which to measure the unisexist denial of any inbuilt masculinity and femininity is nature itself. We are, someone said, "half-angel and half-ape": what is certain is our kinship to the warm-blooded, child-suckling mammals. Spiders may eat their husbands, like some feminists, and bees have the matriarchy that feminists vainly seek in man's past; but we are mammals and have lived in close association with other mammals that we have domesticated. Our ancestors, whether in the wild or on farms, lived, in fact, close to nature: consequently, to a farmer or farmwife, unisexism would, I think, have seemed ridiculous—and, above all, *unreal*. Unisexism, indeed, could only have sprouted, I think, in the monster cities cut off from nature and mother earth.

At all events, let us look for a moment at our fellow mammals to see what we are. The stallions, the dogs, the bulls, the tomcats, certainly, haven't been 'conditioned' by Daddy saying, "Grow up to be a real bull, lad!"—but that's the way they *do* grow up: the fighting bulls. Or the stallions, hard to break and full of fight. The great war horses of the proud knights were stallions, for in battle the fierce stallions would also fight with teeth and hooves. Male dogs are the adventurers; tomcats make the night hideous with their battles and their conquests of females. No, not models—but what the male is. He fights, he is the hunter, he protects his females and the young. The gallant gentlemen on *Titanic*, the Light Brigade charging the guns—they were doing what males, animal and human, have done for millions of years. But the unisexists say that women will be just as good in combat. But *their* heritage—the patient cows, the gentle mares so safe to ride, the often-ladylike bitches: they take care of the young, as they have done for millions of years; they accept the authority (headship) of the males; they do not fight, unless, with no male about, they must fight to protect their calf or puppies. Not adventurous hearts, not fighting hearts, no challenges flung on the winds—but nurturing, protective hearts. All of this man has always known; perhaps the city-dwellers, growing up in the wilderness of brick, living in an apartment with one "fixed" cat, are forgetting who they are, what they are. At all events, the whole point with respect to our fellow mammals is that, although we may improve on their behavior (some male mammals are lamentably inclined towards rape or towards dining on their children), we learn from them what is *in our nature*—what is in our genes.

One school of feminists with pleasing realism admit the differences are innate—*but* urge conditioning towards androgyny anyway. And towards a race of neurotics? Or towards a state like that portrayed in H. G. Wells, *The Time Machine*: the horrifying picture of girlish little weaklings of both sexes in the far future? Androgyny might well end that way.*

---

*The Time-Traveller in A.D. 802,701 finds a decadent, childish race kept alive by the planning of remote ancestors. It is the descendents of what we should call the middle-class (unisexism is a middle-class thing) that he describes in "their Dres-

Not surprisingly, in view of the stallions and stags, the psychologists find that men have a built in propensity for risk-taking—which is of course the reason that young men are so lethal behind the wheel. (Despite skill, they have far more wrecks than girls because of taking chances—or showing off to the female of the species.) The psychologists have a good deal more to say about the real differences between the sexes, particularly that men are goal-oriented and women socially-oriented and nurturing.

The common judgement of mankind, the description of primitive man, the genetic heritage of mammals, and the findings of psychology have been proposed as ways of measuring the claims of unisexism. It may also, I think, be shown to be an excess in a historical perspective. I have often observed what might be called a pendulum swing from the extremes of one age to the opposite extremes of the next. For instance, in the eighteenth century, the age of the drawing room and elegant manners and dress, gentlemen occasionally drew the curtains in their coaches while crossing the Alps so that they might not be offended by all that untamed nature. That age was succeeded by Romanticism—all skylarks and wild torrents and nightingales. The pendulum. Again, sexual attitudes in Tudor England were merry and sane; under Cromwell's Puritans, theatres were shut and merrymaking repressed. With the succeeding Restoration both the court and the theatres became licentious, and things loosened up for a century. But, then Victoria, who was not amused, and excessive prudery became the order of the day. Now, a century or less later, the opposite excess: a virtually sex-saturated age. The pendulum.

But there's more to it: a relationship between sexual repression or sexual license on the one hand, and the position of women on the other. Sexual license cannot flourish when women aren't available except in brothels. In the Victorian Age 'nice women' were notably *not* available, unless of course one married them, for keeps. Lots of lasting marriages, therefore, often felt to be a good thing by women. The ideal of virtuous womanhood, though, required that women be put on a pedestal, sequestered from temptation and unseemly tempting, taught to faint (gracefully) at a risqué remark, and chaperoned against male impulsiveness, which was in any case curbed by innumerable petticoats and corsets. All of this, while most effective in preserving virtue, tended to suggest that females were rather brainless, a

den-china type prettiness"; and he continues: "Then, in a flash, I perceived that all had the same form of costume, the same soft hairless visage, and the same girlish rotundity of limb... [I]n all the differences of texture that now mark off the sexes from each other, these people of the future were alike."

view contradicted by certain wise and commanding dowagers. It is perhaps worth emphasizing that this treatment of the female is not typical of the past in general but of the Victorian Age which was an extreme. As our day is.

As a passing thought, if the pendulum swings from extreme to extreme, does it pass the point of balance (sanity?) somewhere in between? Could that point of balance, assuming that 1880 and 1980 represent the extremes, have been in the 1920s, when women obtained the vote in both England and America and were admitted to women's colleges at Oxford as degree candidates?

Whatever may be the truth as to a point of balance, there seems to me not a doubt in the world that we represent the equal and opposite excess to that of the Victorians. What could be more an excess than that Feminist Bible? Nineteenth-century Oxford didn't admit girls, but then women's colleges were built among the men's colleges in that university, just as in America completely separate women's colleges, like Smith and Vassar, were founded. When I was at Oxford, I thought the system there—women's and men's colleges in the same university (rather like Harvard-Radcliffe), the girls in the life of the university (lectures, clubs, societies) yet separate—was ideal, balanced between all-one-sex and completely coed. But now Oxford, hearing the Spirit of the Age—and for once *not* examining a fundamental assumption—has gone beyond that beautifully balanced system in a panic rush to mix the individual colleges. As Harvard-Radcliffe have done by, in effect, destroying Radcliffe. Balance or excess? Even more excessive, girls at West Point marching about with especially-made *little* rifles looking very absurd indeed. Does it seem precisely balanced, or even sane, for West Point to have rejected frail or short young *men* on the grounds that for an officer of the United States Army a man's strength and stature might be decisive in battle, and then to admit still-frailer, still-shorter *women* who themselves need protection? Or, again, while it seems entirely sensible to welcome women into the ranks of doctors and the other learned professions (as they were, without too hearty a welcome, back in the 1920s), it seems entirely insane to make them policemen.

To make women policemen and firemen and sergeants in the Marines, to send girls to West Point and Annapolis are all related to my earlier remarks about the male runner and the female newscaster in that all of these are a denial of obvious physical differences between the sexes. A denial of reality. The ancient Greeks are justly admired for their fine effort *to see things as they are*. No future age will admire us for that. What would the lucid intelligence of Aristotle—and Aristophanes!—make of our denial of 'the undeniable'? When they'd done laughing, that is? The Victorians, aware of women's frailer bodies and lighter voices, may have decided that their less-visible minds were also frail and light; but *we*, aware now of women's able minds, decide that their *quite* visible bodies and audible voices can do anything men's can. Seeing things as they are?

And yet the feminists, notably Betty Friedan before the Women's Lib Movement even began, have made one valid point. The traditional job of the woman's role is a shrunken one. Fewer children, for one thing. And it is industry that now makes the clothes, churns the butter, preserves the fruit and makes the jam, and bakes what may doubtfully be called the bread. But, however shrunken, the role of homemaker has *not* disappeared and is still *essential*. The differences that psychology discerns between the sexes—men being goal-oriented, women being nurture-oriented—powerfully suggest that homemaking should remain primarily the woman's responsibility. By and large, if there is going to *be* a home—that is, something more than a place to sleep—woman will make it so. Otherwise *home* will become a word found only in history books. It is the house*wife*, not the housebond (husband) who can make a domicile into a home.

But what if the woman has to work outside the home, as millions do, to make ends meet? There's no single answer to this complex problem.

One partial solution occurs to me: that business should accept—or be pressured into accepting—for *any* job (assembly line, teacher, secretary) *two-woman teams* at one full salary. The team would share the responsibility, arrange what hours each would work on a given day (sometimes morning, sometimes afternoon, one day more, one day less), and the employer could count on somebody (whether her hair were red or brown) being there. Very possibly with far less absenteeism. One woman would, so to speak, relieve the watch, as naval officers do, be filled in on what was happening, pick up typing the letter if a secretary or take the next class if a teacher. Actually quite like nurses. The employer would be guaranteed a full-time employee; the team would have a stable job between them. I think millions of women would like such an arrangement very much indeed. A lot better than any feminist solution I've heard. A realistic solution to the problem of the shrunken but still vital role of homemaker in relation to the need for supplementary family income.

I believe that a great many women would feel themselves to be truly liberated to be allowed to be homemakers without pressure from either the feminists or the economy. It has been said that in a good marriage the man is the head and the woman the heart. If there's truth in this, there's a corollary: in an individual, the head works for what the heart longs for—not a question of which rules.

And thus it is in the mystery of "one flesh" of Christian wedlock.

I am not, God knows—and as anyone who has read *A Severe Mercy* knows—hostile to women. I do not for a moment believe that men are superior to women—only different. To me, one of the God-given joys of this life is the radiant, for ever intriguing, complementary difference of man and woman, not just superficially sexual but deep and awesome. Man and woman are equal, yes, but equal in importance and value; and not, thank God, identical. Equal in importance as a nut and bolt are entirely equal in importance without being identical—and doing a job together that neither two bolts nor two nuts could do, holding something together. Man and woman do what two men or two women cannot do: they hold humanity together. A man and a little pseudo-man won't do it either. A man and a *woman*. I can fall on my knees, figuratively at least, before the mysterious wonder of womanhood, even as a true woman sees a splendour in manhood. Masculinity—that which initiates and leads, as the eternal masculinity of God does—needs femininity, feminine response, to complement and complete it. Help*meet* is the biblical word: a suitable or fit help, a completion. Thus man and woman together in that awesome mystery of one flesh is what Our Lord hath ordained for us.

It is in the Name of God and His will for us that I challenge the dragon of unisexism: and my lady's glove is pinned to my lance.

CHAPTER IX

The English Channel

Almost from the hour that I came to belief in Christ, I began to wonder about the Mother Church. If, after all, the claims of Christianity were true, perhaps hers were. The pilgrimage to God begun in Oxford thirty years ago—or begun in boyhood at Glenmerle when I rejected my childhood religion in the name of truth—led on to what has been told in this book: the falling away in the wildness (perhaps the wilderness) of the Angry Years of the '60s, the gentle nudges from God, the sudden return to the Obedience and repentance under the Mercy, and the vocation to write *A Severe Mercy*.

And now it leads me—"farther in"—to the Catholic (the Universal) Church.

But this chapter (the text of the chapter) is no more than a brief preface to the essay of the same title: the essay is the real chapter, for it tells the story very completely. The essay, at least in my own mind, is also something else. Before he submitted to Rome, John Henry Newman, leader of the Oxford Movement, published in 1841 his "Tract 90", demonstrating that the 39 Articles of the Church of England are quite consonant with Catholic belief. The ensuing storm was the prelude to his becoming Catholic. So, since "The English Channel" (the first part, now called "The White Cliffs") was written a year before I even knew that I would submit to Rome and was published in an Anglican journal, causing a certain amount of shock and controversy of its own, I can't help but think of it as *my* 'Tract 90'.

The English Channel of my title is not only that body of water—the Narrow Seas—that separates England physically and spiritually from Europe, it is, figuratively, what separates Anglicans (whether Church of England or Episcopalian) from the Catholic Church under the Successor to Peter. Or, more succinctly, what separates Canterbury from Rome. It is the *English* Channel.

Since the Church of England (and its American and Scotch Episcopal branches) possesses the historic episcopate (the Apostolic Succession) and recites the historic creeds expressing belief in "*One* Holy Catholic & Apostolic Church", Anglicans (unlike other Protestants) often try (as I once did) to persuade themselves that, though not under the Successor to Peter (the Pope), they are somehow 'in' the Catholic Church. Similarly, the United States possesses the historic language, common law, literature, and apple pie of the Mother Country, England, yet Americans, not under the Queen, are *not* in the British Empire/Commonwealth.

Thus a steady and broadening stream of Anglicans, uneasily aware of Newman and, in America at least, uneasily aware of Episcopalian secularism, come sooner or later to recognise that they are *not* in the Universal Church unless they are in communion with the Successor of Peter and that calling themselves 'Anglo-Catholic' does not make them *Catholic*.

Although the pilgrimage to God is life-long, and beyond death, too, there must be times of marching and times of standing still to spy out the Way and times of sleeping. The slow and difficult ascent of a mountain may end in a grand vista of the road ahead and very swift progress indeed. Such a slow ascent was that which culminated in Oxford, the city of my soul, where Davy and I found our faith, a faith that was nurtured in the Church of England by our Rector, by our friends, by C. S. Lewis, and by the Book of Common Prayer. Despite all this, I came some years later to a rocky place (the late '60s) where for awhile I lost my way. But only for a little while, for the God I had sought nudged me back to the road; and then, again, movement became swift and decisive and joyful. I could see where I was going.

The very first of these nudges it will be recalled, a good hard one, was the threat to the beloved Book of Common Prayer that, among other things, took me back to St Stephen's. It was, indeed, though I didn't think of it so, a threat to Anglicanism itself—or mine, at least. I fought hard for the Prayerbook against the clerical 'conspiracy' to remodel it instead of merely revising as they were supposed to be doing. The position was simplicity itself: as shown by countless polls, the people in the Episcopal Church wanted the Book of Common Prayer; the clergy, scorning the people's wish, wanted change and variety—the new 'Book of Varietal Prayer'.

The '*vested* interests' won, of course, giving rise to a certain amount of anti-clericalism. My own sentiments towards them are suggested by my limerick (*New Oxford Review*):

> There were some old clerks who said, "Oh!
> The Prayerbook's a bore and must go:
>   For the spirit of prayer
>   As to fun can't compare
> With our NEW 'Church Variety Show'."

Although the fight to save the Prayerbook was lost, the nudge had in the meantime led on to other nudges and the return to the Obedience: *that*, for me, was the important thing. But, also important, one great link to the Anglican Church, the Book of Common Prayer, was weakened (not destroyed, for the new book had something of the old). And then, having had their will with the Prayerbook, the same 'Pisky' (Episcopalian) leaders, faithfully heeding the secular Spirit of the Age, brought us priestesses. If, indeed, women's 'ordination' denied the Incarnation, then perhaps it was time to go.

C. S. Lewis, needless to say, was a factor in the decision, albeit an extremely confusing one. I ought perhaps to say a little more here than I say in the essay to follow. At Oxford we all used to remark when questions arose, "Well, what does 'St Clive' have to say about that?" But on the Question of Rome he was silent and, moreover, would not be drawn. (I tried.) He was very Catholic (though not high church or 'Anglo-Catholic') doctrinally and imaginatively. There was 'Mother Kirk' in *Pilgrim's Regress* and a boy named Peter as high king in Narnia, and the grey city in *Great Divorce* was Purgatory for those that left it. He believed in prayers for the dead and frequent confession. Nowhere in *Mere Christianity* or his other writings is there any mention of either of the two great Protestant doctrines of salvation-by-faith-alone and *Sola Scriptura*. But—he did not, like Newman and Chesterton, become a Catholic. Very puzzling. Indeed, a mystery. But a journey to Ireland in 1979 brought home to me how much his Ulster background—the deadly hatred there between Catholic and Protestant—would make it difficult, even impossible, for him to become a *Catholic*. One of 'them'.

And yet he prepared my mind for the Catholic Church. And if *my* mind, then other minds?

I once proposed to write an essay on "C. S. Lewis as Moses". A Moses who led people *towards* the 'promised land'—the Mother Church—that he himself could not enter (and to which he had no intention of leading them). The ones thus led might be, in particular, Anglicans, like me, and others, again like me, without ingrained Protestant prejudices, brought to the Faith by him. They might see, as Lewis presumably did not, that the Question of Rome had *got* to be answered. And, indeed, a great many devoted readers of Lewis have become Catholic.

With "C. S. Lewis as Moses" in mind, I wrote to a lot of them— all I could find—and got some fascinating replies that tended to support my idea. One woman wrote: "C. S. Lewis dispelled most of the prejudices that I, as a very Protestant Episcopalian, had against the Catholic Church." A Virginian who later became a Catholic lay brother wrote: "What Lewis did for me was to make me willing to take a second look at Rome." A young man who hopes to become a monk said: "He influenced the Catholicity of my mind...and gave me the capacity to think in terms of Universals and Wholeness." A woman wrote: "By incorporating in his books distinctly RC doctrines, he led me to consider them on their merits and not dismiss them as concerning only RCs." A man wrote: "He showed me how utterly coherent and cogent were the claims and teachings of the Catholic Church; and, like the man in Molière who was astonished to find that he had spoken prose all his life without realising it, Lewis, I'm convinced, was a Catholic apologist all his life without realising it." And a clever woman said: "After reading deeply in Lewis, I had the sudden shock one day of finding that the Catholic Church agreed with *me*."

So there in a paragraph is my unwritten essay on "C. S. Lewis as Moses". I gave it up: it would have taken more research than I cared to give it. But, vouching for the accuracy of the above quotations, including my own contributions in the rest of the chapter, I offer it to anyone casting about for a PhD or book thesis.

The old rhyme about the three positions in the Church of England ran: High and crazy / Low and lazy / Broad and hazy. Davy and I experienced both the high church (St Mary Magdalen) and the low church (St Ebbe's) there in Oxford. (The Episcopal Church in the '70s was the broad church.) Although I loved the faith and holiness of St Ebbe's, I was drawn to the high church, Davy less so. But, indeed, after reading *Brideshead Revisited*—the almost terrible faith of Lord Marchmain's family, despite their sins, as contrasted with the decent unbelief of Anglican Charles—I was already on the road to Rome.

To my regret, I cannot, somehow, recall what Davy thought of *Brideshead*, though we certainly talked about it. But she was less excited by Rome, and of course we took it for granted that we should go that way together or not at all. The question was never decided, owing to our being caught up in the beautiful and terrible ordeal of her dying. And yet her faith, like mine, was in many ways Catholic, as is suggested, perhaps, by her poem to Father Julian in *A Severe Mercy*.

Enough of preface. "The English Channel" essay that follows was first published (or the first part of it was) in an Anglican journal; then slightly abbreviated and including the second part in the Catholic *Communio*; and here the whole of it, revised.

THE ENGLISH CHANNEL
Between Canterbury and Rome

1. *The White Cliffs*

The spires of Oxford, long ago, directed my thoughts successively to two great questions. Although nominally an Anglican, a 'highchair Anglican' (as one says 'cradle Catholic'), I was, in fact, a vaguely theistic agnostic. It had never occurred to me, not since childhood, to *believe* in fairies at the bottom of the garden or all that old stuff about Jesus's being the Son of God. But now I suddenly saw that the towers and spires of Oxford had been raised in heart-lifting beauty by men who *had* believed: and I perceived that the question—the Question of Jesus—that I had never asked had got to be answered: *Was* Jesus, in fact, God? God incarnate crying forsaken upon the Cross? I saw that the world might hinge upon this Question. Thus I became 'an Anglican with leanings towards Christianity' by setting myself, as I have told in my book, *A Severe Mercy*, to finding the answer. Here I need say only that, after much writhing about, I finally answered: Yea, my Lord and my God.

Not long after this life-&-death affirmation, being now astonishingly a Christian, I realised that if the towers and spires of Oxford spoke in stone of deep Christian faith, it was the *Catholic* faith they spoke of. And I perceived that logically a further question followed the Question of Jesus, followed it so logically indeed that I marvel that all converts to the Faith do not at once ask it: If Jesus is God the Son, a fact that very naturally (or very supernaturally) casts a new light upon His words, then what of His words about His Church, founded so clearly upon the Rock that was Peter? What of the mere existence of the Catholic—the Universal—Church, twice as large as all the splinters of Protestantism put together? Twice as large, too, as the faithful Eastern Orthodox, which for centuries had accepted the primacy of the successors of Peter in Rome before the unhappy separation. Rome was the centre of the ancient unity, the centre of Christendom. Logically (and C. S. Lewis had taught me to be logical) the claims of Rome came *first*, that is, before I as a new Christian could decide whether Anglicanism's *Via Media* or any other separated church was a legitimate offspring and a valid way, I had to decide whether the *Mother* Church—as unmistakably the Mother Church as England is the mother country of English-speaking North America—was exclusively what she has always, whilst empires rose and fell, claimed to be: the *visible* One, Holy, Catholic, & Apostolic Church that Christ founded. Logically that was where one *began*. First things first. I was already an Anglican, loving the Book of Common Prayer; if *any* separated church was legitimate, then I would remain an Anglican. But first, logically, there was the Question of Rome.

In a booklet, *Encounter with Light* (1961), written about my conversion to the Christian faith, I put the Question of Rome as it had presented itself to me at Oxford.

I began to think seriously of the mother church and to ask myself the question that every Christian must sometime ask: Is that enormous church, so full of faith and learning, so full of variety except in the strong, unchanging faith, is it, after all, *The* Church? The True Vine? The question, essentially, seems to be: *What is the Church?*

...[Thus,] once the earlier question—is Christ God?—has been answered in the affirmative, one must face up to the further question posed by the existence in history and the undeviating assertion of the Catholic Church.

I looked at the glorious spire of St Mary the Virgin there in Oxford, conscious of the missing spire of Osney Abbey, destroyed by the reformers; and I looked at the melancholy ruins of Godstow Nunnery and Tintern Abbey and Great Glastonbury with thoughts about the less-than-inspiring origin of the semi-detached Church of England [hereafter: C of E]. I knew of course that we—we Anglicans—asserted daily in the creeds that we believed in (and, hence, were in) that One, Holy, Catholic, & Apostolic Church; and we handsomely admitted that Rome was, too. And we asserted that our church—the "Bridge Church" or the *Via Media*—had valid apostolic orders and the Catholic Faith, even though we had cleverly seen through the pretensions of the Papacy, which previously, for a thousand years, we had accepted; and we cut off the heads of Sir Thomas More and Bishop Fisher and others who were willing to die for the ancient loyalty. But the fact that our moment of keen insight into the governance of the Catholic Church had come about through a pope's refusing the self-willed Henry VIII, not perhaps a *good* man, a divorce to marry his doxy (a not-uncommon cause of others leaving Christ's Church ever since) didn't suggest a *holy* insight. And I was not persuaded by those who claimed, pointing to Wycliffe and the Sarum Rite, that the C of E had 'really' had an earlier, nobler origin. Not only Sir Thomas More, Saint, but the Pilgrimage of Grace argued against it.

Once in Southern France in Oxford years, I slipped into the rank kneeling for communion at the altar rail of a Catholic church. God in the hands of a wrinkled French priest. As I received the Host, I thought: Whatever may be the validity of Anglican orders, now at least I have truly eaten Christ's body.

One might suppose from the foregoing that I was near to answering Yea to the Mother Church also. Perhaps I was, but *near* is not *there*. Both Newman's *Apologia* and *Brideshead Revisited* (which one read at Oxford) haunted my mind; and my wise mentor, C. S. Lewis, had instilled in me an essentially Catholic vision of the Church, incidentally making that "Romish Doctrine concerning Purgatory" (Article XXII of the 39 Articles) not only believable in *Great Divorce* but necessary. But, at the same time, Lewis, who had, I presumed, thought deeply on the Question of Rome, remained C of E. And I myself wished the Question of Rome would go away. I loved the C of E: it was at once beautiful and homely: and there was holiness in it. Besides, I was having enough trouble just *being* a Christian without venturing into 'foreign' RC (Roman Catholic) country. I continued, therefore, to follow the beloved Anglican way with one eye upon C. S. Lewis and with occasional bouts of uneasiness.

So the years passed—I was caught up in various kinds of crisis that made deep thought on the matter impossible—but the Question of Rome did not go away. In reading of theological and ecclesiastical disputes I found myself invariably on the Catholic side. The real question for me (as for Newman) was not whether Catholicism was right but whether I as an Anglican *was* a Catholic. In the mid-'70s, I was impelled (by, I believe, Our Lord the Spirit) to write *A Severe Mercy*, which brought the Oxford years and later spiritual developments into focus. In it I spoke of the "unswerving faith of Rome: the place of last resort." And a journey to Ireland and Ulster made me aware as never before of what C. S. Lewis, who grew up in Ulster, would have had to overcome to convert to Catholicism: his remaining C of E became less significant. These events turned my thoughts anew to the Question of Rome.

Today in the last quarter of the twentieth century the vital issue in Christendom is not Catholic v. Protestant but the orthodox Christian Faith (Catholic, Eastern, and Evangelical) v. secularizing heterodox Neo-Modernism—both ecumenical. Or Supernaturalism v. Naturalism. The very essence of Modernism, whether paleo (early twentieth century) or neo (the '70s & '80s), is *the denial of the Supernatural*—hence the Incarnation and the Resurrection: *the Faith*. C. S. Lewis, penetrating as usual to the heart of the matter, described himself as a Supernaturalist: one who believes that a transcendent God is able to reach into His creation with miracles. But indeed Incarnational Orthodoxy needs no clarification: it is, quite simply, the *Faith*; and those who hold it may be called, quite simply, *Christians*. The sort the lions ate. The Secularizing Modernists, many of them, are, in fact, *not* Christians (though they may be priests or even bishops) because they have abandoned the Faith in Incarnation and Resurrection without, of course, openly admitting it. They represent treason in the Church, a secular Fifth Column; and a lion with a taste for genuine raw Christian would not care for them.

Modernism (condemned by St Pius X in 1907 as "the synthesis of all heresies") is often spoken of as a past phenomenon only; but what we have today, best called Neo-Modernism or Secularizing Modernism, has become more respectable but is, all the same, the final poisonous fruit of Modernism (short of leaving the Church altogether): an empty husk, form without faith, except an exaggeratedly humanistic faith in Man as the creator of 'god' as well as the builder of heaven on earth (so far not very heavenly). Neo-Modernism is secularizing in that it seeks earnestly to conform the Church to its own disbelief as well as to every with-it worldly trend; its biblical critics interpret the New Testament, not only by means of honest scholarship but on the basis of unadmitted secular assumptions or presuppositions, especially that the miraculous cannot be accepted. It is perhaps the deadliest heresy of the centuries because of its intellectual dishonesty: the lying pretence of faith even as it undermines the faith of others. The secularists are this-world-ers, serving the Prince of this World, though they no longer believe in the master they so truly serve.

· Yet this very danger, threatening Protestant and Catholic alike, caused the Question of Rome to re-present itself to my mind with a fresh vigour. If all of Evangelical and Eastern Orthodox faith were united once again to the tremendous power of the Catholic Magisterium, what a force for Christ! Not a Church, as Chesterton said, that will move *with* the world but "a Church that will move the world." Unity that would make the Faith more credible to non-Christians. Unity, I was beginning to see, that could *only* be brought about in and through the primacy of the Successor of Peter and the teaching authority (Magisterium) of Holy Church.

Even as I was seeing the Magisterium in this new light, not as an obstacle to becoming Catholic but as the true centre of the defence of the Faith, my deep love for Anglicanism was being jolted as I saw that it was falling helplessly into the hands of the Secularizing Neo-Modernists. It used to be said that whatever might happen in the Anglican Communion, two things would always remain to bind it together: the beloved Book of Common Prayer and the Apostolic Orders. But now the Prayerbook, which Chesterton (again in *The Well and the Shallows*) called holy and powerful "not in so far as it is the first Protestant book, but in so far as it was the last Catholic book", was not merely revised but virtually rewritten. That tie was weakened: the people wanted the old book; the clergy, the new; the old book perished. Then the Episcopal Church, not waiting for the rest of the Anglican Communion and without even a consensus vote, hearing only the voice of the Spirit of the Age, recklessly and with almost indecent haste compromised its claim to valid orders and Catholicity by 'ordaining' women as priestesses. And the tie of the orders was weakened. Thousands left the church. Approval of divorce and of homo*sex*—shown vividly by the 'ordination' of a known, practicing lesbian as a priestess—further proved that Anglicanism, at least in America, was controlled by men who subscribed to the values of the trendy secular world, not those of Christianity. Whether I was to leave the Anglican Church or not, I began to see it as leaving me.

I am not—fortunately perhaps for my faith—one of those would-be shepherds of the flock, the academic theologians who (some of them) present themselves, not at all modestly, as the new 'Magisterium'; but, like C. S. Lewis, I am educated in other ways (history and literature, including the classical), which allows me, as a scholar myself—hence aware of the limitations of scholarship—to keep the relationship between theological scholarship and faith in perspective. Neither a shepherd nor a would-be shepherd, I am merely one of the sheep. But it is, after all, the sheep that, inadequately fed, may nerve themselves to bolt away into other pastures. This sheep, as a result both of the Question of Rome re-presenting itself and of the melancholy decline of Anglicanism, read deeply in the works of those great Anglican Catholics, J. H. Newman, G. K. Chesterton, and Ronald Knox, whose road to Rome I was treading. And I entered into discussions with other thoughtful sheep, including a French Catholic philosopher in Québec, a Lutheran convert to Catholicism in Australia, and a sturdy Anglican in England, all undermining my irresolution from different directions. Whilst all this was going on, it was given a certain impetus by the joyful radiance of John Paul II's appearance among us, giving this sheep intimations, however faint, of what the Second Coming might be like.

More months passed. Suddenly I found myself on the brink of the precipice, the very edge of the white cliffs of Anglicanism. The wide, dark Channel lay below: the English Channel that lies between the Canterbury of Anglicanism and the Rome of Holy

Mother Church. One more step and I'd be gone. Paling slightly, I drew back a trifle and sat down, one leg dangling over the edge, staring across the Narrow Seas towards Peter's dome. Impulses— were they suicidal?—to leap off and start swimming clashed with desires to turn away and go home. It seemed impossible either to take the plunge or to turn firmly away. I continued, therefore, to sit there, not very cheerfully.

Some examination of what, by courtesy, may be called my thinking at this point—and my feelings—may be of interest to other sheep. I saw no doctrinal obstacle to becoming Catholic, least of all, as I've said, the Magisterium or the infallibility of the pope in his rare *ex cathedra* pronouncements. It was altogether clear that, just as Christianity itself stood or fell upon whether Jesus was all God as well as all man, so the Catholic Church—defined as the Successor of Peter and all those in communion with him—stood or fell upon whether it was *The* Church, the visible Church that Christ founded. The Question of Rome. What did Christ, doing the will of the Father, *mean* by 'Church' when He said, "I will build my Church"? Did He mean the Church in the singular or in the 10,000-sect plural? He *spoke* of His Church in the singular (and those who believe in an inerrant Bible may well contemplate that singular).

Protestants, to be sure, have an answer: *The* Church, they say, is the invisible church of the faithful: this is appealing (though it may be confusing the Church and the Kingdom), but the fact that the invisible church was never heard of until after the Protestants broke away, fifteen hundred years after Christ, does rather suggest rationalizing after the fact. I, at all events, could not escape the impression that He did *not* intend the incredible splintering of Protestantism. Moreover, that very splintering showed the inadequacy of the major Protestant doctrine of *Sola Scriptura* and the necessity of the teaching *authority*—the Magisterium—of the Church Catholic. Even a relatively simple document like the U. S. Constitution requires a 'teaching authority', the Supreme Court, to interpret it: How infinitely more does the Bible and the Tradition need it! How *obviously* necessary, if we, many of us, were not blinded by old hostilities! Just as the Apostles under Peter—long before there was a New Testament—interpreted Christ's truth, so their successors, the Bishops under the Successor of Peter, have ever since interpreted that truth. Protestantism (probably the first known instance of throwing out the *mother* with the bath water) has no 'Supreme Court'—hence the continual splintering. The Catholic Church has the Magisterium.

Moreover, although Protestants will not squarely face the fact, we must, if we are to rely upon the New Testament, accept that the Church, which guided by the Holy Spirit defined (chose the canon of) the New Testament, was *then* infallible. The question, therefore, is *not* whether the Church can be infallibly guided by the Spirit in matters of Faith (as she has always claimed to be) but, rather, when did the Spirit leave off the infallible guidance—if it did? When men, when popes, became sinful? But when were they not, even Peter? Their fallenness is, precisely, why the guidance is needed.

Three arguments in particular convince me that the Holy Spirit did *not* leave off His guidance of the Church of Peter in matters of the Faith. The first of these concerns that very period that Protestants rightly point to as having the most corrupt of popes: the hardly-Spirit-filled popes of the Avignon 'Captivity' and the Great Schism as well as the not-noticeably-religious popes of the Renaissance who triggered the Protestant revolt. Lots of sin. No question about that—the sin—but the Protestant critics fail to notice the really significant fact: not one of those wicked popes altered doctrine. To this historically-minded sheep, that fact is quite the most remarkable proof that the Holy Spirit was on the job, guiding His Church away from error. In the very year that Henry VIII's obedient Parliament named him head of the English church, Pope Paul III went through the streets of Rome in sackcloth and ashes for the sins of his predecessors—but not for their errors in doctrine. That is the significant fact: not what the good popes did, but what the bad ones *didn't* do.

The second argument for the continued guidance of the Holy Spirit is the *timing* of the pronouncement of the long-believed-in doctrine of papal infallibility (the infallible Church saying infallibly that the pope is infallible). Springing from the Tradition, it was formally defined as dogma by Pope and Council a little over a century ago. Newman, though not disagreeing with it, thought the definition "premature". That it was not. It was just *before* the unforeseeable inroads of Secularizing Modernism. Imagine the howls from the likes of Hans Küng if it were defined today! As it is the Catholic faithful (and all the faithful everywhere) know that, if need be, out of the depths of Parnassus the oracle will return into the world: the *ex cathedra* utterance of the Magisterium. The Church has the bomb.

The third indication to me of a Spirit-led Church guided beyond the vision of men is the series of events that made possible the pontificate of John Paul II, the pope we need at this moment of history, the white knight of Christendom. First, following the beloved John, a reserved, seemingly timid and cold pope, Paul VI. Then the cardinals met, determined, it is reported, to choose an elderly pope who wouldn't live too long but would project an image of warmth. Cardinal Wojtyla had no chance—too young and vigorous, as well as non-Italian. The cardinals had their way. John Paul I: warmth indeed, captivating the world; and dead in a month. Now the weary cardinals re-assembling wanted a younger man, and now perhaps a non-Italian. So John Paul II strode forth from behind the Iron Curtain, where, like the early Christians, he had dwelt under the shadow of martyrdom (which wonderfully concentrates the mind upon the *Faith*), to become the intellectually powerful Defender of the Faith. No mortal—no cardinal—could have foreseen this chain of events that alone could have led to John Paul II: but the Holy Spirit could.

But doesn't the Holy Spirit dwell within us all, guiding us if we permit? Of course. But does anyone really see the *Holy* Spirit, as opposed to the Spirit of the Age, guiding, say, the Episcopal Church—*as a church*—away from all error? Come on!

God's revealing Himself in the Incarnation for man's redemption is often called the Revelation. But it was not hidden from God—who knows what we call past and future in His eternal Now—that fallen man, *because* he is fallen, will corrupt any truth. How was that once-given Revelation to be kept from corruption? By the Spirit-led Church interpreting the Bible in the light of Tradition, say the Catholics. By the Bible alone—*Sola Scriptura*—with individual enlightenment from the Spirit, say the Protestants. Moreover, say the Protestants, Rome itself has corrupted doctrine: the Assumption (of Mary), for instance. Here a study of Newman's *Development of Doctrine* would be enlightening. Analogically, the Supreme Court (the guidance of the Holy Spirit is not suggested) has developed constitutional doctrine, and the Constitution might not have survived if it hadn't. Similarly, the Magisterium has functioned like a strict-constructionist court for twenty centuries. The question, then—one must ask the right questions—is *not* the validity of the doctrine of the Assumption; the question is the *Church*: Is it Christ's Church, prevented by the Holy Spirit from doctrinal error? If so, one simply accepts the Assumption. One does not argue with the Holy Spirit. And the Faith has remained whole, if in some ways developed, in the Catholic Church.

On the other hand, the Protestant dependence on the Bible alone—*Sola Scriptura*—with individual enlightenment from the Spirit: How has that worked since the Reformation? The truth is, the Bible, divine though it is, is simply *not* enough to guard the truth. The three great Reformation churches—Lutheran, Calvinist, Anglican—have splintered into thousands, yet they all, even the Mormons and the Christian Scientists, have the Bible—and they can't all be right. The Bible, in the absence of the teaching authority of the Magisterium and the Tradition of the visible Church, is being asked to do what a book, however holy, cannot do. Hence the countless sects.

Even as the Reformation Protestants rejected the teaching authority of Holy Mother Church—a rejection that led to *their* authority being rejected and the splintering of Protestantism ever since—so today in the Catholic Church, notably the American and Dutch branches, there are men in the universities who, in their pride of intellect and enfeebled faith, hold that *they*, not the shepherd-bishops and the Holy Father, ought to be the modern 'shepherds': an intellectual 'magisterium', not the old spiritual one. These men are, whether they know it or not, on the road to ever-more-secular Protestantism. Contemplating that intellectual pride that not only destroys their own faith but that of others, I think of a man who was at once an intellectual giant and a spiritual giant and withal humble.

John Henry Newman of Oxford, one of the finest, most powerful minds of the last century, wrote some words in his *Apologia Pro Vita Sua* that have haunted me since my own Oxford days. Describing his own conversion from high Anglicanism to Holy Church, he says that there is a "fitness" to the idea that it might be the Will of God to provide for "retaining in the world a knowledge of Himself, so definite and distinct as to be proof against the energy of human skepticism." And then he says that "when I find that this is the very claim of the Catholic Church...I find no difficulty in admitting the idea."

Neither do I. I cannot believe that God's Revelation was for the first century only. There *is* a "fitness" to the idea that the truth of it should be guarded. I cannot imagine the state of Christendom today if all the early heresies, springing from that "energy of human skepticism", had not been extinguished by the *visible* Catholic Church. But if that Revelation was for all time, its truth must still be guarded by the Magisterium of the Church against the ferocious "energy of human skepticism", manifested in this century by Modernism and Neo-Modernism, which is precisely "human skepticism" or the failure of faith: *the very essence of Modernism is the denial of the Supernatural.* The *Faith* is supernatural or it is nothing. Literally nothing. Nothing that needs faith.

The fact that we (most of us, anyway) have never even seen a miracle in this materialistic age (would we believe it if we saw one?) may make us doubtful of stories about healings or of Sister Marie finding her second-best thimble by the aid of the Blessed Virgin. It is possible to be too credulous—or, today especially, too incredulous. But one truth should be kept in mind: however rare miracles may be today, it is not proof that at the supreme occasion of man's history by *any* reckoning there were not miracles. As St Paul said (I Cor 15:14): "If Christ was not raised, then our gospel is null and void, and so is your faith."

But there are men in the Church, many of them theologians (or, more precisely, atheologians), and their intellectual fellow travellers (especially the social scientists) in the university, who, in fact, disbelieve in the Bodily Resurrection, yet, concealing their loss of faith, they still presume to speak for the Church. They speak in learned and often opaque language, and they are a particular danger to the faith of the less learned (Christ's "little ones") who suppose that men so learned must have authority and wisdom as well as some hidden source of knowledge. But, in fact, in great matters like the Bodily Resurrection of Jesus they do *not* have a scrap of secret knowledge (evidence) hidden from the rest of us.

I would not be thought to oppose legitimate biblical scholarship or the faithful theologians; but I know that the Catholic theologian's job is to inquire into and clarify the mind of the Church; and if he goes beyond that to 'explain away' the miraculous that both Scripture and the mind of the Church attest to, he is as dishonest in doing his job as a chemist who falsifies an experiment or an historian who suppresses a document. If, to be sure, there is valid, ancient, documentary evidence against a particular miracle, it should be brought to our attention; and if there were evidence against a miracle that is an article of faith, it should be quietly presented to the Magisterium for decision, not rushed into print. The burden of *proof* rests upon those who would *disprove* a prophecy (prediction) or a miracle. The truth of Revelation—God Incarnate and the Bodily Resurrection—is for the Christian theologian a given. But what these Neo-Modernist theologians are, in fact, doing—but never honestly admitting—is bringing *to* the New Testament, not faith but assumptions or presuppositions from secular thought: *unverified and unverifiable assumptions*. They *assume*, merely assume, that the miraculous—the intervention of transcendent Supernature into nature—cannot occur, an assumption for which there is not an atom of proof in all science (since science is exclusively concerned with nature). Christianity is a *supernatural* faith, or it is not faith at all.

If a biblical critic says that a prophecy by Jesus of the destruction of Jerusalem or the Temple (which, in fact, happened in 70 A.D.) was inserted by the gospel writer after the event, that is, 'proving' that Jesus never said it and further 'proving' that the Gospel was written after the event, he is merely exhibiting his assumption that prophecy cannot happen. What a refreshment it would be if biblical critics stated all their secular assumptions on page 1! But then of course Christians wouldn't buy the book if the assumptions denied the Faith. But the assumptions are usually not stated, though they are easy enough to spot.

Many of the Neo-Modernists assert belief, especially in preaching, but then speak of New Testament events in a way calculated to shake their listeners' belief. The preacher may say he has deep faith in the Resurrection (in a Pickwickian sense no doubt), but then speak of it as a "faith-happening", a code-word meaning that what *he* believes is that those naïve apostles *really* believed that they had seen the Risen Lord, but of course we know they didn't. How we know that they didn't is not made clear.

The Christian reader and churchgoer needs to train himself to look for the unstated assumptions behind what he reads and hears. Otherwise his faith can be undermined and destroyed by men who, too secularized to believe the Faith themselves, are yet unwilling to do the honest thing of throwing up their jobs as priest or theologian and leaving the Church. Instead, they try to reduce the faith of others—if they could destroy everybody else's faith, that would prove that they were right and comfort them. There are of course splendid Catholic scholars who see with the eye of faith, but it is the secularized intellectuals and theologians who have lost their faith that I am concerned with; often they are the very ones who hold that *they* should be the shepherds of the flock. My poem is about them.

The Shepherds' Reformation

The new apostates' breath
Shrivels divinity up.
Unproved assumptions gauge
Their scholarship: their lord's
The Spirit of the Age.
They stab with secular swords
    The wounded side
    Of the Crucified,
And holding the holy cup
They urge the ultimate death.

As suavely they speak the Creed,
With every word forsworn,
    From His Father's side
    And His fainting Bride
The Son of God is torn.
The flung´stone´shatters
The blue´stained´glass´:
The Light of Heaven scatters
Upon the pitying grass.
—But what if He's risen indeed?

I saw, then, the real war within the churches, the war of Supernaturalism (the Faith) v. Naturalism (the World); and I saw that the best hope of all the churches was the Successor to Peter and the Magisterium of the Catholic Church. There was no doctrinal obstacle to my becoming a Catholic: intellectually I already was a Catholic. And I saw more clearly than many confused members of that Church the vital necessity of the Magisterium in confronting the terrible "energy of human skepticism". But seeing the way clear to becoming Catholic is not quite the same thing as being willing to follow that way.

Indeed the reader, especially the Anglican reader, may be asking when I shall be coming to the case for Anglicanism. It can be argued that it is more Catholic than other Protestant churches and more Protestant than the Catholic Church and so deserves its nickname of "the Bridge Church." But bridges are usually to be *crossed*, by people going one way or the other.

I myself clung to the fond delusion of many Anglicans, especially the high-church ('Anglo-Catholic') ones, that we were somehow *in* the Catholic Church, even if we were not in communion with the pope and even though our own church was becoming less and less 'catholic'. Nevertheless, this unrealistic assumption or delusion that we, unlike other Protestants, are somehow *in* the Universal Church because we retain the Apostolic Succession in the Orders (at least until a bishopess queers it) gives rise to the peculiar difficulty of Anglicans in contemplating Holy Mother Church. The difficulty that I call the *English* Channel that lies between Canterbury and Rome. As a result of it, the Question of the Church, the precise question itself, becomes for us rather elusive; and we tend to live in a somewhat unreal world, shutting our eyes on the one hand to the heresies of the Episcopal Church and shuddering on the other hand at the commonness of the Catholic Church; and comforting ourselves with the beauty of liturgy and incense.

But my love for Anglicanism was not exclusively high-church but was based on the Book of Common Prayer and on Englishness, and I found it ever more difficult to keep my eyes shut and to sustain the delusion that I was, somehow, a Catholic. The number of Anglican priests queued up to become Catholic priests as well as other Anglicans going the same way indicated that others were having the same difficulty and that the 'Bridge Church' was indeed a bridge. Newman, in the end, had decided that the *Via Media* of the Oxford Movement (later to be called 'Anglo-Catholic') that he had done so much to create was simply not valid, and he had become a real Catholic. As did Chesterton and Knox (and more recently Malcolm Muggeridge). Ronald Knox, an Anglican priest like Newman, was steeped in Anglicanism, being the son and grandson of Anglican bishops. Yet in his book, *A Spiritual Aeneid*, about his journey to the Mother Church, he wrote that Anglicanism itself

is not a system of religion nor a body of truth, but a feeling, a tradition, its roots intertwined with associations of national history and of family life; you do not learn it, you grow into it; you do not forget it, you grow out of it.

Yes. Precisely. I had been an Anglican long before I was a Christian, and that feeling he speaks of and that tradition can be very strong indeed. Moreover, when I became a Christian, my faith was nurtured in the Church of England. I hadn't yet quite grown out of it. I wanted to be a Catholic, but I wanted the whole Church of England (and its American branch) to come with me and remain Anglican. I did see, though, that it wasn't a question of opposing arguments, RC v. C of E: it was a question of whether one accepted or rejected the arguments for Rome. One of the arguments is implicit in defining a Catholic as one in communion with the Successor of Peter.

One familiar argument against the Catholic Church troubled me for awhile in a vague way until I realised how intellectually disreputable and *ad hominem* it is. An argument by innuendo. In a veiled way it will be hinted that anyone even considering submitting to Rome (born RCs are exempt because they can't help it) is, if not quite fascist, at least yearning for authoritarian answers and intellectual chains, not brave enough to accept uncertainty and wanting in the valiant questing spirit of man. Needless to say, the suggestion could only come from an essentially-secular humanist, though possibly a secular humanist in sheep's clothing. But, surely (one may reply), the questing spirit of man seeks in order to *find*? Otherwise, dear friend, would there not be something genuinely absurd—something a bit *silly*, in fact—about a valiant seeker determined *not* to find lest he should lose his 'Seeker's Status'? Or lest the finding impose an uncomfortable awareness of his creaturely position?

Indeed, apart from these 'professional seekers' who value their Seeker's Status more than truth, most of us would be only too glad to have some certain answers straight from the ultimate authority, God. We should welcome an angel very warmly indeed should one stop by. "Ask me anything you like," he would say kindly, folding his wings. "Oh, thank you, sir!" we would reply. "Do you mind if I put on my sunglasses—the, er, brightness, you know? Ahhh, that's better! Now, please sir, just what *is* the Church? And would you say a few words about—well, birth control, you know? And divorce. Oh, and homo*sex*. Just for starters. —Oh, some whisky?

No, I suppose not. You don't mind if I do?" — "Not at all," the angel would say. "Now, first of all, about the Church..."

However unlikely an angelic visitant, the question about the Church, though seldom asked with an open mind by Protestants, is *there*. It is implicit in the very existence of the two-thousand-year-old Catholic Church. Logically it *must* be asked. I asked it—and so arrived on the edge of the white cliffs.

Why have I stopped on the brink? [I shall leave the rest of part one, "The White Cliffs", in the present tense as originally written.] I have not stopped because of intellectual difficulties ahead but because I am being pulled in opposite directions. There's no question but that it would be right to go on to Rome, but would it be *wrong* to stay? *Must* I go?

In my faith and worship I am a child of the Church of England. C. S. Lewis, who shaped that faith and was my counsellor and friend, was Church of England. My wife's ashes lie in two Anglican churchyards, one in England and one in Virginia. When I nerve myself to leap off the white cliffs, I hear voices in my ears— gentle, courteous Anglican voices—saying: "Stay! Stay with us. We are your people. We are *your people*, and you speak our language. Do not leave us. You don't want to be a—Catholic!"

I—a *Catholic*! Loving the English thing in prayerbook and history, I feel it to be almost like treachery—and real pain, too. The English ships stood out under Howard and Drake, Hawke and Nelson, to sink the fleets of their several Catholic Majesties who were minded to conquer England. Anglican Cavaliers fought the Puritan Roundheads; and in the return match Virginian Anglican 'Cavaliers' fought the Puritan Yankees. Anglican poets—Vaughan and Herbert—touched the robe of Divinity. The deep graves in the English earth and the Virginian earth. How does one tear the past away? "If I forget Jerusalem..."

And the present. A country parish, St Stephen's, a century and a half in this place under the blue Virginian mountains. People who are dear to me, living about the county in old country houses, full of old and beautiful things, and with an old tradition of courtesy. Houses with names like Elk Hill and Trivium, Bellevue and Lochwood Hall, where I go to dine. These folk are troubled about the new Prayerbook and other things the secularizers are doing, but they would never leave St Stephen's where their people are buried. How can I?

They would never understand if I converted to popery. I can hear them now, saying—not to me, they'd be too polite, but to each other—saying: "Something damned unsound about a feller who'd do a thing like that!" At the same time, of course, they would remember their second-cousin Randolph's great-great-uncle Charles who stole a horse or fought for the Yankees or some such thing.

Past voices, present voices, saying: "Stay! We are your people."

In England there is an *English* RC tradition. Sir Thomas More, Saint, who died for Holy Church with the words: "I die the King's good servant, but God's first." The old Catholic houses that kept the Catholic faith at the risk—often at the cost—of their lives. The English martyrs like the heroic Campion. The English abbeys that have risen again, and all the stream of conversions stemming from the Oxford Movement. The parish churches themselves built when the Church was one. In England there wouldn't be quite that feeling of treachery perhaps, of abandoning one's roots.

But in America, the Catholic Church looks—well, foreign. Probably collections for the IRA. Maybe the Mafia. Of course I'm exaggerating—I think. And a liturgy that makes even the new Episcopal Book of Varietal Prayer sound good. Still, choosing a church is not like choosing a suit or a house, a matter of taste and comfort. A little matter of truth.

The Episcopal Church, if the Secularizers retain control, may be on its way to some sort of national pan-protestant church with no claim to catholicity—and perhaps not much to Christianity either. But whatever the prospects, including priestesses or even a bishopess, that future doesn't affect St Stephen's now.

In the greatest play of our times, *A Man for All Seasons*, the Duke of Norfolk, speaking of the men who have gone along with the King in the break with Rome, says with dignity and pain to Sir Thomas More: "But damn it, Thomas,...You know those men! Can't you do what I did, and come with us, for fellowship?" The most moving of appeals. It is the appeal to me of the courteous Anglican voices in my ears: "Stay! Stay with us, for fellowship." And, indeed, staying—inaction—is a bit easier than going, if it's not a matter of your neck. Still, I must not conceal More's reply to Norfolk's appeal: "And when we stand before God, and you are sent to Paradise for doing according to your conscience, and I am damned for not doing according to mine, will you come with me, for fellowship?" Not a comfortable remark.

But the truth is—and this is the point of real pain—I do not know what my conscience or the Holy Spirit is saying. I am not unaware that my love of Anglicanism is an earthly love or that the Devil may use our legitimate loves for his purposes. I have not neglected pondering Our Lord's words about leaving father and mother to follow Him. But—which way *is* following Him? Even believing that the Catholic Church is the only possible way of unification, should I do more towards unification by 'poping' or by speaking for it, in an 'Anglican voice', within Anglicanism? But even if I knew the answer, which I don't, it is the wrong question, for it is substituting human reason for God's.

The right question is, what is God's will? But I do not know that, either. Nor how to find out.

Uncannily, at just this point in the essay, not knowing how to end and pausing for coffee and thought, the post arrives with a letter, forwarded by my (Catholic) confessor, from a monk of Ampleforth Abbey in England who knows of my 'point of pain'. He advises me to leave off floundering about in the which-is-God's-will dilemma, but, instead, *step over the dilemma to God alone*. "Anything less than Him is an idol—even the Catholic Church." Yet, by seeking God alone, I shall, nevertheless, discover His will, for "I will reveal myself to him who loves me." It seems that God is speaking to me through this monk of Ampleforth.

I ought, though, to make clear the dilemma. It appears to me to be God's will that the Church be One, in union with the Chair of Peter. And at the same time it appears to me to be His will that we should love the people He gives us to love, with a love as much like Christ's as possible. It follows from the first proposition that I should submit to Holy Mother Church; and it follows from the second that I should stay in St Stephen's, loving the people God has given me to love. And it's no good saying that I could go on loving them even if I did leave—people drift apart. This is the dilemma I turn over to God. My mind says *go*, but my heart says *stay*.

Thus I remain on the very edge of the white cliffs, and the wide, dark Channel lies below. A fine intellectual gallop—or, more appropriately, canter—to the dangerous edge of the cliffs is refreshing; but then one wants to go *home*. Sitting here on the brink, I hear across the English Channel from the distant dome of Peter's Church the trumpets of Rome; but behind me, across the green fields, homely and dear, the change-ringing bells singing from the towers of Canterbury.

2. *Crossing the Channel*

The foregoing essay, under the title "The English Channel" (and subsequently somewhat revised) was published, nearly a year after it was written, in an Anglican journal and produced a storm of letters, praising it and damning it and me. And personal letters, all kindly, both from Anglicans saying, "Do not leave us," and from Catholics saying, "Come on, start swimming!" One Catholic correspondent pointed out that the bark of Peter had sprung some leaks since Vatican II but "Come along and help bail!" Though I was still perched on the white cliffs, that letter appealed to me—the idea of being of some help. And I thought: Yes, leaking a little—but a superb helmsman and straight on course to the East. But that luxurious liner that passed, everybody waving but nobody on the bridge and going in circles—was that Anglicanism? Or perhaps *Titanic?*

I had been on the cliffs, now, for about a year and a half and was growing a little tired of being there. There was some consolation, though, in the fact that Newman and Chesterton and Knox had all, it seemed, come to the very edge of the cliffs of Anglicanism and hung about there for a long time before taking the plunge. And C. S. Lewis, despite a truly Catholic mind, had never come near to leaping. So I said my prayers and waited, for something.

In the May of 1981, a couple of months after the "Channel" was published, I went up to Portsmouth Abbey on Rhode Island, a monastery of the English Congregation of the Benedictines, to see my old friend and Confessor, Dom Julian. Apart from visiting him, my purpose was to help him with a forthcoming book of his deep-Christian poetry, *There Shines Forth Christ*, for which I had written an introduction. At the same time, I was wondering, as perhaps he was, whether some special grace would move me to submit to Holy Mother Church. Just in case, I asked him to examine me in the Faith. But nothing happened. After a week I drove north to the French village of La Pocatière in Québec to talk with another friend, Georges Allaire, a Christian philosopher who had given me many insights into the case for Catholicism—and into G. K. Chesterton as well. But Georges who had sharpened my reason could not assist me in determining my will, or God's. Then I came home to Virginia.

On the fridge a fragment of a yellow poster proclaimed: "Not to decide *is* to decide." A kindly old Austin Friar (Augustinian), Father Robert Regan, had pointed out that in choosing Christ Himself long ago I was in a sense refusing to *reject* the Lord—without any special compelling grace. I had said then: "I *choose* to believe." And yet, I now thought, I had chosen Christ with *enough* (sufficient) grace; and it had been only *after* I chose that I had *felt* myself sustained by grace. It was, or it seemed to be, *my* choice. So now it occurred to me that to expect a special grace in this matter of the Church was perhaps a kind of Anglican hauteur: "Anglicans will receive engraved invitations and enter by the main door." This thought, along with Father Bob's observation, supported by the yellow poster, gave me an uneasy feeling that Someone might be expecting me to make up my mind.

At the Abbey in late May, Dom Julian and I had been visited by Peter Kreeft (the man who'd suggested I come along and help bail the bark of Peter) and Tom Howard. We were all four writers, two Catholics and Tom and me, Anglicans: indeed, Tom read us his then-unpublished essay, "Lead, Kindly Light", on his own approach to Rome. And there was talk of it as well as of the published part of "The English Channel". It was a pleasant afternoon of the "Junior Inklings", as someone suggested we call ourselves. In the course of the discussion Peter suddenly said: "I have a question for Tom and Van. If you knew you were going to die tomorrow, what would you do about the Church?" Tom hesitated; but I said instantly: "I should ask Julian to receive me into the Catholic Church." I was faintly surprised at my own certainty, but then I added: "Because, you know, if I were going to die, I should be leaving St Stephen's anyway."

Now at home that question and my reply came back to me. I hadn't thought much about it at the time, but now it occurred to me that I had, in fact, suggested to God a way to bring me to decision: perhaps I had best decide on my own first. "Not to decide *is* to decide." To decide by drift. Then it came to me that perhaps I could go on drifting, but, if I faced up to decision, I could not *reject* Holy Mother Church—just as, long years before, I had realised that I could not reject Jesus. But if I cannot *reject* the Church, that means that only one way is now possible, for I couldn't finally choose Anglicanism without rejecting the Catholic Church. (I, at least, cannot go on drifting unless I can persuade myself that either way is possible.) Therefore, if I *cannot* reject the Church—if only one way is possible—I *have* decided, haven't I?

So I came to decision. I mentioned this to God in prayer.

It was August now, about the first. I telephoned Dom Julian. He, who for years patiently answered my questions about the Church, as well as being my Confessor, must be the one to receive me. We set August 15th, the Assumption, for the Reception. Julian had never urged me to become Catholic and had indeed seemed almost indifferent (not that I believed he was). Now he wrote me that he had prayed for me to come into the Church every day for thirty years. Eleven thousand prayers!

A fortnight to wait between the Decision and the Act. A fortnight of feeling—what? Joyful? Elated? Peaceful? None of these. Gloom, rather. Pain and sadness about St Stephen's and its dear people. Forebodings about what the Catholic Church would actually be like at the parish level. Feelings of treachery towards all that Canterbury represented: old churches in England, my first vicar there, Anglican friends, the very history of England. I buried myself in studying Rome, not papal Rome but classical and pagan Rome—gloomily. I went to St Stephen's a last time—nobody knew—and it almost undid me. The lovely ancient words of the Book of Common Prayer. The people. Three days later the Rector dropped in, and I told him. It almost undid us both. We hugged each other. And my decision remained firm.

The next morning I flew north.

Portsmouth Abbey and Julian. His welcoming smile and our talks helped, as did the loving-kindness of some of the monks. And Peter Kreeft coming in from Boston to be my sponsor or godfather, bringing me an old Russian cross. It was appropriate that he should be the one, for his question at the Junior Inklings meeting had unlocked my indecision. In a deeper sense of course Dom Julian had fathered my Catholicism, beginning at Oxford thirty years before: his prayers and his friendship and his always being there to answer my questions.

The ceremony itself: Father Julian received me into Holy Church. I chose not to waive the conditional baptism. An old and beautiful monk who was also a bishop, Ansgar Nelson, OSB, anointed me in Confirmation. A few Catholic friends looked on. It was done.

As if to show that I wasn't cut off from all things English, the first man I was introduced to as a Catholic was Cardinal Hume, OSB, of England, paying a brief surprise visit to the Abbey, the Abbey that had begun as a priory of English Abbeys. But I was pretty well past feeling anything. Numb to all I thought I should feel—a resolute numbness. The only feeling I can remember was gratitude for the loving-kindness of everybody.

By the time I left two days later, a sort of chuckle was welling up in me, breaking through the numbness. A small parcel Julian gave me—a book I thought—proved to be, when I opened it at home, his carved-wood, mediaeval crucifix that was with my wife when she died. It is beside me as I write.

A papist now, I went the following Saturday evening to my first Mass in Virginia. Julian had written to the pastor, Father Warner; and he and I had had a talk. At the Mass I was startled—almost believing for one amazed instant that it had been 'fixed'—when the Gospel turned out to be Matthew 16: "and upon this Peter/Rock I will build my Church...and give unto you the Keys..." In his homily, Father Warner spoke of the Faith with his own firm, loving faith in every word; and then he celebrated the Eucharist with moving power. There are two Catholic churches in Lynchburg, Holy Cross where Father Warner is, and St Thomas More, which of course drew me by its name. I had meant to check them both out; but after that first mass at Holy Cross, I looked no further. I felt then, and have not since changed my mind, that I was blessed in my priest.

That Mass was on Saturday evening because I had decided to go to St Stephen's one more time and tell people in person what I had done. I still didn't feel elated or joyful, but I did, now, feel a sort of peace and rightness. And that inner chuckle—at myself, I think— persisted. I thought *God* to be rather amused.

I knew that the service at St Stephen's was Matins (morning prayer, not communion) as it is every other Sunday. Then, between the evening Mass and next morning's Matins, it came to me: There wasn't a reason in the world or in Heaven above why (without neglecting Mass) I shouldn't *always* go to Matins at St Stephen's *as a Catholic*—a graduate Anglican, as it were. Unless they stoned me. This sudden plan might seem a bit like having one's cake and eating it, too; but the motive is love. Moreover, it seemed to me *real* ecumenism, not the muddled sort that says that all varieties of religion are equally true as long as people's hearts are in the right place. Suddenly I had a sense of mission—if only to show that becoming papist doesn't lead to growing horns. (Not so far.)

So, with a sort of astonished happiness added to the peace and the chuckle, I drove out into the country to St Stephen's with Nelly, my border collie, beside me and my pocket bulging with copies of the "Channel" (part one), which explained not only why Rome but why St Stephen's still. And I told people, some before Matins, some after, offering the "Channel", which everybody wanted. When I said I'd become RC, they responded with kindness but looked sad. But when I added that I'd continue to be part of St Stephen's at least for Matins, their faces brightened. The Rector gave me a faint, possibly wry, smile at that Petrine Gospel. And in the months [now years] since, I have continued to go to St Stephen's as well as Holy Cross.

What is, to me, so amazing about this whole thing is that in all the years since perceiving my dilemma of doing God's will—either by becoming Catholic *or* by loving the people He gave me to love in St Stephen's—and in all the talks and letters about it, *nobody* saw that I could go to St Stephen's *as a Catholic*. Not even I with my sometimes ingenious (not to say tricky) mind—not even in that fortnight of gloom. No wonder God seemed amused! Now Dom Julian wrote that he thought my going to St Stephen's was "exquisite charity". That shocked me: I was doing it because I wanted to. —But why did I want to?

It seems to me that I had to be willing to leave—actually, in fact, *leave*—'father and mother' *before* they could be given back to me in a new way. An Irish nun, Sister Hilary, who knew of the dilemma said, in response to my note about the Reception, "You will find that you will not lose your friends, for God is not to be outdone in generosity." The words leapt out at me. In pain and sadness I had bidden farewell to St Stephen's and all the Anglican things in my heart, but—"God is not to be outdone in generosity." I could not—I cannot—but believe that this resolution of my anguished dilemma was a gift of grace, the grace of a most loving Lord. A merry gift. It was a deep confirmation of my decision to submit to Holy Mother Church.

Remembering, now with laughter, my gloom on the eve of reception, I thought of that beautiful Catholic poem, "The Hound of Heaven" by Francis Thompson:

Is my gloom, after all,
Shade of His hand, outstretched caressingly?

CHAPTER X

The Examined Life

The unexamined life is not worth living. So said
wise Socrates twenty-five centuries ago. The idea
is worth examining. He evidently thought that most people didn't
examine their lives. Ever since schooldays I have tried, though
sometimes failing or forgetting, to stand back and really look at my
life. *A Severe Mercy* was the result of years of examining what had
been with Davy, until with distance the foothills sank into the plain
and the essential mountains boldly stood forth. What I have had to
tell in this present book, as I said at starting, does not have the distance in time that gives the truest perspective; and yet, especially
since the impulsive '60s, I have subjected the years after Davy to
intense examination.

And I am, after all, trained as an historian. The step-by-step development of my analysis of feminism in time and seeing it as pervaded by unisexism is an illustration of my examining; and so, no
less, is the development since Oxford of my thought on the
Church. I have attempted, when possible, to tell this story in the
writings of the times, for the essays and letters and poems are
themselves concentrated examination and meditation: and the book
itself, pulling them all together, showing that the Faith and the
Obedience are linked in the truest way with joy of life as well as
with the questions relating to women and the Church, is the truest
examination that I am as yet capable of.

Incidentally, quite by chance, while writing this story, I have
read, a bit every day, the charming little book, *A Legend of St Dis-
mas & Other Poems* (just re-published by Ignatius). I wonder how
in tiny ways its spirituality and gentle devotion may have affected
my writing.

The most recent major event prior to the writing of this book was
my becoming a Catholic at the very beginning of the '80s in the
pontificate of John Paul II; and "The English Channel", written

both before and after that event, examined my motives and insights with some thoroughness. Still, because the essay was close to the event in time, the reader may wonder whether there have been regrets, tensions, afterthoughts. Certainly no regrets, especially since my link through St Stephen's to Anglicanism remains: I continue to go to Matins at St Stephen's and feel, somehow, a part of it; I shall always indeed feel myself an Anglican within Holy Mother Church and pray for reunion of all who love the Lord. Faith in the Incarnate God is so overwhelming a bond that the differences among believing Christians of whatever denomination are relatively insignificant: we brethren are.

The only tension resulting from my becoming Catholic—a momentary thing—was when a high-church Anglican ('Anglo-Catholic') wrote to a journal in which I had reviewed a book, taking me to task—me especially, since as a former 'Anglo-Catholic' I knew "full well" what I was doing—for referring to "the Catholic Church" instead of "the *Roman* Catholic Church." Replying I pointed out that 'Roman Catholic' is *not* the name of the Catholic Church and that it is, in fact, "a bit of an insult to the Church as well as a contradiction in terms: if it is only Roman, it is not Universal. But if *it* is not Catholic, what is?" Finally, I asked whether he could not "see that my speaking of the Catholic Church without a limiting adjective in fact explains, not in a word but in the absence of a word, why I became a Catholic? That is my *apologia*: precisely the same as Newman's."

But that was not tension really—just jousting. And there have been no afterthoughts about becoming Catholic except a sense of the inevitability of it and some mild wonder that it took me so long to do it. And I've yet, despite my Anglican fears, to hear so much as a mention of the IRA or Mafia. What I do hear about is the reality of sin and the Divine sacrifice, which is what Christ's Church is about.

One thing I have come to realise since becoming Catholic is that converts to the Mother Church see her in essentials more clearly than most cradle Catholics—see more clearly than some modern Jesuits do—that the Holy Father and the Magisterium are what make the Catholic Church Catholic.

Moreover, despite Feminism-First nuns, faithless theologians, and confused Jesuits, I believe that Christ the King is winning. The Church, I believe, is about to burst forth into a new glory of strong faith.

No one who lives stands still. The mind looks for answers, and there is continual change and development, sometimes slow and barely perceptible but followed perhaps by a sudden leap. So it was with the development towards Holy Church; and so it was, too, with the development towards the moment when I could write *A Severe Mercy*: the fact that the vocation to write it came *after* the meditation of years on the meaning of our life together is itself something to meditate on.

No life stands still, but some people seem to change only with the changes in the proclamation of the Spirit of the Age. "The greatest part of mankind," said Dr Johnson, "have no other reason for their opinions than that they are in fashion." I do not exonerate myself, especially in the '60s. Since then I have been much more conscious of the *Zeitgeist*—and much more critical of it. It is, surely, one aspect of wisdom to be aware of the Spirit of the Age and, remembering how wrongheaded it has been in the past, to look critically at its often specious urgings. A letter that I wrote to the magazine *Commonweal* in reply to a Notre Dame theologian expresses this caution.

The Spirit of the Age

I should like to ask him and the thoughtful readers of this journal whether the McCarthy era in the '50s would have been the best time to re-evaluate the principle that a man is innocent until proved guilty? And whether Nazi Germany of the '30s would have been quite the time and place to propose that no race is superior to another? The *Zeitgeist* or Spirit of the Age of those periods, it may be thought, might well have prevented a just perspective.

Then let me pose two further questions: Is the most sex-saturated age since late Imperial Rome (probably as the result of the swing of the pendulum from that other excess, Victorian prudishness) the ideal moment to re-evaluate the two-thousand-year tradition of clerical celibacy? And is the period when our own Spirit of the Age is uttering soprano shrieks to the effect that women must be everything, including marine drill sergeants, precisely the moment to re-evaluate that other two-thousand-year tradition of the male priesthood—even if the 'pool' of males is only half our immense population? Wouldn't it be wise (though we so seldom are) to table them both until, say, 2082?...

One word more on change and development, which is another way of saying the zigs and zags and the farings forward on one's pilgrimage to God. Readers of *A Severe Mercy* know what change and development were recorded there in the journey from high paganism to Christ—and what constancies, such as my love of Davy, were also recorded. The readers of that book ought not, then, to have expected me to stand still (if any did) for the rest of my life. Anyway, I didn't, as this book has made clear. No one who lives stands still. One begins to ask questions as soon as one can speak. Indeed, my first utterance, if I am to believe Mother, was not a single word but a coherent question: "Where's Daddy?" I must have wanted to know. The young, at least, always want answers. And I was young—nine months.

The *only* reason for asking is to get an answer. The *only* reason for seeking is to find (*not* to maintain one's 'Seeker's Status'). The *only* reason for an open mind is to fill it with truth—as open eyes are to see with. Or an open mouth to snap at a bit of steak. Otherwise, a mouth that just hangs open indicates vacuity; and a mind for ever open on all the great questions is no less a mark of vacuity.

But when one finds—finds love or finds truth—it becomes (or ought to become) a constancy in one's life. Those questions are answered, and one needs no longer be concerned with them, except to help others seeking answers. But new questions pose themselves. If one discovers that the meaning of existence is to be found in Christ, then the question of what is the Church, irrelevant before, may become urgent. So a further answer must be sought.

Not only did I feel that I must answer that question after thorough examination of what Christ's Church is and has been thought to be, but I increasingly felt that Davy's turn to deep wifeliness in the last, and perhaps holiest, year of her life posed for me the absolute necessity of reconciling that turn with the wholly different direction of the feminism I had embraced. Either she had taken a wrong turning by following an 'outdated' St Paul or the feminists had not only taken a wrong turning but were diverging ever further from the *Tao* or the true path. My insight, discussed on an earlier page, and experimentally proved again and again, that the presence of even one woman in a male group—and the confirmation by women that the presence of even one man in a female group—alters the character of that group whatever its *raison d'être* established for me the falsity of the feminist insistence that men and women are, apart from a few physical irregularities, identical. I should be the last to suggest that mixed groups are not a delight but only that they are not—not ever—the *same* as an all-one-sex group. The difference, as I said earlier, is not unlike the difference between champagne and claret. Life would be poorer without either.

The reader has by now seen the answers I arrived at, after much thought, to both the question of the nature of the Church founded by Christ and the question posed by Davy's turn to wifeliness as opposed to my feminism. The reader may not like my answers to one or the other, or both, of the two questions ("Something to offend everybody!"), but at least the reader has seen that the answers were not lightly or quickly arrived at and may see as well exactly how those answers were determined. I hope the readers who disagree and believe me wrong (I've been wrong before) will in their charity forgive me.

If nothing else, the examination of my life represented by this book, as well as the earlier one, has convinced me that I have lived—and shall live and die—under the Mercy. The title of the book is utterly right. The Mercy, which is to say the Love, is *there*. Undeserved. We are *all* under the Mercy, the deserving and the undeserving alike. With utmost sincerity, I rate myself among the latter. But then, although I should not agree, I suppose Davy would so have rated herself. The Mercy—that word that means so much to me, having such need of it—is simply the charity of God. The forgiving love when we know not what we do; and the more gladly forgiving love when we do know and are penitent.

I should like to tell a story at this point, the story of a few days in my life in the '80s. It was published in *Fidelity Magazine* in 1983, and it gives a glimpse of the effect of Catholicism on my life. More to the point of what I've been saying about the Mercy, it shows God's Mercy and loving action in three lives, one of them my own: three lives that became linked through His action. It is, with reference to chess, called "The Knight's Move", I being the piece called the knight, moved by the Player, God. Those few days haunt my meditation still, so I have saved the story for this final chapter. [The reader is asked to forgive or skip the repetition of my background in the third and fourth paragraphs.]

The Knight's Move

The knight in chess does not move in a straight line as all the other pieces do. In each of his moves the knight makes two bounds, the second at right angles to the first, often to the sudden dismay of the opponent.

At the beginning of June the position was that an old and dear friend, George, had an inoperable cancer wrapped round his neck. There appeared to be no immediate danger to his life, but sometime in the next few months I must go to Cincinnati to visit him. But, also in Cincinnati, a young man, Tracy—I had never met him but he had read my books and written me intelligent letters—had just asked me to be his godfather (sponsor) at his reception into Holy Mother Church. Although hundreds of readers had written me about my books and essays, Tracy was the first to ask me to be his sponsor: I felt an immediate delighted responsibility. He would be glad to come to my church in Virginia for the reception; but there was George. Both Cincinnati. Tracy had originally thought of delaying his move because his girl, Sandy, a member of a small Protestant sect, was bewildered—a "whirlwind of confusion"—at his wanting to become a *Catholic*; and he hoped to make her understand why he must. But then, it seemed to him, God had spoken: "*Now*, Tracy! Act, be not afraid." And Sandy, he told me, had said: "Tracy, I love you; and whether I understand or not I'll *always* support you." From the moment I read that, I honoured her—both of them indeed—in my heart.

In order to make clear the spiritual bonding of Tracy and me, I must mention that I myself had come to the Catholic Church from Anglicanism, as Tracy was doing, only a year before. Long decades earlier, when I was at Oxford, my paganism had been challenged by the sweet reason of that great Oxford don, C. S. Lewis. I was truly a pagan, not a materialist or secularist: I had worshipped love and beauty and held a vague theism—some Power behind the suns that was, at least, intelligent and aware of beauty. But then at Oxford I accepted the Christian Faith: the Faith that Jesus was nothing less than God Incarnate: that the Power that made the suns had, in fact, come down from Heaven, and was made man. C. S. Lewis, my guide, was Church of England, nominally my church, too. At the same time, there in Oxford where the ancient spires, raised by the Catholic Church, split the sky, I could not be unaware of the Question posed by the very existence of the Mother Church. Reading Waugh's *Brideshead Revisited* (which one did at Oxford) made me more aware. Then, too, Lewis himself, though C of E, was very Catholic in his mind and practice—praying for the dead, believing in Purgatory, going often to confession—so much so indeed that some of us wondered whether he might not be a crypto-Catholic.

All this is told in my book, *A Severe Mercy*, which Tracy read. And writing that book, only a few years ago, had focussed my mind anew upon the still-unanswered Question of Rome. Eventually I wrote an essay, "The English Channel" (*New Oxford Review,* March, 1981), showing that intellectually, for me, the road led to Rome: that, despite all counter-arguments, Holy Mother Church was the Church founded by Christ upon the Rock that was Peter. But for an Anglican (C of E or Episcopal), unlike other Protestants, there is another question: is he *already* a Catholic? is he *in* the Church? After all, when England broke with Rome back in the troubled 16th century, it retained and still retains in unbroken succession its bishops and archbishops: is it, as some insist, still Catholic? That is the peculiar Anglican difficulty—the 'English Channel' of my title. But I came to see that it is the Chair of Peter that is the mark of the Catholic Church, the essence of Catholicity: where *it* is, is the Catholic Church. To break with it is to cease to be Catholic. Moreover, I saw that, just as the U. S. Constitution, short as it is, needs a Supreme Court to interpret it, so the enormous complexities of Scripture and Tradition desperately need a supreme court to preserve the true Faith against what Newman called "the energy of human skepticism," which has led to the incredible splintering of Protestantism into thousands of sects. But the Catholic Church *has* that 'supreme court': the Magisterium. So, despite pain at leaving my homely and dear Anglicanism, I was received into Holy Church on the Feast of the Assumption, 1981, by my friend and confessor since Oxford days, Dom Julian OSB, at Portsmouth Abbey on Rhode Island. My Channel essay was graced with another chapter, "Crossing the Channel" (*Communio*, Spring 1982). And now Tracy would swim that same Channel, from Canterbury to Rome.

Tracy had been brought up Baptist and had learnt then the importance of personal conversion and of Scripture. But he sensed limitations in the Baptist view, especially after he became an eager reader of every C. S. Lewis book he could lay hands on. He broke away from the Baptists and, for a while, didn't go to church at all. Then one day a burst of magnificent music through an open church door drew him within. It was an Episcopal church; and its kindly Rector— along with the beauty of the services—led him to become an Anglican. That church has always understood what too many Catholics have forgotten: the beauty of holiness, the role of great art in leading man towards God. For Tracy, a music lover, deeply versed in music theory and counterpoint, the church was a haven. By now he was in university, soaking up knowledge. He had a double major, history and literature—perhaps the best of all combinations in the liberal arts—with emphasis upon the Mediaeval and Renaissance. But he was also reading philosophy and, on his own, the classics, being a reader of both Latin and Greek. He was getting, in truth, an *education*, not a mere degree free with the purchase of a box of crackerjack.

He continued to read Lewis and now Thomas Merton as well; and he talked deeply with a Catholic friend. Not yet ready to think of becoming a Catholic, he found himself becoming *aware* of the Catholic Church, despite lingering Protestant prejudice. Once indeed he had gone to a tired-looking Catholic priest and asked about Catholic belief—"just for a paper, you know, just for a *paper*." The priest told him, then interrupted his nervous thanks to say: "You know, young man, I think the Lord might be leading you somewhere...." That remark lingered in Tracy's mind. And now he met Sandy, and love grew between them.

Early in 1982 he wrote to me: he (and Sandy) had just read my book, *A Severe Mercy*, and it had had a strong impact upon them both. After that first letter there were others, to which I replied, as I usually do, with rather concentrated postcard-letters, that is, a couple of thoughtful paragraphs. By now he was becoming aware of certain troubling aspects of the Episcopal Church: its increasingly secular values and 'with-it' trendiness. Moreover, very perceptively, he had seen a significant truth: the truth that Protestants, including Episcopalians, were defensive in their attitudes towards the Catholic Church, while the Catholics he knew seemed serene and undefensive within a veritable Fortress of the Faith.

At this point I remarked in one of my card-letters that I wished I were a Pied Piper and could "play a marvellous song to ALL genuine Christians causing them instantly to see that the Catholic Church is *really* the bulwark of Christendom and John Paul II really *their* leader in the war against secularism and heresy; so then they'd all become Catholic and we should get on with the war." Tracy's reaction to that, he later wrote, was: "WHAT!?! Everyone become WHAT?! Vanauken must be CATHOLIC!" I had thought he knew, and now I sent him the "Channel" essays: the case for Catholicism. Later I said in a card-letter: "You are right to wish Sandy to see that '*This* is the Great Inheritance'—the fullness of the Faith. But I would urge: Don't waste time on that lovely but lost fragment (Episcopal), shot through with heresy: Rome is the heart." And Tracy, quoting that back to me, said: "At that moment it was as if I were freed of something—prejudicial Protestantism: everything came into sharp focus after that." One other card-letter was significant to him. He had spoken of Protestants trying to worship simply as in New Testament times; and I said: "You are quite right about the attempt (even among some Catholics) to imitate the early Church: the life of the Church did develop and deepen over the centuries, and that beauty and power should not be lost. It's like abandoning a civilised dinner table—linen cloth, silver, bone china—to go back to dipping hands into a common stew-pot." That, he said, made him thoughtful.

Then Tracy decided to make a retreat at Gethsemini Abbey, across the river in Kentucky. There, although he had not intended to arise for the 3:15 a.m. office, Vigils, he was awoken by a peal of thunder and made his way barefoot to the church as the great spring storm broke: the thunder crashed and the windows flashed with lightning: and the chanting monks prayed on serenely, unperturbed. The serene peace within, the violence without: the Church and the world. Tracy prayed in the night. "Now," he wrote, "now I knew that the Church was my home." —And would I be his sponsor? I would, gladly.

Tracy was willing to come to my church in Virginia to be received—but there was my doomed friend, George, whom I must visit. George need not be visited right away—but there was Tracy with that "*Now!*" from God. Consequently I flew to Cincinnati.

Tracy turned out to be a lively young man of middle height with fair hair and an engaging smile, his eyes bright with intelligence. He was slightly nervous at first, but that soon passed. We spent an afternoon together, driving about Cincinnati and having a beer or two; we were comfortable and at ease together. He felt, he later said, as though he had known me for years—which, in a way, through my book, he had done. And I became not only glad but proud that he would be my godson, especially since I have no son of my own. I also met his sweet-faced girl, Sandy, whose lovely and hearteningly womanly words of trust I have recorded.

Meanwhile George was happy that I had come to be with him for five days. Up to the previous week he had been working at the newspaper where he was a feature writer—all his life had been in radio, television, and more recently the newspaper—but he had had to stop working, temporarily, owing partly to a new chemical treatment his doctor was trying. His wife, though, the vivacious and affectionate Shirley or 'Shirl'—herself a popular entertainer, playing the piano and singing—told me at the airport that George might have to write me notes, for the cancer had penetrated his jaw. This prospect filled me with foreboding for our time together, if I were to have to do all the talking. It also gave me a sense of sad irony that George—George of the deep and magnificent voice—should be reduced to silence.

And indeed, when we met and clasped hands, George, tall but a little stooped though his blue eyes were as keen as ever, could only mumble. But by the end of that first evening he was talking strongly and well, with all the old resonance. He and I had always talked the night away; and now he *would* talk; and he did. Shirl thought it a 'miracle,' almost. But, more strictly, it would not be I who would deny God's hand in that. So much healing or, at least, renewal in so short a time. All those five days were to be lively talk: but dialogue, not, thank God, monologues by me.

George was not a Christian: his gently cynical scepticism was the same as the scepticism we had shared in our youth. He had known of course of my deserting that scepticism and becoming a Christian and later a Catholic. We had corresponded steadily over the years, both fluent writers, and met from time to time. I had told him, in letters from Oxford, of each step in my thinking that led me to the Faith; and more than once I had put the Case for Christ to him as powerfully as I could. He didn't mind my doing so; he rather enjoyed arguing and scoffing; he had a certain image, I think, of the slightly cynical news-hawk to live up to. And of course he had read my books, where the argument for Christianity is presented in detail. But George was not convinced—or, if he was, a little, he wasn't admitting it; especially now when he felt he must be brave enough—honest enough—to go into the night as he walked in the day, not knowing. He was not an atheist, not hostile, merely an agnostic.

And he wanted to be honest: honesty meant more to him than to almost anyone I've ever known. Even in our youth he had spoken of "beautiful honesty": that was the key to George, the *mot juste* for him. And yet, astonishingly—it was the last thing I ever expected him to say—he had written in a letter less than a month before that maybe his thought had remained immature. It was said in the context of some discussion of Christianity. Was that remark, that realisation or half-realisation, the prompting of grace? He didn't elaborate, nor did I try to pin him down: it was that "beautiful honesty." At all events, now that I was here with him, I felt that these days together were not the time for preaching or pressure: they were the time for loving, that happy, undemanding, and mellow love that is friendship. My Cincinnati visit must be mainly devoted to my old friend.

The day after Tracy and I had driven about and talked together was his reception at St George's Church: I was aware of course of the co-incidence of names—George and St George—and thought of it as another small link, in addition to me and to Cincinnati itself, between the young man at the beginning of his road and the old friend nearing the end of his: the curious knight's move. Tracy's priest, Father Paul Desch, gentle and intelligent, whom I liked at once, explained the simple procedure. And I gave Tracy the ancient Russian cross of bronze that *my* sponsor had given me at my reception—for Tracy to pass on in his turn. (This indeed he has already done, and I now have a godgrandson; but that is another story.) Now Tracy was being received into Holy Mother Church. The God who had said to him, "Act, be not afraid," now spoke to him in the Gospel: "And, lo, I am with you always, even unto the end of time." I stood behind Tracy, my hand on his shoulder, and Sandy watched with big eyes. It was a moving little ceremony; and we were indeed moved. Perhaps, I thought, Sandy would be next. God grant her grace. It was over. And then I must go back to George.

Night after night, late nights, he and I talked the hours away (Shirl at work, thankful I was there to be with George). We talked of everything, including the cancer without pussy-footing round the subject. Our talk on that was not altogether hopeless; after all, there was the new treatment; death did not seem imminent, but we were realistic. Death, or the end of the road, was a thread woven through our conversation. But the talk, and the laughter, ranged far afield. We recalled funny tales from our days as young radio announcers together; and we talked of the Navy years—often together—in the Pacific war against Japan, talking of ships and friends and far islands, George with the same old grin—one grin when I quoted his brief but immortal war poem: "Over some far table top / I lop."

And we talked with absorbed interest of the current Royal Navy action against the Falklands invaders. Naturally we talked of the girls, young and fair, we had known, including the fascinating and mysterious English girl he had loved, whom I subsequently had sleuthed about London in search of—a dramatic little search, reported in a series of aerogrammes to George, that led from the slums of London to a posh Pall Mall club to one of His Majesty's prisons.

One night we talked a bit about *Brideshead Revisited* in the television version a few months before: I had urged George to see it, partly because of Oxford, but also because of the sceptical C of E Charles's encounter with believers. George was impressed with the death of Lord Marchmain—as acting, he said. But Lord Marchmain, the apostate, dying, past all speech, had made the sign of the Cross. I wondered but did not ask what George had made of that.

Then George showed me a film he particularly wanted me to see, *The Shadow Box*. It was about a group of terminally ill people, and even more about their families and friends and lovers: their painful, desperate inability to accept and come to terms with dying. Agony—and agonizing to watch: the inadequacy of secular philosophy up against the final and ineluctable mystery. After it was over and we had sat in thoughtful silence for a few moments, George told me matter-of-factly of his own friends who did not come to see him now or, if they did, came only briefly and uncomfortably. It was not necessary for either of us to point out that I was comfortably there and had been for several days, during which we had talked and joked in the old way for endless hours. I wondered then, and I have wondered since, whether he related my being easily but not indifferently there to my being a Christian. I think he must have had an awareness: after all, George knew that five minus one equals four. And my not urging the Faith: George would know that it was implicit in my silence. Once, in speaking of Davy, my dead wife whom George had known and loved, I said with quiet conviction something of my certainty that she and I should meet again.

There was one surprising turn in conversation. There was some chance reference to the Shroud of Turin; and it evoked an astonishing eager interest in George—almost as though (I have thought since) he was hopeful that modern science could give him grounds for belief. And I, by good chance or grace, had read a thorough account of all the scientific tests only a week or two before I came. I was able, therefore, to give him a lucid account of the investigations and their results and the probabilities. And to answer his questions. Was his eager interest a sign of some love for the Man supposed to be impressed upon the Shroud? A wish for honest justification of belief? He did not scoff at all in his usual doubting-Thomas way; he really wanted to hear. Was that not-scoffing an infant faith? At all events, I thanked God, then and now, that I had chanced to read the book (someone had sent it to me) when I did.

It was, for both of us, a grand five days—and for Tracy and me as well. I left George, promising to return in a month. Tracy, seeming by now an old friend himself, drove me to the airport. A handshake, and then I was flying back to the blue mountains of Virginia.

A few days later I rang George up. In the course of the ten-minute talk, he said—not once but three or four times—that "words cannot express" how much the visit had meant to him. I said, with perfect truth, that it had meant a great deal to me, too. Then at the end he said that my being there had been "one of the great things" of his "whole life."

I felt this last to be a bit extravagant, from George—indeed, I could scarcely believe he had said it—George was simply not given to superlatives and extravagances. Therefore he *meant* it, which was amazing. I wrote to him next day about how good it had been to be with him. Two or three days after he read my letter—precisely a fortnight from the day of my flight to Cincinnati—he died, sitting alone in the study with a half-finished drink beside him: the cancer had torn the carotid artery. Death would have been swift, though perhaps a moment of awareness. Did he think fleetingly of Lord Marchmain and the sign of the Cross? It cannot be known. What I did know was that, if I had delayed going to see him, as I certainly should have done but for God's "*Now!*" to Tracy, I should not, ever, have seen him: the visit with its warmth of love and its consequences known only to God—and now to George—would never have occurred.

My first act when I heard that he was dead was to thank God that I had gone to Cincinnati. My second act, with the ceremony at St George's in mind, was to tell God that I would be *George's* sponsor in the City. Having done this with a sort of terrible urgency, I suddenly wondered if God's purpose in sending me to Cincinnati might have been so that George would have some member of the Church to wish to be his sponsor: someone to bear witness that George, as a lover of truth and honesty ("beautiful honesty" was probably his name for God) was worthy to be numbered among the lovers of Truth Himself. I knew, somehow, that he *was* worthy. Of course God would know even better; but a prayer—and I was praying—is a channel for the action of grace.

Ten days later, reflecting on all this, I became convinced that *lovers*—real lovers of something outside themselves, lovers of another person without thought of self, lovers of honesty and beauty and decency—are given a chance to know Christ as that which they love. (But woe to them that do not *love* outside themselves!) George was a lover—he loved his Shirl and his daughter; he loved that "beautiful honesty"; indeed, he loved me. I rest easy in the conviction that he and I shall again clasp hands.

To have one's petitions granted in this life is a bit dangerous: there may be a sense of one's own virtue or power, even something of magic. But in all this journey to Cincinnati I was not the petitioner (except when it was all over). I didn't go because I had sensitively perceived George's need—perhaps he didn't himself—and of course I didn't know that death was near. Tracy could have come to Virginia—except for George. George could have been visited later (I thought)—except for Tracy's "*Now!*" from God. I didn't want to go just then, but I went.

It seems to me that I was simply moved like a chessman. Moved, too, to prime myself on the Shroud. It is not often that we catch so much as a glimpse of God's hand in the moves of our lives. This once, because of the peculiar interaction of Tracy and George— Tracy causing the time to be at that moment, George causing the place to be in that city—I was given such a glimpse; and I find it awesome.

It was the knight's move. Christ was the player.

One of the chief joys of college teaching is to discover and encourage the bright girl, like Helen whom I helped to Oxford, or the bright young man, like Jim Hunter. About the time I became Catholic, I ceased to teach; but there have been more young men and young women than ever through correspondence resulting from my book, and many of them have come to see me. Tracy of "The Knight's Move" is of course one of those, and the godfather-godson relationship has deepened and become very real to both of us. Another young man, James, clearly on the road to Holy Mother Church, wrote to me; and eventually was received into the Church with Tracy as godfather; and he holds, therefore, the old Russian Cross. A strong vocation is taking him to the cloistered life as a Benedictine. Then there are two fine young men—the Tims—on their way to priesthood at Mt St Mary in western Maryland; they have come to visit several times, while friendship and affection have grown.

"The Knight's Move" is the best answer I can give to the question I'm often asked: What of the good man who dies without committing his ways to Christ Our Lord? Must he be damned? And sometimes the questioner goes on to ask whether there *is* such a thing as damnation and Hell? Must not a loving and merciful God save us all? Again, I can do no more than offer an opinion. Once, when *Christianity Today*, in defining Evangelical belief, said, "The only hope of heaven is through personal faith in Jesus Christ," I was moved to reply. I wrote: "Shouldn't we say perhaps 'the only hope, *as far as we can see*'? Otherwise it's too like limiting God."

C. S. Lewis, one of the wisest of Christians, touched upon salvation in the last of the Narnian tales. There the good man, Emeth, who believes in the false (and actually evil) god Tash, finds that he has really been, in his love of good, serving Aslan, the great lion who is Christ, all his life without knowing it. And Aslan tells him that a man who does "a cruelty in my name, then, though he says the name Aslan, it is Tash whom he serves..." And then Aslan says: "For all find what they truly seek." *Truly* seek—that says it all. And what a man truly seeks can rarely be seen by another, and often not by the man himself. I said in "The Knight's Move" that George's "beautiful honesty" was probably his name for Christ.

As to damnation and Hell, I do indeed believe that Hell exists (even beginning in this life, though not yet irrevocable); and that a man may damn himself *if* he insists. In Lewis's marvellous *Great Divorce*, most of the people on the bus to Heavensgate are *urged* to stay in Heaven but prefer to go back to the grey city, the Hell of their own choosing. Of course, if they had stayed—the mother, the painter, the Modernist bishop—they would have had to give up whatever they wanted more than God. One man, whose sin is lust, allows it to be killed and stays in Heaven: for him, the grey city was Purgatory. Ironically, he is the one most Christians would nominate for Hell first of all.

I have never known a man, either male or female—since I cannot know what he *truly* seeks—that I could pronounce damned; or any man, including myself, certainly saved. But I think there are churchmen, not excluding bishops and theologians, who have ceased to believe, ceased to love—who, like that bishop in *Great Divorce*, simply *will not* make the act of faith or even recognise that they are apostate—and I have little difficulty in supposing that they, along with many self-possessed seculars, will prefer Hell. God will not stand in their way, I think. On the other hand, I believe that there are lovers of Christ who have never heard of Him except as a figment of an 'exploded superstition': *they* will choose Heaven when confronted with Reality.

Hell, on Christ's own authority, exists. And the Evil One. There are those who feel that Heaven would be marred by the knowledge that even one soul was damned and, therefore, say these people who are nicer than Christ, everyone must be saved. But we shall have to wait and see, shan't we? We cannot know, cannot go beyond Christ. I was amused, reading something about universal salvation, by a thought that popped into my mind—half-amused and half-impressed. What if everybody does indeed go to Heaven, where loving-kindness rules and no sin is possible and *nothing* can mar the deep courtesy? —And to *some*, though they cannot show it in any way at all, such pure light and goodness and love is Hell.

The words of Socrates on the examined life began this chapter, which then went on to the words of Lewis, rather a Socrates himself, on all of us finding what we *truly* seek. Let us put them together. Surely it is by examining our life that we learn what we truly seek. Is it important to know? Perhaps for him who truly seeks Christ, though he does not know the Holy Name, it may not be so important to know consciously: he shall find Him all the same. But if a man think he seeks Christ first and, in fact, does not, it may literally be damned important to realise it before the night comes.

Moreover, it is through the examination of one's life that one recognises sin. Nobody *feels* like a sinner, especially in these days of easy psychiatric 'absolution'; or, if he does feel sinful, he may be on the way to repentance. Certainly it was through deep, and in the end sorrowful and penitent, examination that I saw my grave sin of the '60s. The pain was terrible but it was outweighed by the gratitude to God for His showing it to me (convicting me) now rather than at some awe-ful moment later, and by the gladness (there's no other word for it) of confession both to God and to those I'd harmed, and, finally, by the pure joy of known forgiveness. Penitence and forgiveness, whether one is forgiving or being forgiven, is one of the most joyful things a mortal can know.

Examination of one's life goes hand in hand with contemplation: first the seeing it as it is and then the thinking about it. When Davy died, there was first the intense seeing that I called the Illumination of the Past, and then, with it and for twenty years after, the contemplating. Similarly, after seeing, the contemplation of both the sin of the '60s and the happy dance with Christ of the '70s. It was through that contemplation that I realised that *A Severe Mercy* had bridged the two halves of my life and made them one.

Something still deeper was suggested to me through contemplation. When Davy's illness came upon her with the shadow of death, I prayed as did a multitude of others for her healing. But my over-riding prayer was for *her* best good whatever that might be, death or life. She, a year before, had offered-up her life that my soul might be fulfilled. Now I offered-up what *I* wanted—her recovery—and all the years that remained to me for *her* best good, whether that were her life or her death.

In the life that remained to her after we became Christian at Oxford—only four years—she touched but a handful of people, Oxford friends, a dozen or more students, a few Lynchburg friends and nurses, though she touched them deeply. In the last year of her life, she painted a picture, described in detail in *A Severe Mercy*, that I interpreted as a painting of her soul and mine: *The Obedient Soul and the Disobedient Soul*. In it her soul at the behest of her guardian angel was shooting obediently off towards a low door, while my soul argued with my guardian angel who was motioning imperiously towards a high door. I recognised all too easily the truth of her portrayal of me, and I was touched by her humility in assigning only a low door to herself. Needless to say, I saw no 'high door' awaiting me, neither then nor in the future.

It was twenty years later that God, as I believe, commanded me to write *A Severe Mercy*. Publishers estimate an average of two readers for each book sold. On that basis, a million people in a dozen countries know Davy now, know the depth of her love of her Lord. If she had recovered all those years ago, there would never have been a severe Mercy, and that book would not have been written. I cannot presume to speculate as to the 'best good' for her that may have lain beyond the curtain of death, but in the last years of her life her 'best good' was one with the Kingdom's good. And so, as I contemplate all this, I ask myself whether the book (and what preceded it in the way of my repentance) was that 'high door' she dimly discerned for me, and, even more, whether her touching all those million lives through the book was indeed some part of that 'best good' I prayed for her. I cannot know, but I find the working out of the pattern not a little awesome.

Very naturally in contemplation I compare my life in the years since Davy (however much she is in my mind and heart) with the years of our being together. Sometimes readers ask, almost shyly, whether, just possibly, there has been a little happiness since her death. Life then with her had the freshness of morning—and I have ever loved the dawn and the morning hours. It was morning and adventure, a schooner under the wind, and laughter, and a hand in mine; it was more fun, then; it was joyous to be alive. And, finally, it was tragic depths (though not truly tragedy because of the hope).

Now it is afternoon. There is a calm, even a serenity, in afternoon—a mellowness. And it's not without fun, certainly not without gaiety and humour. Few days, if any, without a smile, sometimes at myself. And, indeed, not without adventure. Heaven knows that writing *A Severe Mercy*—writing any book, including this, but that especially—was one of the greatest adventures of my whole life. So was entering the Mother Church. As to happiness, the reader of this book will know by now that there has been much happiness in the years recorded here. And joy, too. The joy of forgiveness. The joy of carrying out the vocation God gave me to write *A Severe Mercy*—of doing His will.

The reader may wonder whether the writing of *Under the Mercy* is vocation, also. Not, certainly, as dramatically and unmistakably so. But I am *doing* it, though I had thought I would not, ever. I have prayed about it, I have enjoyed writing it, and, in the writing, I have felt it to be in harmony with His will. But I shall contemplate it further in the years to come.

Something should be said of my life now. It is a good life. Vancot, full of the lovely old Glenmerle furniture—sleeping in the bed

I slept in as a boy—is small, but it is all I need. All, that is, if I can't have Glenmerle itself. There is not much I wish for, but, curiously enough, I find myself longing for Glenmerle, its woods and meadows, the individual trees, the very contours of the land—but all that is gone beyond recall. Unless, indeed, among the "many mansions" there is a heavenly Glenmerle—the bridge and lily pond, the same hills, the great beech—with Davy waiting by the lily pond, and Flurry and Laddie and the rest running through the grass. I have no doubt in my own mind that we are lord and saviour of individual animals as Christ is Saviour for us.

But my life now. There are good friends for conversation, and the grey Morgan, kept running smoothly by Jim Ottinger, with his ready smile (the sort of man I'd like as a shipmate if going off to war) for drives in the Virginian countryside—with Nelly full of infectious joy at a 'RIDE'. Shirley Rosser, with his stately Virginian courtesy and his deep knowledge of physics, is one of those friends. He figured in *A Severe Mercy*, as did the cheerful and brave Belle Hill, one of my dearest friends. Dick Seymann, a sturdy agnostic with a sense of humour, and a fellow sailor, is another. With these and others, a good dinner with the right wine, the quiet talk by the fire. And the wide world of friends I write to: my old, life-observing college roommate, old friends from Oxford days, and friends made through my books, including the blithe lady Barbara, a guide in the ways of the Church. And friends I go to see in England or New England. Loving the people God gives me to love. And Davy to talk to in prayer sometimes. For she is not lost to me: that faith makes all the difference.

Yes, a good life, alone but not lonely. Not with Christ near. And sometimes the Sacred seems all round me. Very unlike the '60s, but, strangely, *not* unlike Glenmerle as I roamed the woods and fields. I didn't then call it the Sacred, but that is what it was.

Although, like Glenmerle, Davy is gone from me in this world, except in prayer, and has been gone for decades, I know at all times that, though she is 'out of the country', the separation is but temporary. *Temporary* (lasting for a time only)—that is a word for contemplation. Temporal things are temporary. We bear up under a cold because we know it's temporary. But so is a broken hip. Indeed, *all* things in time—even life-long illness or blindness from birth—*all* are temporary. Eternity is our home. And, as we bear temporary pain, so we can bear temporary parting. My parting from Davy—that last parting at dawn in the hospital—was only yesterday; and tomorrow is coming. Thus with that temporality in mind, even though Davy is temporarily away, I have enjoyed the present moment as I drift down the stream of time. Towards her. Towards my Lord.

And I have particularly enjoyed writing, for writing has something of the timeless about it—a breath of eternity. That little poem on an earlier page about the cardinal in scarlet flight seems to me to be touched by eternity—but so does *A Severe Mercy*. In my novel I was in the eternity of my created characters in my created world. None of this has to do with merit, only with the process of writing that touches the writer with the eternal. At all events, I have loved writing, and I have always been writing something since my teens (and even before: I won some sort of state prize in the third grade for a story about a dog). When Davy was still alive, it was scholarly articles and the book *The Glittering Illusion*, and tales of sailing for *Yachting Magazine*—and of course the Journal, quoted so often in *A Severe Mercy*. And in the '60s the novel, *Gateway to Heaven*, I living the adventures I created. And from the mid-'70s on, writing became more my occupation—it had always been my vocation—than teaching, though I had to cram it into the vacs and dawns.

Thus, when I left the college in the early '80s, it seemed merely a prolonged summer vac when I could really get on with things, and I was hardly aware of not going up the hill to classes. I had always hated the lovely crepe myrtle that blooms in August because it meant that my precious summer vac was almost gone. That first summer after I quit teaching, I thought, "Why, that's a right pretty tree."

I had never thought of myself as primarily a scholar—one who deals in footnotes—although I had, perforce, done my share of scholarship; and I didn't really like to be called one, or 'Professor' either. And despite thinking the occasional thought, I disliked being referred to as an 'intellectual'. All these rejections result from the examined life: the discovery of who and what one really is. And isn't. And though I haven't written a score of books or a thousand verses, in my own mind what I really am is a *writer*, a writer of prose and poetry. These titles—writer or poet—I accept. Aquinas said it was better to deliver to others contemplated truths than just to contemplate. And so I have endeavoured, in teaching but more in writing, to do. But it is the contemplation that takes the time, not the writing. The writing is pleasure—hard pleasure, to be sure.

A poet, then, and a writer. And a lover whilst my beloved dwelt with me. And a Christian—Christ's man, a *Christ*-ian. I think I might claim (proclaim) *that* title even if the lions were waiting, growling. Still, perhaps not: I might develop a sudden allergy to cats. One never knows till one is put to the test. It's like that with any sort of dying. One would like to die well, not howling; but only the event will show.

Death, too, is a thing to contemplate. Death as opposed to dying.

The great, ineluctable mystery of death, death perhaps this evening after dinner, waits for every man. It is where the secularist's philosophy fails: he can only try, a bit frantically, to banish thoughts of it; he may even succeed, for awhile. But death is for the Christian, by faith, something more.

In a way both this book and the earlier one are a contemplation of death. In *A Severe Mercy* I contemplated it as the one left behind. And in this book, though I haven't spoken much of my dying, the thought of it has, quietly and even tranquilly, underlain much of the writing—as well as having underlain the years written about. In writing *A Severe Mercy* I prayed often to be allowed to live to finish it, though I had no least reason to suppose I mightn't. But I well knew how often death drops in quite casually and unexpectedly.

It was not long after I did finish it and the manuscript had gone to the printer that it came to me that Davy was nearer to me *ahead* than behind. The book was written twenty years after her death; and, unless I lived a very long life indeed, chances were that I should be with her again twenty years after the book. A curiously pleasing thought. The past is where one cannot dwell (though some try), but day by day with unhurried pace we move *towards* the future. And if death means I shall clasp her again, there is a dawn-brightness ahead, the brighter as the distance lessens. So fare forward, voyager!

I am comfortable about death. Dying—the failing breath, the darkening eyes—is another matter, a grim but *temporary* ordeal. I fancy babies being born find birth a terrifying experience. But birthing and dying will alike be forgotten. Perhaps as I die her hand will creep into mine. For me Robert Browning's poem "Prospice" (which of my own choice I memorised in schooldays) speaks truly of dying and of death. Far more than exploring darkest Africa in the last century or exploring the Galaxy in centuries to come, death if our faith be not false is *the* splendid adventure. And, finally, coming *home*. "And with God be the rest."

In contemplating death I think often of the idea that Heaven and Hell are retroactive: that for one man, however painful his life, he will see it from Eternity as having been a part of Heaven; and for another, perhaps wealthy and successful, his life will have been a part of Hell or the smooth slope that leads to Hell. I try to look at my life, including the sins (and the repentance), as if from Eternity: and I feel hope.

Under the Mercy.

THE END

A SEVERE MERCY

Sheldon Vanauken

A real-life love story full of wonder and hope, tragedy and ecstasy, despair and comfort. A Severe Mercy tells of the young love of Sheldon and Davy Vanauken, their quest for meaning, encounter with C S Lewis, discovery of the living Lord and Davy's untimely death. A widely acclaimed classic.

'The joy and tears of human life and love are here in depth, and burning through them all is the strength of faith and the love of Christ.' – *Baptist Times*

'Love, God and death, the spiritual profundities of human experience . . . Irresistible – and frightening. – *Church Times*

'Can stand with "Pilgrim's Progress" and C S Lewis's "Screwtape Letters" . . . I am proud to recommend it unreservedly.' – *Maurice Wood, Bishop of Norwich.*

BLESSINGS

Mary Craig

Blessings tells of profound suffering and grief, yet also of hope that pierces and transcends the darkness and renews faith in a loving God.

'The most moving book I have read in years. A record of courage, compassion and personal growth through the experience of almost intolerable tragedy. I believe it will strike a responsive chord in the hearts of men and women everywhere in the world.' *Morris West*

'A brave, poignant and inspiring account of how the author has faced and overcome double tragedy . . . it is a beautiful little book that will bring comfort and understanding to anyone who is suffering, bereaved or just sad . . . I beg you to read this book.' *Sunday Express*

'A truly remarkable book in every way.' *Sunday Express*

'A precious insight into the positive uses of personal suffering.' *Church of England Newspaper*

A QUESTION OF GRIEF

Elizabeth Heike

When cancer robbed Madeleine Fisher of her life, few understood the grief of her close companion, Liz Heike. But for Liz, her friend's death was a bereavement of the deepest kind and shook her world to its core.

Her feelings overwhelmed her: anger, guilt, bitterness that her grief didn't seem legitimate to those who set store only by family relationships, confusion that her Christian faith still left her questioning and in pain. 'Bereavement has to be lived through,' she writes, 'but it can eventually bring us a resurrection: we can grow through it and indeed find peace and a curious kind of joy.'

A Question of Grief will extend a hand to the isolated and lonely, those who are grieving or in pain. It will also bring insight and understanding to people caring for the bereaved.

'A wise and beautiful book.' *Mary Craig*

'A most challenging and helpful contribution to all who grieve, a book of unusual depth.' *Dame Cicely Saunders*

'Elizabeth Heike's book is one of the most moving I have read.' *Gilbert Kirby*